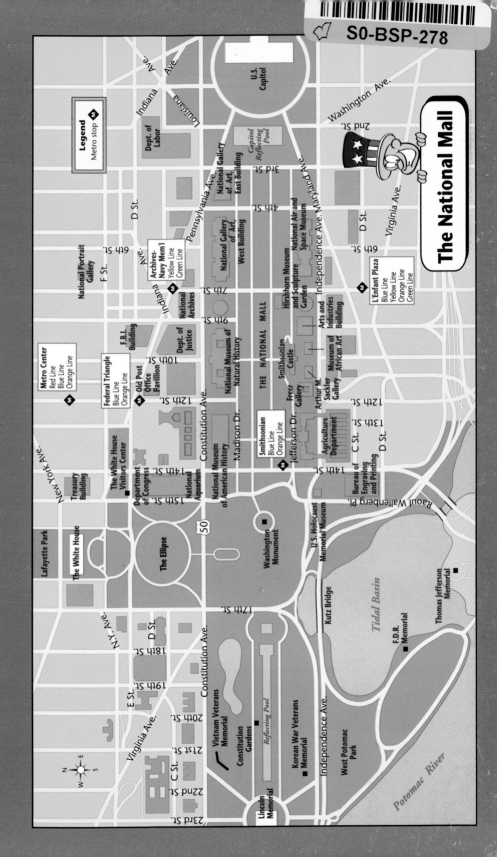

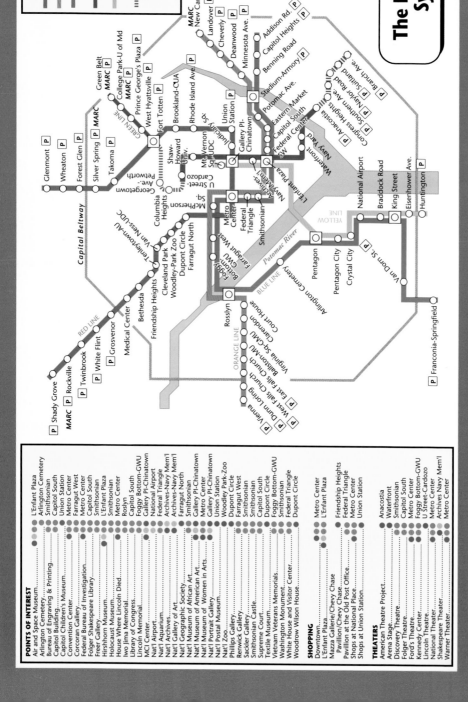

The Metrorail System

Legend

- Wheaton/Shady Grove
- New Carrollton/Vienna
- Addison Road/Franconia–Springfield
- Anacostia/U-Street–Cardozo Greenbelt/Fort Totten
- Mt. Vernon Sq–UDC Huntington

- RED LINE
- ORANGE LINE
- BLUE LINE
- GREEN LINE
- YELLOW LINE

- ┊┊┊O Future stop
- **P** Parking
- O Transfer

POINTS OF INTEREST

Air and Space Museum	L'Enfant Plaza
Arlington Cemetery	Arlington Cemetery
Bureau of Engraving & Printing	Smithsonian
Capitol Building	Capitol South
Capitol Children's Museum	Union Station
Convention Center	Metro Center
Corcoran Gallery	Farragut West
Federal Bureau of Investigation	Metro Center
Folger Shakespeare Library	Capitol South
Freer Gallery	Smithsonian
Hirshhorn Museum	L'Enfant Plaza
Holocaust Museum	Smithsonian
House Where Lincoln Died	Metro Center
Iwo Jima Memorial	Rosslyn
Library of Congress	Capitol South
Lincoln Memorial	Foggy Bottom–GWU
MCI Center	Gallery Pl-Chinatown
Nat'l Airport	National Airport
Nat'l Aquarium	Federal Triangle
Nat'l Archives	Archives–Navy Mem'l
Nat'l Gallery of Art	Archives–Navy Mem'l
Nat'l Geographic Society	Farragut North
Nat'l Museum of African Art	Smithsonian
Nat'l Museum of American Art	Gallery Pl-Chinatown
Nat'l Museum of Women in Arts	Metro Center
Nat'l Portrait Gallery	Gallery Pl-Chinatown
Nat'l Postal Museum	Union Station
Nat'l Zoo	Woodley Park–Zoo
Phillips Gallery	Dupont Circle
Renwick Gallery	Farragut West
Sackler Gallery	Smithsonian
Smithsonian Castle	Smithsonian
Supreme Court	Capitol South
Textile Museum	Dupont Circle
Vietnam Veterans Memorials	Foggy Bottom–GWU
Washington Monument	Smithsonian
White House and Visitor Center	Federal Triangle
Woodrow Wilson House	Dupont Circle

SHOPPING

Downtown	Metro Center
	L'Enfant Plaza
Mazza Gallerie/Chevy Chase	Friendship Heights
Pavillion at the Old Post Office	Federal Triangle
Shops at National Place	Metro Center
Shops at Union Station	Union Station

THEATERS

American Theatre Project	Anacostia
Arena Stage	Waterfront
Discovery Theatre	Smithsonian
Folger Theatre	Capitol South
Ford's Theatre	Metro Center
Kennedy Center	Foggy Bottom–GWU
Lincoln Theatre	U Street–Cardozo
National Theater	Metro Center
Shakespeare Theater	Archives Navy Mem'l
Warner Theater	Metro Center

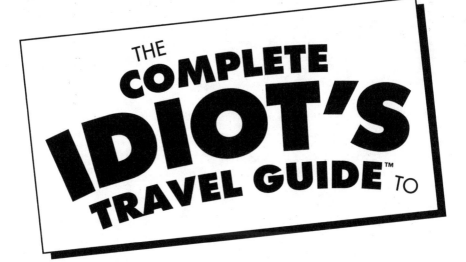

Washington, D.C.

by Beth Rubin

Macmillan Travel USA
A Pearson Education Macmillan Company
1633 Broadway
New York, NY 10019

MACMILLAN is a registered trademark of Macmillan, Inc.
FROMMER'S is a registered trademark of Arthur Frommer. Used under license.
THE COMPLETE IDIOT'S GUIDE name and design are trademarks of Macmillan, Inc.

ISBN 0-02862859-4
ISSN 1520-5592

Editor: Vanessa Rosen
Production Editor: Tammy Ahrens
Design by designLab
Page Layout: Melissa Auciello-Brogan, David Pruett
Proofreader: Laura Goetz
Staff Cartographers: John Decamillis, Roberta Stockwell
Additional Cartography: Raffaele DeGennaro
Illustrations by Kevin Spear

Special Sales

Bulk purchases (10+ copies) of Frommer's and selected Macmillan travel guides are available to corporations, organizations, mail-order catalogs, institutions, and charities at special discounts, and can be customized to suit individual needs. For more information write to: Special Sales, Macmillan General Reference, 1633 Broadway, New York, NY 10019.

Manufactured in the United States of America

Contents

Maps

About the Author

Beth Rubin's love affair with Washington, D.C., began when she moved here as a student in the '60s—before the Kennedy Center, Watergate, and Metro. Since then, she has survived eight presidential administrations while escorting countless relatives and friends (and her own two kids) around this idiotic city. She has parlayed her knowledge of the nation's capital into print for 20 years and is the author of *Frommer's Washington, D.C. with Kids*. When writer's block hits, she is only too happy to shut down her computer and head for a museum on the Mall.

An Invitation to the Reader

In researching this book, we discovered many wonderful places—hotels, restaurants, shops, and more. We're sure you'll find others. Please tell us about them, so we can share the information with your fellow travelers in upcoming editions. If you were disappointed with a recommendation, we'd love to know that, too. Please write to:

The Complete Idiot's Travel Guide to Washington, D.C.
Macmillan Travel
1633 Broadway
New York, NY 10019

An Additional Note

Please be advised that travel information is subject to change at any time—and this is especially true of prices. We therefore suggest that you write or call ahead for confirmation when making your travel plans. The authors, editors, and publisher cannot be held responsible for the experiences of readers while traveling. Your safety is important to us, however, so we encourage you to stay alert and be aware of your surroundings. Keep a close eye on cameras, purses, and wallets, all favorite targets of thieves and pickpockets.

The following abbreviations are used for credit cards:

AE	American Express	EU	Eurocard
CB	Carte Blanche	JCB	Japan Credit Bank
DC	Diners Club	MC	MasterCard
DISC	Discover	V	Visa
ER	enRoute		

Introduction

The *Complete Idiot's Travel Guide to Washington, D.C.,* shows how even the least important person in the world can snag some VIP passes to the White House, as well as sit in on a session of Congress, eat at the city's best restaurants, find great hotels that cost next to nothing, gain free access to some of the best attractions in town, and even see the Supreme Court in action.

I understand that when it comes time to do things such as get hold of a White House schedule of events, find your way around the city, ride the Metro, catch a glimpse of the president, or tour the FBI, even the best of us can feel like an idiot. That's where this easy-to-use guide comes in. Instead of overwhelming you with information coming from a million different directions, I give you everything you need to know straight and simple.

How to Use This Book

The book is divided into six sections, devoted to giving you an overview of the city, getting you here, finding you a comfortable and affordable nest, steering you toward the top attractions and restaurants, and showing you a good time.

Part 1 supplies the building blocks for planning your vacation. You'll learn when the busiest and least-crowded months are, what the weather is like, how to get here, and where to gather more information. There's also a calendar of events in this part of the book to help you decide when's the best time to see the cherry blossoms or catch one of the many festivals that take place here. I've included useful addresses, phone numbers, and Web sites that'll help you organize your trip, as well as money-saving tips and worksheets that will help you balance your budget (even when the federal government cannot).

Part 2 is all about hotels. I give you the lowdown on neighborhoods and share some tips on finding the best rates. As you read through the hotel listings, my sidebar boxes—which categorize hotels by special interests ranging from the best hotels for celebrity gawking to the hotels with the most breathtaking views—will help you decide which is the place for you.

Part 3 gets you from the airport, train, or Beltway to your hotel, with specific information on shuttles, taxis, and rental cars. After that, you'll learn where things are and how to navigate the city. Thumbnail sketches of the major neighborhoods will help you plan your itinerary efficiently.

Part 4 is all about my favorite four-letter word: *food*. You'll learn where to get grub when hunger strikes, from a hot dog on the Mall to a leisurely multicourse meal at one of Washington's finest dining establishments. Once again, to help narrow your choices, I've indexed the restaurants in categories ranging from the best places for kids to the spots that are best for whispering sweet nothings.

Part 5 describes the sights, from the major Smithsonian museums to the best parks, and shopping meccas. To help you plan your days without keeling over, I've provided some sample itineraries and planning tips.

Part 6 is devoted to the nighttime scene. It covers dance clubs where you can get down to a local band and shake your booty and explains how to mine the cultural landscape for a show, concert, or dance performance. I'll even help you get dressed, order discount tickets, and recommend places where you can kick back with a cocktail and listen to a tinkling piano.

Extras

This book has several features you won't find in other guidebooks—features that will help you make maximum use of the information (and find it faster!).

As mentioned above, indexes cross-reference information so that you can see at a glance your options in a particular subcategory. For example, Italian restaurants, Georgetown hotels, Dupont Circle shopping, etc.

I've also boxed tidbits of useful information in sidebars, which come in five "flavors": D.C. Dirt, Hear Ye! Hear Ye!, Tourist Traps, Balancing the Budget, and Time Savers.

D.C. Dirt

Here you'll find interesting facts or trivia about the nation's capital.

Hear Ye! Hear Ye!

Check these boxes for handy facts, hints, and insider advice.

Tourist Traps

These boxes steer you away from rip-offs, activities that aren't worth the trouble, shady dealings, and other pitfalls.

Balancing the Budget

These boxes will give you tips on saving money, which will make your trip affordable as well as enjoyable.

Time Savers

Here you'll find ways to save time, avoid lines and hassles, and streamline the business of traveling.

The best way to remember something is to write it down. With that in mind, I've provided worksheets to help cement the facts in your head. I recommend underlining or highlighting as you go along. Since this book is yours to keep, you have the green light to write in it without guilt.

A **kid-friendly icon** (**Kids**) is used t-hroughout the book to identify those activities, attractions, restaurants, and hotels that are especially suited to people traveling with children.

Appendices at the back of the book list important numbers and addresses covering every aspect of your trip, from reservations to emergencies.

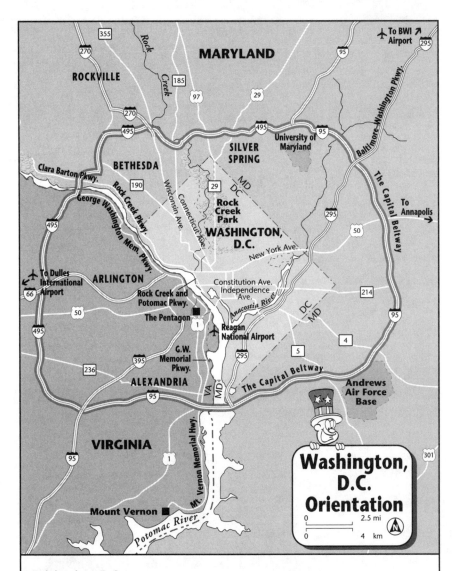

Driving into D.C.

Note that all of the following highways lead to the **Capital Beltway (I-95/I-495)**, which is a wheel (or noose) around the D.C. area, with spokes leading into the city. Talk to your hotel to find out which spoke is right for you.

- If you're driving into D.C. from the north, **I-270**, **I-95**, and **I-295** are the main links to the Washington metropolitan area.

- From the south, **I-95** and **I-395** are the most direct and quickest routes.

- From points east, such as Annapolis and the Eastern Shore of Maryland, the road of choice is **Route 50**, which becomes New York Avenue in the District.

- West of D.C., coming from Virginia, motorists should cruise down **I-66**, which leads into both Constitution Avenue and Rock Creek Parkway.

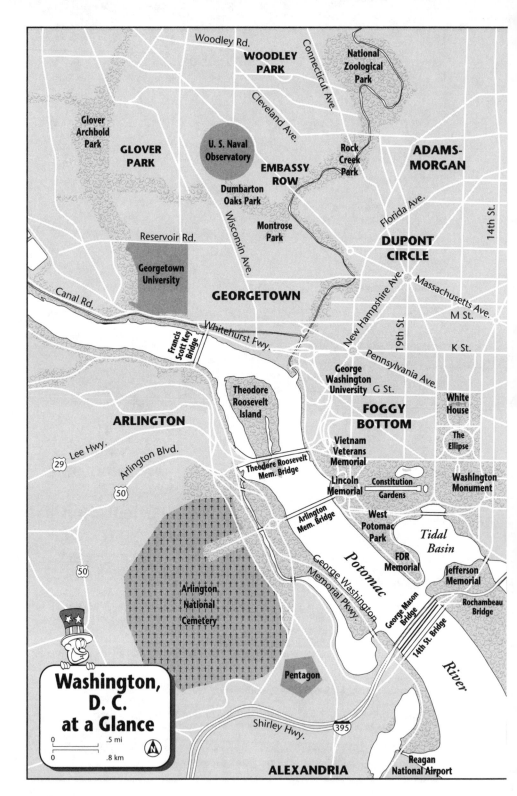

Washington,
D. C.
at a Glance

0   .5 mi

0   .8 km

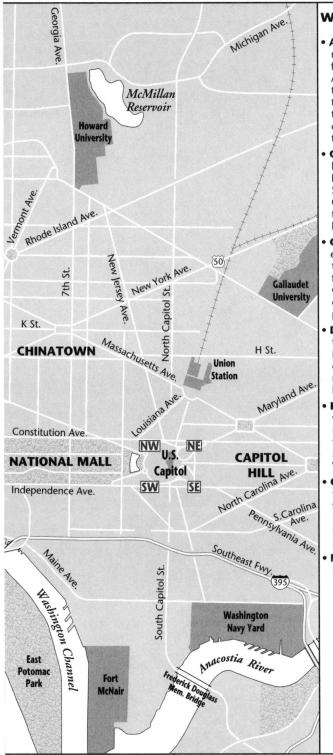

WHAT'S DOING WHERE?

- **Adams-Morgan** This neighborhood gets its flavor from the large Latino and African-American populations that live here. It's a great place to wander around and explore the funky shops, cool bars, and culinary delights from around the world.

- **Capitol Hill** The Capitol is king of the hill in this neighborhood. Visit the Capitol, Supreme Court, Library of Congress, and enjoy restaurants that cater to those with business on the Hill.

- **Chinatown** Before or after an event at the MCI Center, this is the place to eat good Chinese food, buy some tea, or find that Chinese folk medicine that you can't get at your local pharmacy.

- **Dupont Circle** Day or night, there's always something to do in Dupont Circle. Just pop into one of the many galleries, restaurants, movie theaters, or boutiques that abound here.

- **Foggy Bottom** Within walking distance of the White House, Foggy Bottom is home to the Kennedy Center, State Department, and George Washington University.

- **Georgetown** Here, in one of the oldest parts of town, you'll find Georgetown University, Dumbarton Oaks Gardens, historic homes, and great shopping and restaurants.

- **National Mall** You can spend hours here exploring the Lincoln Memorial, Washington Monument, Air and Space Museum, National Museum of Natural History, (and numerous other Smithsonian museums), or just lounging in the 2-mile park-like space extending from the Capitol to the Lincoln Memorial.

Part 1

What You Need to Do Before You Go

Watergate, Zippergate, the District of Columbia, the nation's capital—however you think of it, Washington, D.C., is a vibrant, multicultural city. You want history? This is where history is made. You want museums? It would take $2\frac{1}{2}$ years of round-the-clock viewing to take in everything housed in the Smithsonian Institution's 16 museums. But the fun doesn't stop there. 21 million visitors a year flock to Washington and its Broadway-caliber theater, flourishing music and dance scene, international restaurants, and great shopping—along with a beautiful riverfront setting, wide boulevards, and those famous cherry trees.

Washington is busy throughout the year, so you may be in for a nasty wake-up call if you arrive unprepared. Which brings us to the purpose of Part 1 of this book—planning ahead. If you keep up with your homework and follow my instructions, you should have it made in the shade. Part 1 will guide you through the process of deciding how to get to Washington and when to go, as well as divulge all the important things you need to know before you go. For example, you can't just waltz into the White House. In fact, if you want to take the VIP tour of the president's home, you best write away to a very important person as far in advance as possible. In Part 2 I'll help you find restaurants, shopping, and lodging. I'll also give you the bottom line on entertainment and how to get around the city. Before you know it, other, less-well-informed visitors will be asking you for directions and advice.

Chapter 1

How to Get Started

In This Chapter

➤ Where to get information before you leave home

➤ Planning ahead

➤ When to go

➤ Who do you think you are? (Evaluating your special needs and interests)

Information, Please

If you can write, dial, or surf, you can gather a wealth of information about the city in the comfort of your own home. Bear in mind that most brochures are not public service announcements. In fact, most of the visitor information that you find in your mailbox is paid for by private businesses—hotels, restaurants, and the like. For more objectivity, compare what you uncover in those brochures with the information in this book and other, more detailed, guidebooks, like *Frommer's Washington, D.C.,* by Elise Hartman Ford.

A number of nonbiased tourist bureaus are eager to assist you prior to your arrival in Washington. Use the addresses and numbers below to write, call, or surf the Web for brochures, maps, and event calendars—you'll accumulate enough material to open your own travel agency. If you're traveling with children, be sure to grab a copy of *Frommer's Washington, D.C. with Kids.*

Begin your search with the **Washington, D.C., Convention and Visitors Association,** 1212 New York Ave. NW, Suite 600, Washington, DC 20005

(☎ **202/789-7000**), or click onto their
Web site at **www.washington.org**.
Another good source is the **D.C.**
Committee to Promote Washington
(D.C. Government), 1212 New York Ave.
NW, Suite 200, Washington, DC 20005
(☎ **202/724-5644**).

Surfing the Web
For more on-line info, visit thefollowing:

➤ *Washington Post* Web site at
www.washingtonpost.com.

➤ Smithsonian Institution at
www.si.edu.

D.C. Dirt
Before Washington, D.C.,
became the nation's capital,
it was a swampland and
malaria-infested hard-luck
post in colonial times. The
more things change, the
more they stay the same.

➤ Washington Web (a site with links to more than 30 newspapers) at
www.washweb.net.

Putting Pen to Paper & Ear to the Receiver
Here are some other useful resources to contact while you're planning your
trip:

➤ **Washington, D.C., Reservations,** 1201 Wisconsin Ave. NW, Washington, DC 20007 (☎ **800/554-2220; www.dcaccommodations.com**).
This service offers free hotel advice and reservations at a great price.

➤ **Capitol Reservations,** 1730 Rhode Island Ave. NW, Washington, DC
20036 (☎ **800/847-4832**). Book your hotel and find out what type of
rooms are available by contacting this reservation service.

Hear Ye! Hear Ye!
Soon as you know you're coming, write or call your senator or representative to
request advance tickets for touring the **Capitol, Supreme Court, White**
House, FBI, and **Bureau of Engraving and Printing.** With a little help
from your friends in Congress you can bypass long waits in line. The earlier you
put in the request (even 6 months ahead), the better your chances. Since
ticket allotment is limited, there's no guarantee. Send your request to: Name
of congressional representative, U.S. House of Representatives, Washington, DC
20515; or Name of your senator, U.S. Senate, Washington, DC 20510. While
you're at it, don't forget to give the dates of your D.C. visit, and flattery might
get you somewhere.

3

➤ **Bed 'n' Breakfasts of Washington, D.C.,** P.O. Box 12011, Washington, DC 20005 (☎ **202/328-3510;** www.bnbaccom.com). Thinking of making your trip to Washington a romantic getaway? Bed 'n' Breakfasts will find the B&B that's right for you.

If you're planning on visiting Washington during the **National Cherry Blossom Festival** (which runs from late March into early April), write for a schedule of events to **National Cherry Blossom Festival,** P.O. Box 77312, Washington, DC 20013-7312, or call the hot line at ☎ **202/547-1500.**

For information on Metrorail (D.C.'s subway), write to the **Washington Metropolitan Area Transit Authority,** 600 5th St. NW, Washington, DC 20001 (☎ **202/637-7000**), and request the free *Metro Pocket Guide.*

When Should I Go?

There is never a *bad* time to visit Washington, although some times are better than others. Tourists pour in like Niagara Falls from mid-March to mid-June. Everyone and his uncle comes to see the cherry blossoms and Washington abloom in the spring. That means hotels and restaurants are more crowded and it takes a little longer to do some things. It also means that traffic can be worse than usual.

The HHH Factor—Heat, Humidity & Haze

Summer brings truckloads of tourists, along with stifling heat and humidity. Fortunately, all public buildings are air-conditioned. And, many museums and galleries have extended hours, eliminating "crush hour."

Summer visitors can find great deals at hotels. Because of the heat and lack of business travelers during the summer, hotels trip over each other with cost-saving packages.

But summertime doesn't bring Washington to a halt. Even locals, like myself, participate in a number of summer events, like free band concerts on the Washington Monument grounds and other sites. And we're often among the half-million or so who fill the Mall for the Fourth of July fireworks.

Fall—(Shhh!) The Best-Kept Secret

Although the heat and humidity can hang around for a while after Labor Day, fall is gorgeous, especially October, when the air is crisp, downtown is less crowded, and the leaves are changing color. With the crispness of the weather comes the crisp sound of dollar bills exchanging hands, as hotel prices spring back up.

D.C. Dirt

Besides its notoriety as the nation's capital, center of the Free World, and site of the annual Cherry Blossom Festival, Washington enjoys another, more dubious, distinction. Without a doubt, outside of Rome, it is the home of the world's worst drivers. There is a reason for this. "Native Washingtonian" is practically an oxymoron, since a large chunk of the population hails from other states, other countries, and maybe even other galaxies. Many learned to drive in Keokuk or Katmandu (or are learning on D.C.'s streets); visiting hordes are often lost ("Dear, we've just driven around Dupont Circle for the 15th time . . ."); and everyone, regardless of political persuasion, is in a hurry. So it's a jungle out there. Add a few drops of rain or dusting of snow and you have major gridlock. During rush hour—which, in truth, *is most* hours between 5am and 9pm—inclement weather can triple or quadruple commuting time.

A Winter Wonderland

Winter means fewer tourists, and hotel rates (theoretically at least) are lower than in spring or fall. Decked out for the holidays, the city is lovely. Sometimes a light frosting of snow adds glitter to the scene. (But be advised, the white stuff can be heavier than "light.") One thing you need to know: *No one in this city knows how to drive in the snow.* Thank goodness for Metro.

Average Monthly Temperatures

	Jan	Feb	Mar	Apr	May	June	July	Aug	Sept	Oct	Nov	Dec
Avg. High (°F)	45	44	53	64	75	83	87	84	78	68	55	45
Avg. Low (°F)	27	28	35	44	55	63	68	66	60	48	38	30

Average Monthly Rain and Snowfall

	Jan	Feb	Mar	Apr	May	June	July	Aug	Sept	Oct	Nov	Dec
Rain (in.)	2.76	2.62	3.46	2.93	3.48	3.35	3.88	4.4	3.22	2.9	2.82	3.18
Snow (in.)	5	5	2	0	0	0	0	0	0	0	1	3

When Shouldn't I Go?

Remember, if it's a national holiday, the nation's capital will probably celebrate it. On the following legal national holidays, banks, government offices, and post offices are closed. Subways (Metrorail) and buses (Metrobus) operate less frequently, usually on a Saturday or Sunday schedule (☎ 202/

5

637-7000). Museums, stores, and restaurants vary widely in their open/closed policy. To avoid disappointment, call before you go.

National Holidays

➤ **New Year's Day:** January 1

➤ **Martin Luther King Jr.'s Birthday:** Third Monday in January

➤ **Presidents' Day:** Third Monday in February

➤ **Memorial Day:** Last Monday in May

➤ **Independence Day:** July 4

➤ **Labor Day:** First Monday in September

➤ **Columbus Day:** Second Monday in October

➤ **Election Day:** In election years (2000, 2004, etc.), the Tuesday following the first Monday in November is a legal holiday.

➤ **Veterans' Day/Armistice Day:** November 11

➤ **Thanksgiving Day:** Last Thursday in November

➤ **Christmas Day:** December 25

Washington, D.C. Calendar of Events

Go ahead. Consider your vacation schedule. Figure out if you'll have an extra day or two before or after a business conference. Find out the dates of the kids' school breaks. See what's closed or open on which holidays. Deal with factors over which you have no control. After you've done all that—throw a special event or two into the mix to clinch the ideal time for your visit.

Information about current and upcoming events appears in the "Weekend" section of the *Washington Post* every Friday. Some changes and cancellations are inevitable, so a simple phone call can prevent disappointment. Admission to the following events is free unless otherwise noted.

January

➤ **Martin Luther King Jr.'s Birthday** (☎ 202/619-7222). King's birthday is celebrated the third Monday in January with speeches, musical performances, and choral presentations citywide and a wreath-laying ceremony at the Lincoln Memorial, sight of King's "I have a dream" speech. The **Martin Luther King Memorial Library** (☎ 202/727-1186) hosts a variety of events to celebrate King's life.

➤ **Robert E. Lee's Birthday Bash** (☎ 703/557-0613). The birthday of the commander of the Confederate Army is observed January 19 at Arlington House in Arlington National Cemetery with 19th-century music, food, and exhibits of Lee memorabilia.

➤ **Inauguration Day.** On January 20 of every fourth year, the president is sworn in at the West Front of the Capitol. The next presidential inauguration will be January 20, 2001. A colorful (and endless) parade follows the swearing-in from the Capitol to the White House along Pennsylvania Avenue.

February

➤ **Black History Month** (☎ 202/357-2700). The contributions of African-Americans are noted at museums, libraries, and recreation centers with special exhibits, events, and performances. Contact the **Martin Luther King Library** (☎ 202/727-1186) for information about additional activities.

➤ **Abraham Lincoln's Birthday** (☎ 202/619-7222). A wreath-laying ceremony and reading of the Gettysburg Address mark our 16th president's natal day at the Lincoln Memorial on February 12.

➤ **George Washington's Birthday** (☎ 202/783-6832). Knee britches, white stockings, and powdered wigs are in order February 22 at the Washington Monument.

March

➤ **Washington Flower & Garden Show** (☎ 202/789-1600). Herald spring—and not a moment too soon—at the Washington Convention Center, 9th and H streets NW. You'll have to pay to sniff the flowers.

➤ **St. Patrick's Day Parade** (☎ 202/637-2474). On the Sunday closest to St. Paddy's Day, it's top o' the mornin' as an emerald green parade winds down Constitution Avenue, from 7th to 17th streets NW, with floats, bagpipes, bands, and dancers.

➤ **Ringling Bros. and Barnum & Bailey Circus** (☎ 703/448-4000). The greatest show on earth pitches its tent at the D.C. Armory with lions and tigers and bears, oh my! The morning before the circus opens, you can watch the animals shuffle through city streets from the circus train to the Armory. Usually in late March and early April.

➤ **Smithsonian Kite Festival** (☎ 202/357-2700). Kite lovers breeze over to the Washington Monument grounds for this annual event where prizes are awarded for homemade creations. Pray for wind. Usually the last weekend in March.

April

➤ **National Cherry Blossom Festival** (☎ 202/619-7222). As long as an ill-timed freeze hasn't put the cabosh on the blossoms, the sight around the Tidal Basin is breathtaking.

A parade—with floats of waving princesses from the 50 states, celebrity guests, and concerts—caps the festivities on the final Sunday of the 2-week festival. In past years grandstand seats were $12. For parade

information, call the D.C. Downtown Jaycees (☎ 202/728-1137).
Otherwise, check local newspapers for activities, scattered throughout
the festival like so many falling cherry blossoms.

When all is said and done, however, the main draw remains the trees
themselves. Crowds of strolling visitors throng the Tidal Basin from
dawn until well after dark, when huge floodlights illuminate the trees.
For specific cherry blossom events, check the *Washington Post* or call
☎ 202/789-7038 or 202/547-1500. Blossom info buds on the Internet
at the National Park Service Web site at **www.nps.gov**.

➤ **White House Easter Egg Roll** (☎ 202/456-7041). Kids 8 and
under get egg-cited over the annual Easter Monday roll on the South
Lawn of the White House. Line up early at the southeast gate. Visitors
scramble for tickets beginning about 7am at the Visitor Pavilion on the
Ellipse (the park area south of the White House). Distribution continues until all tickets are gone. It's a mob scene. No yolk.

➤ **Thomas Jefferson's Birthday** (☎ 202/619-7222). On April 13,
Jefferson groupies gather at the memorial honoring the third U.S. president with military drills and a wreath-laying ceremony.

➤ **White House Garden Tour** (☎ 202/456-7041). It's worth the line
to tour the Rose Garden and the Children's Garden, with its bronze
impressions of the hands and feet of White House offspring. Usually
the first weekend of April.

➤ **Smithsonian Craft Show** (☎ 202/357-2700). This glorious 4-day
juried show of fine crafts features 100 exhibitors at the National
Building Museum, 401 F St. (Metro: Judiciary Square). Admission is
required to drool and buy. Usually mid-April.

➤ **William Shakespeare's Birthday** (☎ 202/544-7077). It's "Happy
Birthday to Will" on the Saturday closest to the Bard's April 26 birthday
at the Folger Shakespeare Library, 201 E. Capitol St. SE, with
Elizabethan music, theater, children's events, and food.

May

➤ **Georgetown Garden Tour** (☎ 202/333-6896). Several private gardens in one of Washington's classiest neighborhoods are open to the
public, for a fee, on the second Saturday of May. The fee includes light
refreshments and a bus tour.

➤ **National Cathedral Flower Mart** (☎ 202/537-6200). The first
Friday and Saturday of the month, flowers and plants, along with
entertainment and food, blossom forth on the verdant grounds of the
National Cathedral, Wisconsin and Massachusetts avenues NW. There's
also an extensive selection of herbs for sale.

➤ **Memorial Day** (☎ 202/685-2851). A wreath-laying ceremony and
military music take place at the Tomb of the Unknowns in Arlington
National Cemetery. "Borrow" a blanket on the Sunday of Memorial Day

weekend, when the **National Symphony** (☎ 202/416-8100) sere-
nades an audience of thousands on the West Lawn of the Capitol.

June
➤ **Smithsonian Festival of American Folklife** (☎ 202/357-2700).
Tourists and locals flood the Mall (from late June through July 4) to
enjoy traditional American music, crafts, and ethnic foods reflecting
our nation's rich folk heritage.

July
➤ **Independence Day Celebration** (☎ 202/619-7222). Is there a
more fitting place to celebrate the nation's birthday? I don't think so. A
12:30pm parade along Constitution Avenue, from 7th to 17th streets
NW, kicks off the day's events that climax with a fabulous fireworks
extravaganza on the Mall.

August
➤ **U.S. Army Band's 1812 Overture** (☎ 202/619-7222). The Salute
Gun Platoon of the 3rd U.S. Infantry hammers out the noisy finale of
this patriotic concert by the U.S. Army Band at the Sylvan Theatre on
the Washington Monument grounds.

September
➤ **Labor Day Concert** (☎ 202/619-7222). On the first Monday of
September, the National Symphony bids adieu to summer, even though
it's usually hot as Hell, with a concert on the West Lawn of the Capitol.

➤ **National Frisbee Festival** (☎ 301/645-5043). It's a "ruff" scene
when disk-catching top dogs and their world-class Frisbee masters fill
the Washington Monument grounds Labor Day weekend.

➤ **Kennedy Center Open House Arts Festival** (☎ 800/444-1324 or
202/467-4600). Sometime in early to mid-September, local and national
talents entertain inside and outside
the Ken Cen in this annual salute to
the performing arts. Plan on a wait
for admittance to the inside events.

October
➤ **Greek Fall Festival and
Christmas Bazaar** (☎ 202/
333-4730). Stuff yourself with sou-
vlaki and binge on baklava while
enjoying Greek music, dancing, and
crafts—and get a jump on holiday
shopping—at Saint Sophia Cathedral,
36th Street and Massachusetts
Avenue NW.

D.C. Dirt

In *Money* magazine's 1998
rankings of the "Best Places
to Live in America," the
Washington metropolitan
area took top honors as
No. 1 in the Northeast.
Rankings are based on 37
quality-of-life factors.

➤ **U.S. Navy Birthday Concert** (☎ 202/433-6090). It's dress blues only (denim for you) at the U.S. Navy Band's annual birthday concert held the second Monday in October at the Kennedy Center. The Navy is 224 years old in '99. Did you remember to send a card? Tickets are free, but you need to send away for them by mailing a self-addressed, stamped envelope (in early September) to Navy Birthday Tickets, U.S. Navy Band, Building 105, Washington Navy Yard, Washington, DC 20374-5054.

➤ **White House Fall Garden Tour** (☎ 202/456-7041). One weekend (all day Saturday, Sunday afternoon only in mid-October) the public can view the Rose Garden, South Lawn, and colorful chrysanthemum beds, as well as the White House's public rooms, while a military band plays something suitably stirring. No tickets are required; line up at the Southeast Gate at E Street and East Executive Avenue.

➤ **Taste of D.C. Festival** (☎ 202/724-5430). Food from 50 diverse D.C. restaurants is yours for the tasting on Pennsylvania Avenue NW, between 9th and 14th streets. The tasting takes place Saturday through Monday of Columbus Day weekend, which is the second weekend of October. There's live entertainment too. Food is modestly priced. (I wish I had the antacid concession.)

➤ **Theodore Roosevelt's Birthday** (☎ 703/285-2225). The old rough rider's birthday is celebrated with nature programs and island tours on the Saturday closest to the actual birth date (October 27, 1858). The island is off the northbound lanes of the G. W. Parkway, north of Roosevelt Bridge.

➤ **Marine Corps Marathon** (☎ 800/RUN-USMC). About 16,000 runners take part in the annual 26-mile marathon on the fourth Sunday of the month. The race starts at the Iwo Jima statue of the Marine Corps Memorial in Arlington National Cemetery.

November

➤ **Veterans' Day Ceremonies** (☎ 202/619-7222). An appropriately solemn ceremony honoring the nation's war dead takes place November 11 at Arlington Cemetery's Memorial Amphitheater. The president or another high-ranking official lays a wreath at the Tomb of the Unknowns.

December

➤ **National Christmas Tree Lighting and Pageant of Peace** (☎ 202/619-7222). Early in the month, the president or some other First-Family member throws the switch, lighting the nation's blue spruce Christmas tree and 57 Scotch pine sibs (representing the 50 states, the District of Columbia, and the six U.S. territories) and heralding the 3-week Pageant of Peace. The festivities take place on the Ellipse, behind the White House. Seasonal music is performed most evenings through December from 6 to 9pm.

➤ **Kennedy Center Holiday Celebrations** (☎ 202/467-4600).
Seasonal festivities include a Messiah sing-along, Hanukkah festival,
Christmas Eve and New Year's Eve programs, and concerts by local chil-
dren's choruses. Many events are free.

➤ **White House Christmas Candlelight Tours** (☎ 202/208-1631).
Candlelight tours of the First Family's Christmas decorations are usually
held three post-Christmas evenings from 5 to 7pm. If you don't want
to be left out in the cold, arrive well before 7pm.

➤ **Family Hanukkah Celebration** (☎ 202/518-9400). The Jewish
Community Center, 1529 16th St. NW, hosts a Festival of Lights party
with storytelling, dreidel games, music, and puppet shows. You can't
spin your dreidel until you pay admission.

D.C. Dirt

Pierre Charles L'Enfant, who planned the federal city (and enjoyed a rep as an
ornery, cantankerous son-of-a-gun), died penniless and was buried in a pau-
per's grave in 1825. In 1909, he finally overcame his Rodney Dangerfield status
and got respect. His remains were moved to Arlington National Cemetery,
where his grave has a commanding view of the city he designed. (Too bad he
can't enjoy it.)

We Are Family: Traveling with Your Kids

It's safe to say that Washington is one of the most kid-friendly cities in the
world. Hotels knock themselves out to welcome families, seducing them with
breaks on rooms and food and special activities. In recent years the museums
have moved from a "don't touch" to a hands-on attitude, targeting exhibit
areas to children, and adding more interactive displays and family workshops. At most museums kids can pick up an activity booklet to enhance
their visit.

If your youngsters go ballistic when they're cooped up for too long (and why
should we expect them to be any different from us?), downsize museum
time, or at least break up the brain drain with physical activity. Head for the
zoo, rent a pedal boat on the Tidal Basin, fly a kite or ride the carousel on
the Mall. And think long and hard about staying in a hotel with a pool.

The Family That Plans Together . . .

Get your kids involved in the planning process. Visit the local library or
bookstore for information on Washington. Heck, turn on the news or hand

them a newspaper for information (not always savory) on the nation's capital. Rent a movie that is set in the city (*All the President's Men, No Way Out, Dave,* or *Suspect*) or a travelogue from your local video store. Buy a few jigsaw puzzles of Washington monuments so that your children are familiar with the buildings before they arrive. An excellent resource for D.C. information is **Travel Books and Language Center,** 4437 Wisconsin Ave. NW (☎ **800/ 220-2665** or 202/237-1322). Call for one of their catalogs.

Let your kids look over the brochures and help plan each day's activities. If they've outgrown diapers, they can surf the Web sites listed earlier in this chapter. For a guidebook all about traveling to Washington with children, look for *Frommer's Washington, D.C. with Kids.*

Arriving & Finding Transportation
Sometimes children are even less patient and more fidgety than their parents. If you arrive at National Airport or Union Station and are not too bogged down with luggage, take the Metro, the most efficient way to get around. If you're laden with luggage, strollers, and cribs, take a cab. It may take you longer to reach your hotel in D.C. traffic, but at least you'll have door-to-door service. If you arrive at Dulles or BWI airport and it's long past their bedtime, you may want to take a cab rather than wait for the bus or van. See chapter 8 for more information on getting into the city from the airports.

Finding a Babysitter
If you're looking forward to spending every second with the kids, no problem, mon. You won't need a baby-sitter. If you want to sneak away for a cocktail or cozy dinner for two, you'll need a sitter. Inquire when you make your hotel reservation. Otherwise, ask the concierge. Many hotels provide reliable, bonded sitters.

Or try **White House Nannies** (☎ **301/652-8088**), which has been providing sitters in the area since 1985. "Caregivers" are carefully screened and have first aid and CPR training. For this, a quiet evening out without the rugrats will cost you $8 to $12 per hour, depending on the caregiver's experience and number of children. Oh yes, there's also a 4-hour minimum and a one-time $25 booking fee (ouch!).

Travel Advice for the Senior Set
People over the age of 60 are traveling more than ever before. And why not? Being a senior citizen entitles you to some terrific travel bargains. If you're over 50 and not a member of **AARP (American Association of Retired Persons),** 601 E St. NW, Washington, DC 20049 (☎ **202/434-AARP**), do yourself a favor and join. You'll get discounts on car rentals and hotels.

Mature Outlook, P.O. Box 9390, Des Moines, IA 50306-9519 (☎ **800/ 336-6330;** fax 847/286-5024), is a similar organization, offering discounts on car rentals and hotel stays at many Holiday Inns, Howard Johnsons, and Best Westerns. The $20 annual membership fee also gets you $100 in Sears coupons and a bimonthly magazine. Membership is open to all Sears customers 18 and over, but the organization's primary focus is on the 50-and-over market.

In addition, most of the major domestic airlines, including American, United, Continental, US Airways, and TWA, offer discount programs for senior travelers—be sure to ask whenever you book a flight. In Washington, people over the age of 60 usually get reduced admission at theaters, museums, and other attractions, and they can often get discount fares on public transportation. Carrying identification with proof of age can pay off in all these situations.

The Mature Traveler, a monthly 12-page newsletter on senior citizen travel, is a valuable resource. It is available by subscription ($30 a year) from GEM Publishing Group, Box 50400, Reno, NV 89513-0400. GEM also publishes *The Book of Deals,* a collection of more than 1,000 senior discounts on airlines, lodging, tours, and attractions around the country; it's available for $9.95 by calling ☎ **800/460-6676.** Another helpful telephone number is ☎ 617/350-7500; fax 617/350-6206.

Balancing the Budget

Amtrak (☎ **800/USA-RAIL**) offers a 15 % discount on the full, one-way coach fare (with certain travel restrictions) to people 62 and over. **Greyhound** (☎ **800/231-2222**) gives a 10 percent discount to travelers who are 62 or older.

Grand Circle Travel is one of hundreds of travel agencies specializing in vacations for seniors. But beware: Many of them are of the tour bus variety, with free trips thrown in for those who organize groups of 20 or more. Seniors seeking more independent travel should probably consult a regular travel agent. **SAGA International Holidays,** 222 Berkeley St., Boston, MA 02116 (☎ **800/343-0273**), offers inclusive tours and cruises for those 50 and older.

Elderhostel is a national organization that offers low-cost educational travel programs for people 55 or older. Programs to Washington include week-long residential programs that focus on government and American history, art, and literature. Costs average around $460 per person, including meals, room, and classes. For information, call ☎ **410/830-3437.**

Advice for Travelers with Disabilities

Washington is a dream city for those with special accessibility needs. Every subway station has an elevator. Floor-level lights blink in anticipation of arriving trains for the hearing impaired. Bells chime when the doors are about to open or close, and a bumpy rubber guard has been installed at the edge of the platform, to alert the visually impaired. Columns feature Braille lettering for station identification. The TDD number for Metro information is ☎ **202/628-8973.**

Regular **Tourmobile** trams are accessible to visitors with disabilities. The company also offers special vans for immobile travelers, complete with wheelchair lifts. Call ☎ **202/554-5100** for more information.

Building Accessibility

All public buildings, particularly the Smithsonian Institution's museums, are accessible. Many of the films shown at such facilities as Air and Space have narrated descriptive tapes provided by the Washington Ear, and most, if not all, of the live theaters in town have infrared headsets for those who have vision or hearing impairments. Many live productions also feature at least one performance that is signed. Occasionally, one comes across a slight inconvenience—for example, the wheelchair-accessible entrance to the Archives is located on the Pennsylvania Avenue side, not the Constitution Avenue side. However, if you're taking the subway and getting off at the Archives–Navy Memorial station, then the Archives is right across the street. Some of the older galleries, particularly around Dupont Circle, are less wheelchair accessible than newer ones, but call ahead and they'll work to accommodate you.

Travel Organizations

Travelers with disabilities should consider ordering *A World of Options*. This 658-page book of resources for disabled travelers covers everything from biking trips to scuba outfitters. It costs $45 and is available from **Mobility International USA,** P.O. Box 10767, Eugene, OR 97440 (☎ **541/343-1284** voice and TDD; www.miusa.org). For more personal assistance, call the **Travel Information Service** at ☎ **215/456-9603** or 215/456-9602 (for TTY).

Many of the major car-rental companies now offer hand-controlled cars for disabled drivers. Avis can provide such a vehicle at any of its locations in the United States with 48-hour advance notice; Hertz requires between 24 and 72 hours advance reservation at most of its locations. **Wheelchair Getaways** (☎ **800/873-4973;** www.blvd.com/wg.htm) rents specialized vans with wheelchair lifts and other features for the disabled in more than 100 cities across the United States.

Travelers with disabilities may also want to consider joining a tour that caters specifically to them. One of the best operators is **Flying Wheels Travel,** 143 West Bridge (P.O. Box 382), Owatonna, MN 55060 (☎ **800/535-6790**). They offer various escorted tours and cruises, as well as private tours in minivans with lifts. Another good company is **FEDCAP Rehabilitation Services,** 211 W. 14th St., New York, NY 10011. Call ☎ **212/727-4200** or fax 212/721-4374 for information about membership and summer tours.

Vision-impaired travelers should contact the **American Foundation for the Blind,** 11 Penn Plaza, Suite 300, New York, NY 10001 (☎ **800/ 232-5463**), for information on traveling with seeing-eye dogs.

Advice for Gay and Lesbian Travelers

There's a fairly large and active gay and lesbian population in the Washington area (somewhat focused around the Dupont Circle area), with plenty of activities and resources. The first place to start is with the newspaper the *Washington Blade,* which also has a Web presence at **www.washblade.com**. It has listings of gay and lesbian activities (religious and spirituality, sports, community arts and entertainment, politics, horoscope, employment, vacations, bar guide, etc.) and news of interest to the community. Another good Web site is **www.gayscape.com**. The Web site **www.omegadc.com** provides information about gay nightclubs.

Lambda Rising Book Store, 1625 Connecticut Ave. NW (☎ 202/ 462-6969), has a vast selection of literature and is known for its camaraderie and sense of community. There's an extensive selection of gay and lesbian travel guides as well as gay-themed T-shirts, jewelry, and gifts. **Lammas,** a women's bookstore at 1607 17th St. NW (☎ 202/775-8218), is another source of information, as well as music and gifts. For support group information, contact the D.C. (and national) office of **PFLAG,** 1101 14th St. NW, Suite 1030, Washington, DC 20005 (☎ 202/638-4200).

Chapter 2

Money Matters

> **In This Chapter**
>
> ➤ Money: How much and what kind?
>
> ➤ Budgeting your trip
>
> ➤ Pinching pennies

The government may shut down when it's trying to balance the budget, but that doesn't mean you should too. Visitors who are debating where to spend and where to cut will be happy to know that most of the best sights in Washington are free. Even when there's a once-in-a-lifetime exhibit, you might be required to reserve a timed-entry tickets, but there won't be a charge. Some exceptions are the movies at the Smithsonian's Air and Space Museum, the service charge for the free reserved tickets to the United States Holocaust Memorial Museum, admission to the National Aquarium at the Department of Commerce, and private galleries (the Phillips Collection, for example).

The buck sure doesn't stop here. In fact, in this chapter I'll show you how to make the buck and the credit cards and traveler's checks go farther than you ever thought they could go.

Should I Carry Traveler's Checks?

Traveler's checks are something of an anachronism from the days when people used to write personal checks all the time instead of going to the ATM. In those days, travelers could not be sure of finding a place that would cash a check for them on vacation. Because they could be replaced if lost or stolen, traveler's checks were a sound alternative to filling your wallet with cash at the beginning of a trip.

These days, however, traveler's checks are less necessary because most cities have 24-hour ATMs linked to a national network that most likely includes your bank at home. **Cirrus** (☎ **800/424-7787** or 800/4CIRRUS) and **Plus** (☎ **800/843-7587**) are the two most popular networks; check the back of your ATM card to see which network your bank belongs to. The 800 numbers will give you specific locations of ATMs where you can withdraw money while on vacation. You should withdraw only as much cash as you need every few days and avoid the insecurity of carrying around a huge wad of cash.

Still, if you feel you need traveler's checks and don't mind the hassle of showing identification every time you want to cash a check, you can get them at almost any bank. **American Express** offers checks in denominations of $10, $20, $50, $100, $500, and $1,000. You'll pay a service charge ranging from 1% to 4%, though AAA members can obtain checks without a fee at most AAA offices. The local AAA in Washington is located at 701 15th St. NW (☎ **202/331-3000**).

If you'd like to buy or cash in some traveler's checks while in Washington, head to one of the two American Express travel office locations. One is located at 1150 Connecticut Ave. NW (☎ **202/457-1300**). The other is at Mazza Gallerie, 5300 Wisconsin Ave. NW (☎ **202/362-4000**). You can also get American Express traveler's checks over the phone by calling ☎ **800/221-7282**; Amex gold and platinum cardholders who call this number are exempt from the 1% fee.

Citibank offers **Citibank Visa** traveler's checks at Citibank locations across the country and at several other banks. To find the Citibank closest to you, call ☎ **800/541-8882.** The service charge ranges from 1.5% to 2%; checks come in denominations of $20, $50, $100, $500, and $1,000. For information on non-Citibank **Visa** traveler's checks, call ☎ **800/732-1322.** **MasterCard** also offers traveler's checks. Call ☎ **800/223-9920** for a location near you.

The Green Stuff

Some people like to travel with a wad of green stuff because it makes them feel secure. Frankly, I think it's unnecessary and a liability. Why make the pickpockets' job easier? ATM machines are widely available, and if you have plastic, there's no need to bulge your pockets with bills. Unless you're the sort who likes to pay for everything with cash, $200 for incidentals and emergencies should do it.

ATM Machines

ATM machines are nearly ubiquitous, but just to make sure you can find one, go to the Visa (**www.visa.com**) or the MasterCard/Cirrus (**www.mastercard.com**) Web sites for the location of the nearest machine. If the spirit moves you, call Cirrus (☎ **800/424-7787**) and Plus (☎ **800/843-7587**) for specific ATM locations where you can withdraw your money. Smaller banks may charge for the service, but a warning message should let you know before you complete the transaction, so you can bail out.

17

Hear Ye! Hear Ye!

Need some cash fast? In Washington, bank hours generally run from 9am to 2pm weekdays and from 9am to noon on Saturday. Some banks have Friday evening hours as well. If you're in a real bind, hotels will usually cash guests' personal checks.

Plastic Money

You can save yourself hassle (and bulging pockets) by using credit cards rather than cash or traveler's checks in most hotels, restaurants, and retail stores. You'll need a credit card or debit card if you want to rent a car, make a bank withdrawal, or tap an ATM.

You can also get **cash advances** off your credit cards at any bank (though you'll start paying interest on the advance the moment you receive the cash, and you won't receive frequent-flyer miles on an airline credit card). At most banks, you don't even need to go to a teller; you can get a cash advance at the ATM if you know your PIN (personal identification number). If you've forgotten your PIN number or didn't even know you had one, call the phone number on the back of your credit card and ask the bank to send it to you. It usually takes 5 to 7 business days, though some banks will do it over the phone if you give them your mother's maiden name or some other identification.

Stop, Thief! (What to Do If Your Money Gets Stolen)

Almost every credit-card company has an emergency 800 number you can call if your wallet or purse is stolen. You may be able to receive a wired cash advance off your credit card immediately. In many places, credit-card companies will send you an emergency credit card in a day or two. The issuing bank's 800 number is usually on the back of the credit card. (But that doesn't help you much if the card was stolen, does it? So just call information at ☎ **800/555-1212** to find out the number.)

Balancing the Budget

If you opt to carry traveler's checks, be sure to keep a record of their serial numbers (or the receipts) so that in an emergency you can track those checks down, cancel them out, and get a refund.

Emergency Numbers

➤ **Citicorp Visa's** U.S. emergency number is ☎ **800/645-6556.**

➤ **American Express** cardholders and traveler's check holders should call ☎ **800/221-7282** for all money emergencies.

➤ **MasterCard** holders should call ☎ **800/307-7309.**

Odds are that if your wallet is gone, you've seen the last of it, and the police aren't likely to recover it for you. However, after you realize that it's gone and you cancel your credit cards, it is still worth a call to inform the police. You may need the police report number for credit card or insurance purposes later.

Balancing the Budget

Here are some smart money tips. Free.

➤ Use indoor ATM machines whenever possible. You're a sitting duck on the street and someone is more apt to grab your cash.

➤ Don't leave cash and valuables in your hotel room. Some hotels have in-room safes or safety deposit boxes (ask at the front desk). It makes sense to stash your spare cash, family jewels, and loose change here.

➤ To cut down on cash purchases and keep your credit-card bills to a minimum, debit your account directly.

What's This Sucker Gonna Cost?

Although the best sights in Washington are free, hotels and restaurants are gonna cost ya.

Lodging

A suite usually occupied by heads of state and rock stars at a grand hotel will cost you megabucks. If you can take advantage of special packages and discounts at a chain or small, independent hotel, you'll be able to budget and monitor the cash flow. In chapter 5 you'll find a few hotels for under $100 a night. In the $125 to $150 range, the choices are much greater. If you're going to shell out a lot of money for lodging, it might be wise to look for a hotel with a kitchenette so that you can stock the refrigerator and save on snacks and meals.

Restaurants

While dining options run the gamut from fast food to hoity-toity, there are scores of good, inexpensive restaurants to choose from. If you dine early and opt for the early-bird specials or fixed-price deals, or eat your main meal at lunch when prices are lower, you can save handsomely. Leave room for chapter 9, where I give you the lowdown on some of the best bargains in town.

Transportation

Not even the most confirmed masochist uses a car for sightseeing in Washington. Traffic is thick, and the one-way streets and circles are daunting. Street parking is at a premium and garages and lots charge a pound of flesh. If you arrive in the family buggy, garage it for the duration of your stay. (Be sure to ask about parking rates when you make a reservation.) Transportation via the Metro is relatively inexpensive. Figure $3 to $5 per day per person, and use the Metro during non-peak times to save. If you're a walker, you can put mileage on your feet instead of your wallet.

Attractions

Aside from some private galleries and museums, admission is free to most attractions, including *all* Smithsonian museums.

Shopping

This is a gray area when budgeting. Some people don't feel like they've been away if they haven't filled an extra suitcase with new purchases. If you practice self-restraint, however, and don't bow to the desire to outfit your entire neighborhood in souvenir T-shirts at $15 a pop, you won't have a problem.

Entertainment

What you spend on entertainment is another big variable when apportioning your travel dollar. If you want to catch a show, concert, or major dance performance, you will pay $25 to $60 for a seat. You can have a good time clutching an ice-cream cone and people-watching in Georgetown for under $5 per person.

Balancing the Budget

Look at all that money you're saving by visiting free museums. But beware! When it comes time to visit some privately run galleries and museums, you'll probably be asked for a contribution. No one will hit you over the head for it, but in all fairness 25¢ doesn't cut it when a suggested contribution is sought. Let your generous side show through and think of all the money you're saving by not paying admission at the other museums.

At the end of the chapter you'll find a worksheet to help you budget your trip.

What Things Cost in Washington, D.C.

Taxi from Reagan National Airport to a downtown hotel	$13.00–$14.00
Metro from Reagan National Airport to downtown	$1.10 (nonrush hour)–$1.35 (rush hour)
Taxi from Dulles Airport (Va.) to downtown	$40.00–$45.00
Super Shuttle from BWI to 1517 K St. NW	$17.00
Local telephone call	35¢
Metro ride	$1.10–$3.25
Taxi	$4.00 (within same zone) and up
Movie ticket (adult)	$4.75 (matinee before 6pm)–$7.50 (after 6pm)
Movie ticket (child)	$4.50
Admission to all Smithsonian museums	Free
Glass of wine	$4.00–$8.00
Medium-sized cup of coffee at Starbucks	$1.60
Medium-sized soft drink at McDonald's	$1.31
Medium-sized soft drink at Morton's of Chicago (Expensive)	$1.75
Roll of 100 film, 36 exposures	$6.50

Tipping

Tipping is part of the American way of life, on the principle that you must expect to pay for any service you get. Here are some rules of thumb:

➤ Bartenders: 10% to 15%

➤ Bellhops: $1 a bag

➤ Cab drivers: 15% of the fare

➤ Cafeterias, fast-food restaurants: no tip

➤ Chambermaids: $1 a day

➤ Checkroom attendants (restaurants, theaters): $1 per garment

➤ Doormen (if the doorman hails a taxi for you): $1

➤ Parking-lot attendants: $1

➤ Redcaps/porters (airport and railroad station): $1 per piece

What Do Those Dollar Signs Mean?

Throughout the book you'll see one or more dollar sign symbols attached to items, especially in the hotel and restaurant listings. These are not here for decoration. They are keyed to a scale at the start of the chapter so that you

Balancing the Budget

Be prepared to pay the following D.C. taxes:

Sales tax	5.75%
Restaurant	10%
Hotel	14.5%

can tell at a glance under what price bracket a particular item falls. For example, a restaurant prefaced by $$ will cost between $15 and $25; and one marked $$$$ will cost more than $50.

What If I'm Worried I Can't Afford It?

Are you afraid that you might have to make a risky side trip to the Treasury Department to help finance your trip? Not to worry! Stick with the free guided tours and head over to the budget worksheet at the end of this chapter. If the numbers are too high, think about where you can trim some fat.

There are lots of ways to cut down on costs. The Balancing the Budget boxes scattered throughout this book offer tips on trimming your budget. In the meantime, here are some ways to save money in the capital city.

➤ **Go in the off-season.** Winter is the least expensive season to travel to Washington. However, you can also find some good deals in summer because Congress is on break and business travelers are sparse. Also remember that hotel rates drop on the weekends.

➤ **Travel on off-days of the week.** Airfares vary depending on the day of the week. If you can travel on a Tuesday, Wednesday, or Thursday, you may find cheaper flights to your destination. When you inquire about airfares, ask if you can obtain a cheaper rate by flying on a different day. Staying over on a Saturday night could cut airfares by more than half.

➤ **Try a package tour.** For many destinations, you can book airfare, hotel, ground transportation, and even some sightseeing just by making one call to a travel agent or packager, for a lot less than if you tried to put the trip together yourself. (See the section on package tours in chapter 3 for specific suggestions of companies to call.)

➤ **Reserve a hotel room with a kitchen and eat in.** It may not feel as much like a vacation if you have to do your own cooking and dishes, but you'll save a lot of money by not eating in restaurants three times a day. Even if you only make breakfast and an occasional bag lunch in the kitchen, you'll still save in the long run. And you'll never be shocked by a hefty room service bill.

➤ **Always ask for discount rates.** Membership in AAA, frequent-flyer plans, trade unions, AARP, or other groups may qualify you for discounted rates on car rentals, plane tickets, hotel rooms, even meals.

Ask about everything (corporate rates, family rates, weekend rates) and don't give up easily; you could be pleasantly surprised.

➤ **Ask if your kids can stay in your room with you.** A room with two double beds usually doesn't cost any more than one with a queen-sized bed. And many hotels won't charge you the additional person rate if the additional person is pint-sized and related to you. Even if you have to pay $10 or $15 for a rollaway bed, you'll save hundreds by not taking two rooms.

➤ **Try expensive restaurants at lunch instead of dinner.** Lunch tabs are usually a fraction of what dinner would cost at most top restaurants, and the menu often boasts many of the same specialties.

➤ **Get out of town.** You'll find some bargain accommodations if you're willing to drive a little farther or ride the Metro a little longer. Outer areas such as Chevy Chase, Bethesda, Greenbelt, and Lanham in Maryland, and Arlington and Alexandria in Virginia, are connected to the Metro. You can start by calling the hotel chains such as **Holiday Inn** (☎ **800/HOLIDAY**), **Econo Lodges** (☎ **800/55-ECONO**), or **Comfort Inn** (☎ **800/228-5150**) to see what's available in these towns. Be sure to ask the distance of the closest Metro station. If not within walking distance, ask if the hotel provides complimentary shuttle service; or head to the box "Hotel Bargains" in chapter 6, which lists specific budget hotels that are outside the city but close to the Metro.

➤ **Walk a lot.** A good pair of walking shoes can save you a lot of money in taxis and other local transportation. And as a bonus, you'll get to know the city more intimately.

➤ **Use the Metro.** The Metro system in Washington is safe, clean, convenient, and, oh yeah, cheap. You can buy a **One Day Pass** for $5, which allows you to ride all you want from 9:30am to closing, which is midnight (or all day long on weekends and holidays).

➤ **Skip the souvenirs.** Your photographs and your memories should be the best mementos of your trip. If you're worried about money, you can do without the T-shirts and Washington Monument key chains.

Convenience Costs

Show up at a popular restaurant without a reservation, an hour before a show, and you're a captive audience. Maybe you'll go across the street and, because you're starving and pressed for time, spend double for dinner. Get my drift? Spontaneity has its place in any vacation, but some things require planning, especially if you want to stick to your budget.

Here are some more tips to keep your budget on track:

➤ Eat a big breakfast late morning and get a snack midafternoon to tide you over until dinner.

➤ Skip sit-down lunches and buy street food. A hot dog with the works, small bag of potato chips, and can of soda from one of the vendors on the Mall will set you back $3 or less. Hey, it won't satisfy the major food group requirements, but it will fill you up. Or eat your main meal midday and have a light bite for dinner.

➤ Bypass the expensive "in" places in favor of small local restaurants like the Brickskeller near Dupont Circle or Sholl's cafeteria downtown (see chapter 10). For a quick, inexpensive lunch, you could also try the Smithsonian Museum cafeterias, and the food courts at the Old Post Office Pavilion, Shops at National Place, and Union Station.

➤ Always ask "Do you have anything for less?" when making a hotel reservation.

➤ Don't drink in hotel bars. For the price of a glass of wine and tip, you can buy an inexpensive bottle in a liquor store near your hotel.

➤ With kids, pick up a pizza or have one delivered for dinner and watch a movie.

➤ Watch your watch. The early-bird dinner menu may end at 6:30, the second you realize you're hungry.

➤ Refill your water bottle throughout the day. At $1 or more a pop, bottled water can add up, and you already have the bottle.

Balancing the Budget

If you ignore all my warnings about using a car in Washington and rent one anyway, here's a thought on how to save money. Rental car companies can charge up to an extra $10 a day for collision insurance. But most major credit-card companies cover this. Call your credit card company before you book and see if this $10 is really necessary.

Budget Worksheet: You Can Afford This Trip	
Expense	Amount
Airfare (multiplied by number of people traveling)	
Car Rental (if applicable)	
Lodging (multiplied by number of nights)	
Parking (multiplied by number of nights)	
Breakfast *may be included in your room rate* (multiplied by number of nights)	
Lunch (multiplied by number of nights)	
Dinner (multiplied by number of nights)	
Baby-sitting	
Attractions (admission charges to museums, movies, tours, theaters, nightclubs, etc.)	
Transportation (cabs, subway, buses, etc.)	
Souvenirs (T-shirts, postcards, that antique you just gotta have)	
Tips (think 15% of your meal total plus $1 a bag every time a bellhop moves your luggage)	
Don't forget the cost of getting to and from the airport in your hometown, plus long-term parking (multiplied by number of nights)	
Grand Total	

How Will I Get There?

Chapter 3

In This Chapter

➤ The benefits of using a travel agent

➤ Planes, trains, and automobiles: figuring out the vehicle for you

➤ Advice on whether to take a tour or design the trip yourself

➤ How to fly smart, where to fly to

Getting there used to be half the fun. But heaven knows, travelers face a lot of choices. While pioneer spirits like to make their own arrangements, handing over responsibility to a travel agent can take the hassle out of planning a trip. Where to start? First, ask yourself if you'll be comfortable in a strange setting, finding your way on your own, or if you'd rather receive the kid-glove, spoon-fed treatment afforded by a group tour.

Travel Agent—Friend or Foe?

A good travel agent is like a good friend. Once you cut through the superficial stuff and forge a bond, your travel agent will prove invaluable. The best way to find a good travel agent (and sometimes a good friend) is by word of mouth.

A really good agent not only finds the bargain airfares and hotels but also helps you budget your time in a destination and find a flight that doesn't necessitate changing planes in Vancouver and Cincinnati. A good agent also can find you a better deal for a hotel room, knows the pros and cons of staying in different neighborhoods within a city, and can recommend restaurants and must-see sights.

Agents work on commissions paid by the airlines, hotels, and tour companies—not by you. Some may try to sell you vacations that net them the biggest commissions. Well-informed travelers get the most out of a travel agent and are less likely to be duped. This doesn't mean you have to study world geography, international cuisine, and hotel management for years. It does mean you should read about your destination (you've already taken a giant step by picking up this book!) and choose some accommodations and attractions that appeal to you. Get a more comprehensive guidebook, like *Frommer's Washington, D.C.*, or *Washington, D.C. with Kids.* If you have access to the Internet, check prices on the Web yourself in advance (see "Internet Warfare" later in this chapter for more information on how to do that) so that you can do a little prodding. Then, and only then, take your newfound knowledge to a travel agent, and let the agent make the arrangements. Agents have at their fingertips more information than you or I in a month of Sundays. They can book your hotel room and issue tickets and vouchers (and get better prices in most cases). One key thing to remember: A travel agent is working for you, not vice versa. Of course, you are free to do everything on your own, but it can be very time-consuming and usually is not cost-effective.

Should I Join an Escorted Tour or Travel on My Own?

With more than a million people visiting Washington annually as part of a group tour, you can rest assured there is no shortage of tour operators. Some companies provide fully escorted tours. On these tours, you're escorted from beginning to end. While you eat and while you sightsee, you'll never be alone. The leader (not necessarily a tour guide) is there to make sure everything goes smoothly. Some people like the comfort of being with other people and swapping stories. If you fit into this category, then an escorted tour is for you.

If you do choose an escorted tour, ask a few simple questions before you sign up:

➤ **What is the cancellation policy?** Do you have to put a deposit down? Can they cancel the trip if they don't get enough people? How late can you cancel if you are unable to go? When do you pay? Do you get a refund if you cancel? If *they* cancel?

➤ **How jam-packed is the schedule?** Do they try to fit 25 hours into a 24-hour day, or is there ample time for relaxing by the pool or for shopping? If you don't enjoy getting up at 7am every day and not returning to your hotel until 6 or 7pm, certain escorted tours may not be for you.

➤ **How big is the group?** The smaller the group, the more flexible and the less time you'll spend waiting for people to get on and off the bus. Tour operators may be evasive about this, because they may not know the exact size of the group until everybody has made their reservations, but they should be able to give you a rough estimate. Some tours have a minimum group size and may cancel the tour if they don't book enough people.

➤ **What is included?** Don't assume anything. You may have to pay to get yourself to and from the airport. Or a box lunch may be included in an excursion, but drinks might cost extra. Or beer might be included, but wine might not. How much choice do you have? Can you opt out of certain activities, or does the bus leave once a day, with no exceptions? Are all your meals planned in advance? Can you choose your entree at dinner, or does everybody get the same chicken cutlet?

If you choose an escorted tour, think strongly about purchasing travel insurance, especially if the tour operator asks you to pay up front. But don't buy insurance from the tour operator! If they don't fulfill their obligation to provide you with the vacation you've paid for, there's no reason to think they'll fulfill their insurance obligations either. Get travel insurance through an independent agency. See "What About Travel Insurance?" in chapter 4.

Unescorted Tours

Other tour companies make all the arrangements and then you're on your own. Many people prefer the convenience of having someone else booking airlines, hotels, rental cars, sightseeing, and meals. They also want to enjoy group rates. However, they don't want to travel with a large group and do want more flexibility. If you fit this description, an unescorted or package tour is probably your cup of tea. You'll keep your independence as well as get hotel and airfare reservations at discounted prices that you couldn't negotiate as an independent traveler.

The best place to start looking for information on package tours is the travel section of your local Sunday newspaper. Also check the ads in the back of national travel magazines like *Travel & Leisure, Arthur Frommer's Budget Travel Magazine, National Geographic Traveler,* and *Condé Nast Traveler.* **Liberty**

D.C. Dirt

It's been said that in Washington, D.C., there are more lawyers than anywhere else on the planet. Sixty-nine pages of the Washington, D.C., Yellow Pages are devoted to lawyers, compared to 51 pages for physicians and surgeons. But hey, it's a good business. High rollers in a jam willingly fork over up to $350 an hour for representation by Washington's top defense lawyers. According to a *Washington Post* story in October 1998, only $115.50 of an hourly $350 fee is pretax profit. Yeah, right. And I'm a Spice Girl.

Travel (many locations; check your local directory, since there's not a central 800 number) is one of the biggest packagers in the Northeast and usually boasts a full-page ad in Sunday papers. You won't get much in the way of service, but you should get good deals. **American Express Vacations** (☎ 800/241-1700) is another option.

Some companies offer you a choice of escorted or independent tours. Below you'll find examples of what Washington tour providers have to offer. Prices quoted were for the summer of 1998.

Pick a Peck of Pickled Packages

Yankee Holidays (☎ 800/225-2550; www.yankee-holidays.com) has been offering individual city packages and customized group tour packages for over a quarter century. The trips to Washington include a 2-night, 3-day Capitol Experience with lodging and a 1-day sightseeing pass for $145 to $179 (per person/double occupancy). The Washington Diplomat tour (4 days and 3 nights) includes lodging, dinner at the Hard Rock Cafe, a day of sightseeing, and a choice of tours, from $316 (per person/double occupancy). Other tours and additional nights are available. Groups of 20 or more should call ☎ 800/343-6768.

Globetrotters (☎ 800/999-9696) offers 2-, 3-, 4-, and 5-night packages to Washington with eight different categories of hotels (from Quality Suites to Willard Inter-Continental). Prices start at $147 (per person/double occupancy) for 2 nights at the lowest category and go to $937 (per person/double occupancy) for 5 nights at the upper category during prime season, including all hotel taxes and service charges and some sightseeing fees, depending on the package purchased. If any service is not delivered as described in the brochure, Globetrotters will warrant an appropriate refund. The company also offers a Price Match Guarantee that will honor any competitor's published price at the same hotel, same room category, same length of stay, same travel dates, and comparable flights.

Local Organized Tours

There are a number of local tour bus operations. These are good companies to contact if you'll want to do some specific sightseeing once you're in town. You should note, however, that the best way to see Washington on a guided tour is through **Tourmobile** or **Old Town Trolley** (see chapter 12 for more information).

Atlantic Coast Charters (☎ 800/548-8584) in Hagerstown, Maryland, conducts tours through the heart of the Civil War historical areas. In late 1998, tours included trips to the Kennedy Center, jaunts on the *Odyssey* cruise ship, and shopping trips to Potomac Mills (Dale City, Virginia).

Smithsonian Associates (☎ 202/357-3030; www.si.edu/tsa/rap/tours-dc.htm) offers day and overnight bus trips to nearby areas.

Does It Matter Which Airport I Fly Into?

Washington is served by three airports: **Baltimore–Washington International (BWI), Ronald Reagan National Airport,** and **Washington–Dulles International.** Since the opening of a new facility in July 1997, National has become easier to navigate, but you still have to determine which terminal your flight departs from. All three airports have modern fast-food outlets and decent shopping.

Hear Ye! Hear Ye!

If you're looking for information about how to get into the city from the airport, flip ahead to the "From Air to There" section in chapter 7.

Ronald Reagan National Airport (Reagan National)

If you'll be staying in Washington proper and can find a nonstop flight from your hometown, **Reagan National** is the airport of choice. You can easily catch a taxi into town, or use the subway, now located conveniently close to the new terminal.

Baltimore–Washington International (BWI)

Don't overlook **BWI,** where flights may be cheaper. Specifically, BWI is a hub for no-frills **Southwest.** In most instances, the other airlines serving BWI match Southwest's low fares. And don't worry that this airport is in Baltimore—you can easily catch an Amtrak or commuter train, which will take you directly to Union Station. BWI and Dulles offer international flights, if you're traveling abroad before or after your Washington visit. Of all three airports, you'll have the easiest time getting around BWI—it's shaped

Balancing the Budget

These days with the e-saver fares offered by several airlines on the Internet, you can find a $69 round-trip flight from New York to Washington. Here's how e-saver fares work. Register on the Web sites given below. Every week (usually Wednesday), you'll receive an e-mail notifying you of last-minute airfare discounts. The only glitch: You will have to be flexible with your travel dates— you'll usually be able to get a flight out only on Saturday morning and a return on Monday or Tuesday.
American Airlines: www.americanair.com
Continental Airlines: www.flycontiental.com
Northwest Airlines: www.nwa.com
TWA: www.twa.com
US Airways: www.usairways.com
Epicurious Travel (travel.epicurious.com) allows you to sign up for all of these airline e-mail lists at once.

sort of like a hand, with five terminal wings spreading out from the single initial check-in area.

Washington–Dulles International Airport (Dulles)

Dulles is majestic in its Saarinen design, but you have to contend with the main terminal, the infield terminal, and shuttle vans to the planes. Dulles will continue to be a pain in the butt until the inefficient shuttle vans are history, in theory, at least, by the dawning of the 21st century.

The Shuttlebutt on the Shuttle

If your schedule isn't flexible, but you need to get to or from New York in a pinch, think "shuttle." The shuttles are convenient because you can just show up, buy a ticket, and hop on the next plane out. In both New York and Washington, planes leave every half hour—no reservations required.

The **Delta Shuttle** (☎ 800/221-1212), which flies out of LaGuardia's Marine Terminal in New York to Reagan National Airport, has hourly flights leaving daily on the half hour. To Washington, departures are weekdays from 6:30am to 8:30pm, plus an extra 9pm flight; Saturday from 7:30am to 8:30pm; and Sunday from 8:30am to 8:30pm, plus an extra 9pm flight. From Washington to New York, departures are hourly on the half hour from 7:30am to 9:30pm. Because the schedule has been known to change, please call for the latest information. As we go to press, the fare for the shuttle is $55 one way or $110 (plus tax) round-trip all day on Saturday and on Sunday from 8:30am to 2:30pm. At other times, the fare runs from $209. But before you book your ticket, ask about special advance purchase and promotional fares.

The **US Airways Shuttle** (☎ 800/428-4322) runs from a separate terminal at LaGuardia Airport in New York to Reagan National Airport. Weekday departures from New York are hourly from 7am to 9pm, Saturday from 7am to 8pm, and Sunday from 9am to 9pm. From Washington to New York, there are hourly departures on weekdays and on Saturday from 7am to 9pm, and on Sunday from 9am to 9pm. The weekend fare is $110 round-trip. There's also a student rate (12 to 24 years old)—for $170 you can fly round-trip any time of the week. Otherwise the fare could reach as high as $404 round-trip. Ask about senior (age 62 and over) discounts.

Fighting the Airfare Wars

If you've ever flown, you know there is no such thing as a "typical" or "normal" fare. For every flight there are usually several fares available under three main categories: first class, coach, and discount. Although visitors to Washington benefit from a wide choice of flights, they may grow dizzy deciphering the ever-changing fare structure.

Generally, midweek fares ticketed 21 days or more in advance are the lowest. Holidays (unless you can arrange your schedule around the heaviest travel days) are often subject to blackout restrictions, as in "no bargains spoken here." Winter fares are usually lowest and summer fares are highest. But, as you no doubt know, fare wars spread like swamp fever. Watch for newspaper ads announcing special promotions. They pop up unexpectedly throughout the year and can save you big bucks. If you don't qualify for a promotional or other reduced fare, you could end up paying substantially more for your ticket. To get the most for your travel dollar, plan well in advance and do a bit of comparison shopping by calling the airlines or consulting an accredited travel agent.

Also inquire about money-saving packages that include hotel accommodations, car rentals, tours, etc., with your airfare.

Balancing the Budget

Consolidators, also known as bucket shops, are a good place to check for the lowest fares. Their prices can be better than the fares you can get yourself and are often even lower than what your travel agent can get. You see their ads in the Sunday travel section of your local newspaper. Some of the most reliable consolidators can be reached at ☎ **1-800-FLY-4-LESS** or **1-800-FLY-CHEAP.** Another good choice, **Council Travel** (☎ **800/226-8624**), caters especially to young travelers, but their bargain-basement prices are available to people of all ages.

The airlines frequently offer special **family fares** as well. Children under 2 who do not occupy a seat usually travel free. Depending on the airline, various discounts apply to kids between the ages of 2 and 12. If you will be traveling with an infant, toddler, or active preschooler, when you make your reservation request the seats behind the bulkhead, where you'll have more legroom and they'll have more play room. Many planes have special fittings for bassinets and some will allow you to use your child's car seat. To find out if your particular brand of car seat is approved by the Federal Aviation Administration, request "Child/Infant Safety Seats Acceptable for Use in Aircraft" from the Community and Consumer Liaison Division, APA-400 Federal Aviation Administration, 800 Independence Ave. SW, Washington, DC 20591 (☎ **202/267-3479**).

Internet Warfare

It's possible to get some great deals on airfare, hotels, and car rentals via the Internet. So go grab your mouse by the tail and start surfing—you could save a bundle on your trip. The Web sites below are worth checking out, especially since all services are free (but don't forget that time is money when you're on line).

➤ **Travelocity (www.travelocity.com).** This is one of the best travel sites out there. In addition to its "Personal Fare Watcher," which notifies you via e-mail of the lowest airfares for up to five different destinations, Travelocity will track the three lowest fares for any routes on any dates in minutes. You can book a flight right then and there, and if you need a rental car or hotel, Travelocity will find you the best deal via the SABRE computer reservations system (a huge database used by travel agents worldwide). Click on "Last Minute Deals" for the latest travel bargains, including a link to "H.O.T. Coupons" **(www.hotcoupons.com),** where you can print out electronic coupons for travel in the United States and Canada, including Hawaii.

➤ **Microsoft Expedia (www.expedia.com).** The best part of this multipurpose travel site is the "Fare Tracker": You fill out a form on the screen indicating that you're interested in cheap flights to wherever from your hometown and once a week they'll e-mail you the best airfare deals. The site's "Travel Agent" will steer you to bargains on hotels and car rentals, and you can book everything, including flights, right on line. This site is even useful once you're booked: Before you go, log on to Expedia for oodles of up-to-date travel information, including weather reports and foreign exchange rates.

➤ **Preview Travel (www.reservations.com** and **www.vacations. com).** Another useful travel site, "reservations.com" has a "Best Fare Finder" that will search the Apollo computer reservations system for the three lowest fares for any route on any days of the year. Say you want to go from Chicago to D.C. and back between December 6 and 13: Just fill out the form on the screen with times, dates, and destinations, and within minutes Preview will show you the best deals. If you find an airfare you like, you can book your ticket right on line—you can even reserve hotels and car rentals on this site. If you're in the preplanning stage, head to Preview's "vacations.com" site, where you can check out the latest package deals for D.C. and other destinations around the world by clicking on "Hot Deals."

➤ **Trip.Com (www.thetrip.com).** This site is really geared toward the business traveler, but vacationers-to-be can also use Trip.Com's valuable fare-finding engine, which will e-mail you every week with the best city-to-city airfare deals on your selected route or routes.

➤ **Discount Tickets (www.discount-tickets.com).** Operated by the ETN (European Travel Network), this site offers discounts on airfares, accommodations, car rentals, and tours. It deals in flights between the United States and other countries, not domestic U.S. flights, so it's most useful for travelers coming to D.C. from abroad.

➤ **Priceline.com.** On this auction-like Web site, you decide what you want to pay for your airline ticket or hotel room. Input when and where you want to fly to, the price you want to pay, and your credit-card number. Priceline then does a search to determine if any

33

supplier will accept the price; if the price is accepted, the ticket is immediately bought and charged to your credit card. The Web site offers a similar deal for hotel rooms.

Hear Ye! Hear Ye!

If you have special dietary needs, be sure to order a special meal. Most airlines offer vegetarian meals, macrobiotic meals, kosher meals, meals for the lactose intolerant, and several others. Ask when you make your reservation if the airline can accommodate your dietary restrictions. Some people without any special dietary needs order special meals anyway, because they are made to order, unlike the mass-produced mystery meals served to the rest of the passengers. But whatever you choose, don't expect gourmet fare.

How to Make Your Flight More Pleasant

The seats in the front row of each airplane cabin, called the **bulkhead seats,** usually have the most legroom. They have some drawbacks, however. Because there's no seat in front of you, there's no place to put your carry-on luggage, except in the overhead bin. The front row also may not be the best place to see the in-flight movie.

Emergency-exit row seats also have extra legroom. They are assigned at the airport, usually on a first-come, first-serve basis. Ask when you check in whether you can be seated in one of these rows. In the unlikely event of an emergency, you'll be expected to open the emergency-exit door and help direct traffic.

Ask for a seat toward the front of the plane. The minute the captain turns off the "Fasten Seat Belts" sign after landing, people jump up out of their seats as though Ken Griffey Jr. just hit a home run. They then stand in the aisles and wait for 5 to 10 minutes while the ground crew puts the gangway in place. The closer to the front of the plane you are, the less hurry-up-and-waiting you'll have to do. Why do you think they put first class in the front?

Wear comfortable clothes. The days of getting dressed up in a coat and tie to ride an airplane went out with Nehru jackets and poodle skirts. And dress in layers; the supposedly controlled climate in airplane cabins is anything but predictable. You'll be glad to have a sweater or jacket that you can put on or take off as the temperature on board dictates.

Bring some toiletries aboard on long flights. Airplane cabins are notoriously dry places. Take a travel-sized bottle of moisturizer or lotion to refresh your face and hands at the end of the flight. If you're taking an overnight flight (a.k.a. the red eye), don't forget to pack a toothbrush to combat that feeling upon waking that you've been sucking on your seat cushion for 6 hours. If you wear contact lenses, take them out before you get on board and wear glasses instead. Or at least bring eyedrops.

And if **you're flying with kids,** don't forget chewing gum for ear pressure problems with swallowing, a deck of cards or favorite toys to keep them entertained, extra bottles or pacifiers, diapers, etc.

The Big Engine That Can: Arriving by Train

You can also take **Amtrak** into Washington, a favored means of travel (with dozens of trains daily—not quite as many on weekends—from options ranging from nonreserved to Metroliner) from New York and the Northeast (no worries about inclement weather backing up take-offs and landings, or even about ground traffic getting to and from the airports). Amtrak also has trains coming in from the south and west. From New York City, Philadelphia, and Wilmington, Amtrak is the quickest, most efficient way to reach Washington. The trains arrive at Union Station (on Capitol Hill) with a Metro station and plenty of cabs out front. If you hit it right, you can find a discount fare from New York to Washington for $122 round-trip, or from Boston to Washington (a heckuva long ride) for $124.

Amtrak Vacations also has package tours, with prices starting at $225 from Philadelphia and Wilmington, or $185 from Baltimore (per person/double occupancy). The trip includes round-trip coach rail, 2 nights at the Holiday Inn on the Hill, and a trolley tour with on/off privileges. Other options available include after-dark tours, visits to Mount Vernon or Williamsburg, rental car, transfer to hotel, and an upgrade to premium Metroliner Service. Hotel upgrades are also available. Call your travel agent or ☎ **888/AMTRAK-1,** or log on to Amtrak's site at **www.northeast.amtrak.com/bestbuys**.

Arriving by Car

Having a car in Washington is like having 10 albatrosses tied around your neck. If you must drive, be prepared to garage your car at a cost of up to $20 per day. And forget driving once you've arrived in the nation's capital. While easily accessible on foot and by Metrorail (our subway), Washington is your worst driving nightmare, with confusing traffic circles; poor signage; one-way streets that dead end, only to continue several blocks away; and potholes rivaling the moon's craters. One wrong turn and you can end up in Virginia or one of the less-desirable neighborhoods. But if, after all my warnings, you still insist on driving, head straight to the next paragraph, which discusses the major driving routes into the city.

All of the following highways lead to the **Capital Beltway (I-95/I-495),** which is a wheel (or noose) around the D.C. area, with spokes leading into the city. Talk to your hotel to find out which spoke is right for you. If you're driving into D.C. from the north, **I-270, I-95,** and **I-295** are the main links to the Washington metropolitan area. From the south, **I-95** and **I-395** are the most direct and quickest routes. From points east, such as Annapolis and the Eastern Shore of Maryland, the road of choice is **Route 50**, which becomes **New York Avenue** in the District. West of D.C., coming from Virginia, motorists should cruise down **I-66**, which leads into both Constitution Avenue and Rock Creek Parkway. See the map "Washington, D.C. Orientation," to get a better picture of what I'm talking about.

---

1   Schedule & Flight Information Worksheets

Travel Agency: _____ **Phone #:** _____

Agent's Name: _____ **Quoted Fare:** _____

Departure Schedule & Flight Information

Airline: _____ Airport: _____

Flight #: _____ Date: _____ Time: _____ am/pm

Arrives in _____ Time: _____ am/pm

Connecting Flight (if any)

Amount of time between flights: _____ hours/mins.

Airline: _____ Flight #: _____ Time: _____ am/pm

Arrives in _____ Time: _____ am/pm

Return Trip Schedule & Flight Information

Airline: _____ Airport: _____

Flight #: _____ Date: _____ Time: _____ am/pm

Arrives in _____ Time: _____ am/pm

Connecting Flight (if any)

Amount of time between flights: _____ hours/mins.

Airline: _____ Flight #: _____ Time: _____ am/pm

Arrives in _____ Time: _____ am/pm

---

2 Schedule & Flight Information Worksheets

Travel Agency: _____ **Phone #:** _____

Agent's Name: _____ **Quoted Fare:** _____

Departure Schedule & Flight Information

Airline: _____ Airport: _____

Flight #: _____ Date: _____ Time: _____am/pm

Arrives in _____ Time: _____ am/pm

Connecting Flight (if any)

Amount of time between flights: _____ hours/mins.

Airline:_____ Flight #:_____ Time: _____am/pm

Arrives in _____ Time: _____ am/pm

Return Trip Schedule & Flight Information

Airline:_____ Airport: _____

Flight #: _____ Date: _____ Time: _____am/pm

Arrives in _____ Time: _____ am/pm

Connecting Flight (if any)

Amount of time between flights: _____ hours/mins.

Airline:_____ Flight #:_____ Time: _____am/pm

Arrives in _____ Time: _____ am/pm

3   Schedule & Flight Information Worksheets

Travel Agency: _____ **Phone #:** _____

Agent's Name: _____ **Quoted Fare:** _____

Departure Schedule & Flight Information

Airline: _____ Airport: _____

Flight #: _____ Date: _____ Time: _____am/pm

Arrives in _____ Time: _____ am/pm

Connecting Flight (if any)

Amount of time between flights: _____ hours/mins.

Airline:_____ Flight #:_____ Time: _____am/pm

Arrives in _____ Time: _____ am/pm

Return Trip Schedule & Flight Information

Airline:_____ Airport: _____

Flight #: _____ Date: _____ Time: _____am/pm

Arrives in _____ Time: _____ am/pm

Connecting Flight (if any)

Amount of time between flights: _____ hours/mins.

Airline:_____ Flight #:_____ Time: _____am/pm

Arrives in _____ Time: _____ am/pm

4 Schedule & Flight Information Worksheets

Travel Agency: _____ **Phone #:** _____

Agent's Name: _____ **Quoted Fare:** _____

Departure Schedule & Flight Information

Airline: _____ Airport: _____

Flight #: _____ Date: _____ Time: _____am/pm

Arrives in _____ Time: _____ am/pm

Connecting Flight (if any)

Amount of time between flights: _____ hours/mins.

Airline:_____ Flight #:_____ Time: _____am/pm

Arrives in _____ Time: _____ am/pm

Return Trip Schedule & Flight Information

Airline:_____ Airport: _____

Flight #: _____ Date: _____ Time: _____am/pm

Arrives in _____ Time: _____ am/pm

Connecting Flight (if any)

Amount of time between flights: _____ hours/mins.

Airline:_____ Flight #:_____ Time: _____am/pm

Arrives in _____ Time: _____ am/pm

Chapter 4

Tying Up the Loose Ends

In This Chapter

➤ Insurance: Do you need it?

➤ What to do in case of illness

➤ What to bring to town

Okay, you've booked a flight or train to whisk you to Washington. Now you have to decide where you'll stay (more about this in chapters 5 and 6), what in the heck you'll do once you arrive, make reservations, put a hold on your mail, kennel Fido, remember to pack your toothbrush, and do a hundred or so other last-minute chores. If you save all the last-minute details until the last minute, you'll probably waste those last minutes waiting in line, calling around for tickets, or scouting an all-night drugstore to replace the toothbrush you left on your dresser. Is this any way to start a vacation? I think not. In this chapter I'll help you get organized and make sure you've covered all the bases, from ordering tickets for a pre-Broadway show at the Kennedy Center to packing comfy walking shoes. The worksheet at the end of the chapter will keep you on track.

Do I Need to Rent a Car in Washington, D.C.?

There are three answers to this question: No, no, and no. If you have any doubts, see the section on this subject under "Arriving by Car" in chapter 3. This is one area of your visit you don't have to prearrange. Taxis and/or shuttles are plentiful at the three airports (Reagan National, Dulles International, and Baltimore–Washington International) and train station (Union Station) serving D.C. Metro serves Reagan National Airport and

Hear Ye! Hear Ye!

The best (and many think the only) way to tour the White House is on a special VIP tour Tuesday through Saturday between 8 and 8:45am. Yeah, I know it's early, but the tour is more extensive than the cattle-call tour that the not-so-important who don't write away ahead of time are forced to go on. Besides, you'll have plenty of time to sleep when you're dead. Write as far in advance as possible to your congressperson. Only 10 tickets per week are given to each senator and congressional representative.

Union Station. Some hotels provide complimentary shuttle service, so be sure to ask when booking your room.

What About Travel Insurance?

Travel insurance falls into three broad categories: trip cancellation, medical, and lost luggage. Trip cancellation insurance is a good idea if you have paid a large portion of your vacation expenses up front. Also note that insurance may cover you only for a death in the family or serious illness, not if you change your plans; read the policy carefully.

The other two types of insurance may not make sense for most travelers. Your existing health insurance should cover you if you get sick while on vacation (though if you belong to an HMO, you should check to see whether you are fully covered when

Tourist Traps

Buy film before you leave home. And buy a roll or two more than you think you'll need. Although there are plenty of places to purchase film in Washington, you'll be a captive audience and may pay substantially more than at your favorite neighborhood discount store. Besides, who wants to waste a vacation looking for film?

away from home). It's important to be covered for emergency evacuation as well, in the event that you need to fly home on sudden notice, with a doctor in tow—it could cost $10,000 or more. And your homeowner's insurance should cover stolen luggage if you're covered for off-premises theft. Check your existing policies before you buy any additional coverage. The airlines are responsible for $1,250 on domestic flights if they lose your luggage; if you plan to carry anything more valuable than that, keep it in your carry-on bag.

Some credit cards (American Express and certain gold and platinum Visa and MasterCards, for example) offer automatic flight insurance against death or dismemberment in case of an airplane crash. If you still feel you need more insurance, try one of the companies listed below. But don't pay for more insurance than you need. For example, if you only need trip cancellation insurance, don't purchase coverage for lost or stolen property. Trip

41

Tourist Traps

There are 26,000 hotel rooms in Washington, ample for your family or group if you book well ahead. During the busiest tourist season, from mid–March to mid–June, the pickin's can be slim for those who wait until the last second to make reservations. You snooze, you lose.

cancellation insurance costs approximately 6% to 8% of the total value of your vacation. Among the reputable issuers of travel insurance are:

➤ **Access America,** 6600 W. Broad St., Richmond, VA 23230 (☎ **800/ 284-8300**)

➤ **Mutual of Omaha,** Mutual of Omaha Plaza, Omaha, NE 68175 (☎ **800/228-9792**)

➤ **Travel Guard International,** 1145 Clark St., Stevens Point, WI 54481 (☎ **800/826-1300**)

➤ **Travel Insured International, Inc.,** P.O. Box 280568, East Hartford, CT 06128 (☎ **800/243-3174**)

Aaaachooo! What If I Get Sick Away from Home?

Other than having your wallet ripped off, there are few things more distressing than an ill-timed illness or accident to spoil a vacation. It may be tough to find a doctor you trust at 3am or to reach your physician at home if he's playing the back nine with his buddies. If you're on medications, bring them *all* with you, and a prescription for more should you run out. As one who has popped a lens more than once on a bathroom tile floor, I strongly suggest bringing an extra pair of prescription eyeglasses or contacts too. If you have health insurance, carry your identification card in your wallet and a photocopy in your suitcase. Don't forget over-the-counter medications for common ailments, like a stuffy head or upset stomach.

Hear Ye! Hear Ye!

If you have a medical emergency, take a taxi to one of the following hospitals: **Children's Hospital National Medical Center,** 111 Michigan Ave. NW (near Catholic University and the National Shrine; ☎ **202/884-5000**); **George Washington University Hospital,** 901 23rd St. NW (entrance on Washington Circle; ☎ **202/994-3211**); or **Georgetown University Hospital,** 3800 Reservoir Rd. NW (☎ **202/784-2118**).

CVS has two 24–hour pharmacies in the D.C. area. One is at 14th Street and Thomas Circle (at Vermont Avenue; ☎ **202/628-0720**); and the other is located at 67 Dupont Circle (☎ **202/785-1466**).

If you suffer from a chronic illness, talk to your doctor before taking the trip. For such conditions as epilepsy, diabetes, or a heart condition, wear a **Medic Alert identification tag,** which will immediately alert any doctor to your condition and give him or her access to your medical records through Medic Alert's 24-hour hot line. Membership is $35, plus a $15 annual fee. Contact the **Medic Alert Foundation,** P.O. Box 1009, Turlock, CA 95381-1009 (☎ **800/825-3785**).

If you do get sick, ask the concierge at your hotel to recommend a local doctor—even his or her own doctor if necessary. This is probably a better recommendation than any national consortium of doctors available through an 800 number. If you can't get a doctor to help you right away, try the emergency room at the local hospital. Many hospital emergency rooms have walk-in clinics for emergency cases that are not life-threatening. You may not get immediate attention, but you won't pay the high price of an emergency room visit (usually a minimum of $300 just for signing your name, on top of whatever treatment you receive).

Making Reservations & Getting Tickets Ahead of Time

At peak times, say in spring around the Cherry Blossom Festival, Metro, hotels, museums, and restaurants are crowded. To avoid wasting time in line for special exhibits and hot shows, as well as some of the tonier restaurants, order your tickets or make that Saturday night dinner reservation before you leave home.

What restaurants require advance reservations? The following is a list of restaurants where it'll benefit you to call ahead:

➤ **Coco Loco** (☎ 202/289-2626)

➤ **Galileo** (☎ 202/293-7191)

➤ **Georgia Brown's** (☎ 202/393-4499)

➤ **Greenwood at Cleveland Place** (☎ 202/833-6572)

➤ **Kinkead's** (☎ 202/296-7700)

➤ **La Colline** (☎ 202/737-0400)

➤ **Marrakesh** (☎ 202/393-9393)

➤ **Morton's** (☎ 202/955-5997 downtown; 202/342-6258 Georgetown)

➤ **Obelisk** (☎ 202/872-1180)

➤ **Pesce** (☎ 202/466-3474)

➤ **Prime Rib** (☎ 202/466-8811)

Hear Ye! Hear Ye!

It's the concierge's job to make reservations—at restaurants, hot shows, etc. Chances are, your concierge knows a lot of important people around town. He or she might even have an in at that fancy restaurant that you forgot to make a reservation at. Before you give up and head to the Golden Arches, inquire with the concierge— you never know. And a few dollars tip won't hurt.

Know Where to Go—Washington, D.C. Entertainment

To find out what's going on before you arrive, head for a newsstand selling out-of-town newspapers and magazines. Pick up a copy of the *Washington Post* (preferably on Friday for the inclusive Weekend magazine) or monthly *Washingtonian* magazine. If these are unavailable, click onto the *Washington Post*'s Web site at **www.washingtonpost.com**.

Can't find a copy of the *Post*? Log in to the following Web sites and you'll find out what's happening before all the information hits the press.

➤ D.C. Committee to Promote Washington and Washington, D.C., Convention and Visitors Association share a Web site at **www.washington.org**.

➤ D.C. Office of Tourism Promotions has a Web site at **www.ci.washington.dc.us/TOURISM/tourism.htm**.

➤ Washington Web, a consortium, has links with 36 D.C. area newspapers at **www.washweb.net/washweb/NewsMedia/Newspapers/index.html**.

➤ The National Park Service (with information on annual events, Ford's Theatre, and entertainment at sites maintained by the Park Service) has a Web site at **www.nps.gov/ncro/parklist.htm**.

➤ Also try Netscape's Washington, D.C., information Web site (with numerous links) at **www.nmjc.org/JIAP/wash.html**.

➤ The Smithsonian Institution's home page is at **http://www.si.edu**.

➤ **www.wahington.sidewalk.com** offers a wealth of information about music, sports, dining, nightlife, or whatever else might be happening when you're going to be in town.

D.C. Dirt

You're not the only one who's planning a trip to the nation's capital. About 21 million people visit the Washington, D.C., area annually and pump close to $5 billion into the local economy. That's almost three times the population of New York City all filing into one little city!

Call Now—Information by Phone

In addition to the aforementioned resources, you can call the Washington, D.C., Convention and Visitors Association at ☎ **800/422-8644.** For information on current theater, call Protix at ☎ **800/955-5566** or 703/218-6500, TicketPlace at ☎ **202/TICKETS,** or Ticketmaster at ☎ **800/551-7328** or 202/432-SEAT.

Packin' It In

I'm not sure where this idea originated, but it makes good sense: When traveling, take half the clothing you think you'll need and twice as much money. Definitely words for smart travelers to live by! Start by laying out everything you think you'll need, then put half of it away. In an emergency, you can always wash something in the sink and drape it over a lamp shade to dry.

Even if you forget your underwear and razor, be sure to pack comfortable walking shoes. Washington is a walking city, and your tootsies will be miserable in stylish but too-tight shoes. Pack clothing that you can layer. Washington's weather is fickle, and spring through fall, the thermometer can climb from early-morning comfortable to unbearable by noon. On such occasions, if you're traipsing around the Mall in a sweatshirt with nothing but skin underneath, you'll wish you'd stayed home. A light sweater or windbreaker is a necessity in all seasons, even in summer when the overly air-conditioned buildings may turn your lips blue. By all means, pack a raincoat to handle the precipitation that falls fairly evenly throughout the year (see the charts in chapter 1). To learn the current temperature and the next day's **weather forecast,** call ☎ **202/976-1212** or check out the Weather Channel's Web site at **www.weather.com**.

Don't leave home without some other essentials: a camera, toiletries, and medications (packed in a carry-on bag so that you'll have them in case the airlines "misplace" your luggage in Vladivostok), something to sleep in, and a change of underwear. The packing checklist later in this chapter has other essential packing suggestions.

Leave formal wear in mothballs unless you're invited to a state occasion at the White House. Men should pack a jacket and tie for the fancy shmancy restaurants. Otherwise a collared shirt and khakis or dress slacks will serve you well. Women need only bring a simple dress (perhaps in basic black, which doesn't show the wrinkles), skirt, or dress pants for the posher restaurants.

As for choosing your suitcase, go with what you have and what's worked in the past. I prefer the wheeled carry-on type with a collapsible handle because it's easier on the back. While hard-sided luggage protects breakables better, it weighs a ton empty. I wrap an old towel around breakables in a soft-sided bag and, thus far, have fared well.

Hear Ye! Hear Ye!

After years of packing tasteful, coordinated outfits in every color of the rainbow, I now subscribe to the dictum of seasoned travelers everywhere: Separates in black and neutral white or tan. It works like a charm. Not only can you mix and match, fooling everyone into thinking you have a huge wardrobe, but black shows dirt and wrinkles less than, say, pale peach.

45

Pack the biggest, hardest items, like shoes, on the bottom, and put smaller items in and around them. Pack breakables in between several layers of clothes or keep them in your carry-on bag. Put things that could leak (shampoo, suntan lotion, and such) in zip-seal bags. Locking your suitcase with a small padlock (available at luggage and leather goods stores, if your bag doesn't have one) is a good idea. Also, secure an identification tag on the outside and affix a bright ribbon or tape to the handle for easy identification.

Airline policies differ over whether you're allowed one or two pieces of carry-on luggage, so call for the latest word. Carry-on bags must fit in the overhead compartment or under the seat in front of you. Carry breakable items, a book or magazine, and vital documents (like return tickets, passport, and wallet) with you. Last but not least, carry a snack, in case you don't like the airline food (almost inevitable) or can't wait to eat. It may be an hour after lift-off before meal service begins.

Packing Checklist: Don't Forget Your Toothbrush!

- ☐ Socks
- ☐ Underwear
- ☐ Shoes (try not to pack more than two or three pairs; don't forget a good pair of walking shoes)
- ☐ Pants and/or skirts
- ☐ Shirts or blouses
- ☐ Sweaters and/or jackets
- ☐ Umbrella (the folding kind, so you can carry it with you)
- ☐ A belt
- ☐ A jacket and tie or a dress (only if you plan to go someplace fancy in the evening)
- ☐ Shorts (in warm weather)
- ☐ Bathing suit (if your hotel has a swimming pool or if you're trekking to a beach)
- ☐ Workout clothes (if you plan to use the hotel gym)
- ☐ Toiletries (razor, toothbrush, comb, deodorant, makeup, contact lens solution, hair dryer, extra pair of glasses, sewing kit, and so on)
- ☐ Camera and film
- ☐ Medications (pack these in a carry-on bag so you'll have them even if you lose your luggage)

Part 2

Finding the Hotel That's Right for You

A hotel is your home away from home. When choosing a temporary home (or hotel, as some might prefer to call it), four things are of the utmost importance: price, location, space, and amenities. I cannot tell a lie. Washington, D.C., hotel rooms are not inexpensive. But what else would you expect in a cosmopolitan East Coast city that also happens to be the nation's capital?

That's the bad news. Now for the good. Although accommodations will eat a healthy chunk of your travel dollar, room prices compare favorably with those in other major U.S. cities. And because so many D.C. attractions are free, and most of the recommended restaurants are in the moderate range, you'll come out ahead in the long run. Besides, you won't need a car (in fact, a car is a liability) and public transportation is convenient and reasonable.

The choice is yours. Check into a lavish hotel with all the extras, in a location that's within walking distance of the major sights, or choose a spot less centrally located and forgo the terry robes and room service. Bear in mind, however, that forking over extra bucks for a room in the heart of town can outweigh the time and expense of commuting.

Chapter 5

Pillow Talk: The Lowdown on the Washington, D.C. Hotel Scene

In This Chapter

➤ To be here or to be there? Choosing what neighborhood to stay in

➤ Hotel sweet hotel? Choosing the right hotel

➤ There's room for everyone: Choosing the right room

Of the four considerations—price, location, roominess, and amenities— you're already acquainted with the first, since you worked out your budget with the worksheet at the end of chapter 2. (If you didn't, now's as good a time as any to do it.) If you view this trip as a once-in-a-lifetime splurge, you may want to throw caution to the wind and book a suite at the Four Seasons or another luxurious hotel. I can think of worse ways to dispose of the green stuff! If you're on a tight budget, there's always the Youth Hostel or friends or relatives living in the area.

Location! Location! Location!

Each Washington, D.C., neighborhood has its own distinct flavor and char- acter that will color your experience, should you choose a hotel there. In the following sections, I'll give you thumbnail portraits of all the major D.C. neighborhoods you can choose from.

I have purposely left out neighborhoods like Adams–Morgan that are not eas- ily accessible to Metro.

Capitol Hill

The area known as "the Hill" radiates from the U.S. Capitol and extends east- ward to the D.C. Armory. H Street NE and the Southwest Freeway mark its north and south perimeters. Besides the Capitol, you'll find the Supreme Court, Library of Congress, Folger Shakespeare Library, Union Station, Capital Children's Museum, and National Postal Museum, as well as many restaurants. Safety is a concern, however, after dark.

In a nutshell:

- ☺ You'll be able to walk to many attractions, including the mall.
- ☺ You'll be able to visit your senator and congressional representative.
- ☺ You'll be close to Union Station and Metro.
- ☺ Prices, for the most part, are less than in other areas.

But . . .

- ☹ You'll be far from patches of greenery.
- ☹ You'll be in an iffy neighborhood.

Balancing the Budget

Ask about special promotions, weekend packages, and discounts when you call to make a reservation. It's amazing how flexible hotels can become when they're not filled. It's true what they say: The squeaky wheel gets the oil.

Convention Center/Downtown

A mix of office buildings, shops, hotels, and restaurants, this large area takes in the White House, Chinatown, the Convention Center, MCI Center (for sports and concerts), theater district, 7th Street arts corridor, and D.C.'s business heart around Connecticut Avenue and K Street NW. Lying roughly between 7th and 22nd streets NW (east to west) and P Street and Pennsylvania Avenue (north to south), the area is convenient to several Metro stations and within walking distance of many attractions. Prices for accommodations run from moderate to through the roof.

In a nutshell:

- ☺ You'll be in the thick of things.
- ☺ You'll be able to walk to many attractions, restaurants, shops, and theaters.

But . . .

- ☹ You'll probably pay top dollar.

Dupont Circle

Named for the traffic circle and minipark from which Connecticut, Massachusetts, and New Hampshire avenues radiate like wheel spokes, vibrant Dupont Circle is a melting pot known for its bookstores, boutiques, galleries, restaurants, and hospitable climate to gays. After much of D.C. has rolled up the sidewalks, Dupont Circle is wide awake. Hotels are more reasonable here than in the Downtown sector, but the area is an extra Metro stop or two away from most attractions.

In a nutshell:

☺ You'll be in a stimulating, multicultural neighborhood.

☺ You'll have restaurants, shops, and galleries close by.

But . . .

☹ You may have to contend with street and traffic noise.

Foggy Bottom

The former industrial area west of the White House known as Funkstown is marked by charming row houses and brick sidewalks in the shadow of the Kennedy Center, State Department, George Washington University, and infamous Watergate. You may be in D.C., but a pleasing, European ambience fills the air in this attractive neighborhood located in the West End of the city. Back on the American side of things, you can walk to the White House and Georgetown.

☺ You'll enjoy soaking up the urban village atmosphere.

☺ You'll be close to the Kennedy Center, White House, and Georgetown.

But . . .

☹ You'll have to take Metro to most sights.

☹ You'll have fewer hotel choices.

Georgetown

Established in colonial times and one of D.C.'s most prestigious addresses, the former bustling tobacco port northwest of Foggy Bottom still pulses with activity generated by the many restaurants, pubs, and boutiques along its main thoroughfares, Wisconsin Avenue and M Street. Historic homes line the quieter side streets, and students from D.C., the suburbs, and nearby Georgetown University flood the area evenings and weekends. Visitors seeking peace and quiet are advised to ask for a room off the street, or to stay elsewhere. The nearest Metro station, Foggy Bottom, is about a 20-minute walk or 10-minute bus ride.

In a nutshell:

☺ You'll be able to walk to shops, restaurants, and nightlife.

☺ You'll be close to Dumbarton Oaks, the waterfront, and recreation on the C&O Canal.

But . . .

☹ You may have trouble sleeping, especially on weekends.

☹ You'll be a long walk from Metro and a longer walk to most attractions.

☹ You'll be unhappy if you dislike crowds and hoopla.

Upper Northwest

The site of the National Zoo, many good restaurants, and upscale shopping, the largely residential area has several hotels in all price ranges. The downside of this neighborhood is the longer commute to the downtown sights. Otherwise, travelers—especially families—will find good value.

In a nutshell:

☺ You'll be close to the National Zoo, prime shopping, and restaurants.

☺ You'll find good value, especially on weekends.

But . . .

☹ You'll be several Metro stops away from most major attractions.

☹ You'll spend more money and time commuting.

The Price Is Right

The **rack rate** is the maximum rate that a hotel charges for a room. It's the rate you'd get if you walked in off the street and asked for a room for the night. You sometimes see the rate printed on the fire/emergency exit diagrams posted on the back of your door.

Hotels are happy to charge you the rack rate, but you don't have to pay it, unless the hotel is full. Perhaps the best way to avoid paying the rack rate is surprisingly simple: Just ask for a cheaper or discounted rate. You may be pleasantly surprised.

In all but the smallest accommodations, the rate you pay for a room depends on many factors, not the least of which is how you make your reservation. A travel agent may be able to negotiate a better price with certain hotels than you could get by yourself. (That's because the hotel gives the agent a discount in exchange for steering his or her business toward that hotel.) Reserving a room through the hotel's 800 number may also result in a lower rate than if you call the hotel directly. On the other hand, the central reservations number may not know about discount rates at specific locations. For example, local franchises may offer a special group rate for a wedding or family reunion, but they may neglect to tell the central booking line. Your best bet is to call both the local number and the 800 number and see which one gives you a better deal.

Room rates also change with the season and as occupancy rates rise and fall. If a hotel is close to full, it is unlikely to extend discount rates; if it's close to empty, it may be willing to negotiate. Room prices are subject to change without notice, so even the rates quoted in this book may be different from the actual rate you receive when you make your reservation. Be sure to mention membership in **AAA, AARP, frequent-flyer programs,** and any other corporate rewards program when you make your reservation. You never know when it might be worth a few dollars off your room rate.

What's Off-Season?

Rooms are at a premium and most expensive from mid-March through mid-June. Generally, summer (July and August) and winter are considered off-season in Washington. Except for the influx of visiting families, the city is relatively quiet in summer when congressional representatives are home stumping, catching up on paperwork, and vacationing. This is the best time to cash in on family packages and discounts, but the heat and humidity can be devilishly uncomfortable, and some theaters are dark. In summer, families often receive perks, such as 50% off an adjoining room for the kidlets. Some properties allow kids 12 and under to eat free in the hotel's restaurants. Many allow children under the age of 16 or 18 to stay free in the parents' room. Things are also slower around the Thanksgiving and Christmas holidays, and in January and February. But you may have to contend with rain, snow, or sleet. If the post office can do it, you can too!

Getting the Best Room

Somebody has to get the best room in the house. It might as well be you.

➤ **Always ask for a corner room.** They're usually larger, quieter, closer to the elevator, and have more windows and light than standard rooms, and they don't always cost more.

➤ **When you make your reservation, ask if the hotel is renovating; if it is, request a room away from the renovation work.** Inquire, too, about the location of the restaurants, bars, and discos in the hotel—these could all be a source of irritating noise.

Hear Ye! Hear Ye!

Are you celebrating an anniversary, a promotion, a special birthday? Don't be shy when booking your hotel room. The reservations people often take notes, and you may find a bottle of champagne or some other treat waiting for you in your room when you arrive.

➤ **If you aren't happy with your room when you arrive, talk to the front desk.** If the hotel has another room available, it should have no problem accommodating you, within reason.

➤ **If the smell of smoke bothers you, request a nonsmoking room.** Most hotels have nonsmoking rooms available.

Taxes & Service Charges

As you go through the selection process, don't forget to factor in fees over and above the basic rate you pay. The hotel tax in Washington is 14.5% (ouch!). So a $150-per-night room will cost you $171.75. When you make your reservation, be sure to ask if the quoted price includes the hefty tax.

Tourist Traps

Phonies beware! Some hotels charge 75¢ or $1 (a minute) for making a local phone call from the room. If you put on your slippers and shuffle to a lobby pay phone, you can make the same call for a mere 35¢. And as odd as it sounds, with all the discounted rates offered these days by cell phone companies, it might be cheaper to call from a cell phone than from the hotel phone.

What Kind of Place Is Right for You?

Deciding where to stay is never easy. You want to be sure that you're getting the most for your money and that you're staying in a perfect location. Well, let me tell you—you'll find it all in Washington, ranging from small hotels with kitchen facilities, to suites with an extra room, and flashy deluxe accommodations with all the bells and whistles—and price tags—to match. Washington also has many B&Bs, but most of these are not centrally located.

I've selected hotels that have sufficient capacity, are accessible to Metro, are in reasonably safe neighborhoods, and offer good value for their price category. Even if the decor is plain, they're well maintained or have been renovated in the past few years. In other words, I'm not going to steer you to a 4-room place over an all-night club, with peeling paint, in a far-away, questionable neighborhood. *Capiche?*

Tourist Traps

Some unsuspecting tourists think all those cute little bottles and snacks in the minibar are gratis, a gift from the hotel to thank guests for their business. Uh-uh. You'll pay dearly for every nip you take. Ask the concierge where the nearest package store is and BYO. Or pack a flask. You can pick up ice from a vending machine in the hotel for a nominal sum. In most instances, if you order ice from room service, it'll cost you.

Bed & Breakfasts

While there are some very nice and well-run homes operating as inns, most are in out-of-the-way locations, especially for visitors hoping to cram all the Mall museums into a weekend. If you're visiting Washington with no particular agenda, except for sniffing out the details of the latest scandal, by all means consider staying in a B&B. Most are not within walking distance of Metro and, therefore, are inaccessible except by car or taxi. If you're a fan of B&Bs, here are some helpful services that screen inns and book rooms from $50 to $250 per night.

Hear Ye! Hear Ye!

Having given you my take on staying in a B&B, I offer the Morrison–Clark Historic Inn (see chapter 6).

➤ **Bed and Breakfast League/Sweet Dreams & Toast,** P.O. Box 9490, Washington, DC 20016 (☎ **202/363-7767**)

➤ **Bed & Breakfast Accommodations Ltd.,** P.O. Box 12011, Washington, DC 20005 (☎ **202-328-3510;** fax 202/332-3885)

Hear Ye! Hear Ye!

Even in the finest hotels, strange noises, loud TVs, and snoring partners can wreak havoc with your sleep. If you're a light sleeper, carry earplugs whenever you travel. If you forget, substitute cotton balls or wadded-up tissue. When all else fails, make a salami sandwich of your head with two pillows (it works!).

Hotel Strategies for Families Traveling with Kids

If you're adventurous enough to drag the little darlin's with you, you're in luck. Washington hotels bend over backward to woo families with special amenities ranging from free or reduced-price extra rooms for kids to low-cost children's menus, special activities, and video arcades. (Choices that are especially kid-friendly are starred with a kid-friendly icon in the next chapter.) Ask about the hotel's facilities when you reserve a room. Pools—some are indoor and, therefore, open year-round—are a big plus when traveling with kids. So are in-room cable movies and VCRs, and proximity to shopping and parks. Opt for a hotel that allows children to stay free in the parents' room. Most do. If you can swing it, get a suite with a kitchenette. The way most kids inhale food, you'll save megabucks by having some meals and snacks in your home away from home.

Hotel Strategies for Travelers with Disabilities

When booking a room, discuss accessibility with the reservationist; be sure to ask about stairs, grab rails, and width of doorways. For more information about hotels and accessibility, contact the **Washington, D.C., Convention and Visitors Association,** 1212 New York Ave. NW, Suite 600, Washington, DC (☎ **800/422-8644** or 202/789-7000), or visit the Web site at **www.washington.org**.

What If I Didn't Plan Ahead?

I can't imagine arriving without reservations, unless a personal emergency brings you to the nation's capital, and I definitely don't recommend it. However, if you do arrive in Washington without a reservation, you won't necessarily have to sleep in an airport lounge. You may be able to get a room by calling a reservation service, which buys up rooms in bulk and resells them. Do it as soon as you arrive at the airport or Union Station. Try the following, both in business for about 15 years. Or, you could schlep your luggage around town and inquire in person. But why, unless you're a masochist, would you want to do that?

➤ **Capitol Reservations** (☎ **800/VISIT-DC** or 202/452-1270) works with about 75 hotels. If you have time before leaving home, you can visit the Web site at **www.hotelsdc.com**.

➤ **Washington, D.C., Accommodations** (☎ **800/554-2220** or 202/ 289-2220) is a good resource for information and reservations. Agents act as matchmakers and pair visitors with hotels meeting their specific needs. Visit them on the Web at **www.dcaccommodations.com**.

Chapter 6

Washington, D.C. Hotels from A to Z

In This Chapter

➤ Quick indexes of hotels by location and price

➤ A review of my favorite Washington, D.C.–area hotels

➤ A worksheet to help you make your choice

Okay, it's time to choose a place to lay your head. The chapter starts with lists that break down my favorite snooze sites by neighborhood and price. The reviews that follow give you all the information you'll need to make a decision.

The reviews are in alphabetical order for easy referral, and the hotel's neighborhood appears right beneath its name. Locate them on the maps and you'll know where they are in relation to the sights you want to see. If you want to be near the National Zoo, for example, **Upper Northwest** is for you. If you'd like to walk to many attractions, **Downtown** has your name on it. For a funkier scene that's great for browsing, try **Dupont Circle.** Shopaholic foodies can enjoy primo shopping and a slew of restaurants in historic **Georgetown.** Want to stay in a charming neighborhood far from the maddening crowds, or planning a clandestine meeting with your amour? Try **Foggy Bottom.** See chapter 5 for a more in-depth discussion of Washington neighborhoods.

You'll note that I've attached "Kid-Friendly" icons to hotels with features that are especially attractive to families. But I haven't forgotten those of you without kids who are looking for the best pad for doing business, or having a romance, or bringing the mutt, and so on. Look through the index boxes dotted throughout this chapter to see which hotel best suits your needs.

Price Categories

As for prices, I've noted rack rates in the listings and also preceded each description with a dollar-sign icon to make quick references easier. (Ain't I clever?) As you've probably deduced, the more $ signs under the name, the more you pay. Go to the head of the class. Dollar-sign icons reflect the average of a hotel's high- and low-end rack rates. It goes something like this:

$ = under $100

$$ = $100–$150

$$$ = $150–$200

$$$$ = $200–$250

$$$$$ = $250 and up

In cases where the rack rates flirt with the next higher category, I've been kind and assigned the lower dollar-sign designation.

A final word before you get to work: As you look over the reviews, jot down the ones that appeal to you. I've provided a chart at the end of the chapter for this very purpose. In the meantime, mark an "X" next to the ones you like. Go ahead, release all those pent-up inhibitions and write in the book!

Quick Picks: Washington, D.C. Hotels at a Glance
Hotel Index by Location

Capitol Hill

Holiday Inn on the Hill

Hotel George

Hyatt Regency Washington

Downtown

Days Inn Premier Convention Center Hotel

Grand Hyatt Washington at Washington Center

Hotel Harrington

Hotel Washington

Jefferson Hotel

J. W. Marriott Hotel

Lincoln Suites

Loews L'Enfant Plaza

Morrison–Clark Historic Inn

Red Roof Inn

Renaissance Washington, D.C. Hotel

Washington International Hostel (WIH)

Willard Inter-Continental

Dupont Circle

Canterbury Hotel

Hotel Sofitel

Hotel Tabard Inn

Foggy Bottom

George Washington University Inn

Swissôtel Washington: The Watergate Hotel

Wyndham Bristol

Georgetown

Four Seasons

Uptown

Omni Shoreham

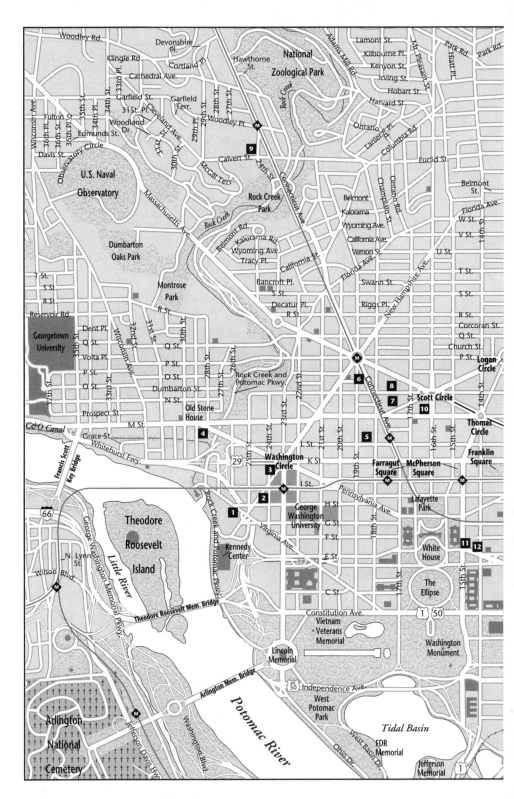

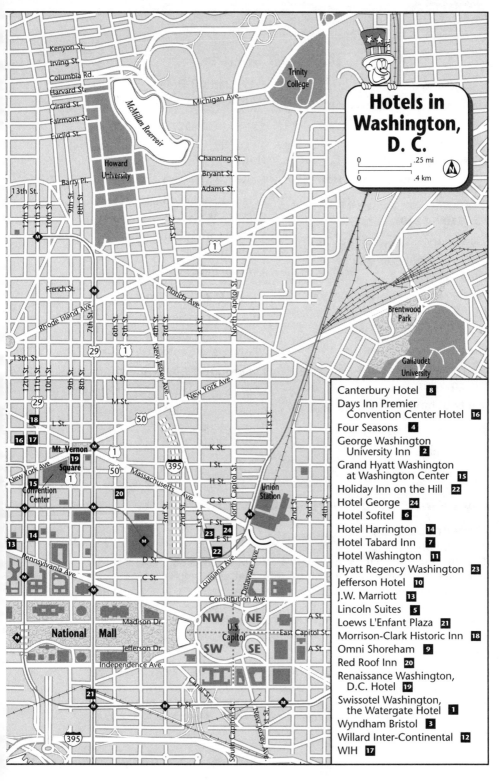

Hotels in Washington, D. C.

0 ——— .25 mi
0 ——— .4 km

Trinity College
McMillan Reservoir
Howard University
Brentwood Park
Gallaudet University

Kenyon St.
Irving St.
Columbia Rd.
Harvard St.
Girard St.
Fairmont St.
Euclid St.
Michigan Ave.
Channing St.
Bryant St.
Adams St.
Barry Pl.
13th St.
French St.
Florida Ave.
Rhode Island Ave.
13th St.
New York Ave.
N St.
M St.
L St.
Mt. Vernon Square
Convention Center
New York Ave.
Massachusetts Ave.
K St.
I St.
H St.
G St.
F St.
E St.
D St.
C St.
Pennsylvania Ave.
Madison Dr.
National Mall
Jefferson Dr.
Independence Ave.
Constitution Ave.
U.S. Capitol
East Capitol St.
A St.
A St.
Louisiana Ave.
Delaware Ave.
Canal St.
South Capitol St.
New Jersey Ave.
North Capitol St.
Union Station

Canterbury Hotel **8**
Days Inn Premier
  Convention Center Hotel **16**
Four Seasons **4**
George Washington
  University Inn **2**
Grand Hyatt Washington
  at Washington Center **15**
Holiday Inn on the Hill **22**
Hotel George **24**
Hotel Sofitel **6**
Hotel Harrington **14**
Hotel Tabard Inn **7**
Hotel Washington **11**
Hyatt Regency Washington **23**
Jefferson Hotel **10**
J.W. Marriott **13**
Lincoln Suites **5**
Loews L'Enfant Plaza **21**
Morrison-Clark Historic Inn **18**
Omni Shoreham **9**
Red Roof Inn **20**
Renaissance Washington,
  D.C. Hotel **19**
Swissotel Washington,
  the Watergate Hotel **1**
Wyndham Bristol **3**
Willard Inter-Continental **12**
WIH **17**

Hotel Index by Price

$ (Under $100)

Days Inn Premier Convention Center Hotel (Downtown)

Hotel Harrington (Downtown)

Hotel Tabard Inn (Dupont Circle)

Washington International Hostel (Downtown)

$$ ($100–$150)

Canterbury Hotel (Dupont Circle)

George Washington University Inn (Foggy Bottom)

Holiday Inn on the Hill (Capitol Hill)

Hotel Washington (Downtown)

Lincoln Suites (Downtown)

Morrison–Clark Historic Inn (Downtown)

Red Roof Inn (Downtown)

$$$ ($150–$200)

Hotel George (Capitol Hill)

Hotel Sofitel (Dupont Circle)

J. W. Marriott Hotel (Downtown)

$$$$ ($200–$250)

Hyatt Regency Washington (Capitol Hill)

Loews L'Enfant Plaza (Downtown)

Renaissance Washington, D.C. Hotel (Downtown)

Willard Inter-Continental (Downtown)

Wyndham Bristol (Foggy Bottom)

$$$$$ ($250 and up)

Four Seasons (Georgetown)

Grand Hyatt Washington at Washington Center (Downtown)

Jefferson Hotel (Downtown)

Omni Shoreham (Upper Northwest)

Swissôtel Washington: The Watergate Hotel (Foggy Bottom)

My Favorite Washington, D.C. Hotels

Canterbury Hotel
$$. Dupont Circle.

This all-suite hotel with surprisingly affordable rates is big in personal service. The 99 suites are decorated in subtle shades to help ease your tensions after a strenuous day of business or sightseeing. Service is key. The staff almost dares guests to find something they can't or won't do (within legal limits of course). The Canterbury has a cozy publike restaurant and is on one of the neighborhood's quieter blocks but close to the action in Dupont Circle.

1733 N St. NW (between 17th and 18th sts.). ☎ *800/424-2950 or 202/393-3000. Fax 202/785-9581. Web site: www.utellhotels.com.* **Metro:** *Dupont Circle, take escalator out of south entrance, left onto Connecticut Ave., left at N St., cross 18th St. to the hotel (in the middle of the block).* **Parking:** *$13.* **Rack rates:** *$130 double. AE, DC, DISC, MC, V.*

Hotel Bargains

You don't need to stay in Washington, D.C., to have a good time. Take the Metro to a nearby suburb in Maryland or Virginia and you'll find some budget accommodations that are only a short distance away from the action. Try the following:

➤ **Best Western Capital Beltway,** 5910 Princess Garden Parkway, Lanham, MD (☎ **301/459-1000**). Complimentary van service (8am–8pm) to New Carrollton Metro, 1 mile away.

➤ **Econo Lodge Metro Arlington,** 6800 Lee Highway, Arlington, VA (☎ **703/538-5300**), 3 blocks to East Falls Church Metro.

➤ **Holiday Inn Chevy Chase,** 5520 Wisconsin Ave., Chevy Chase, MD (☎ **301/656-1500**), 1 block to Friendship Heights Metro.

➤ **Holiday Inn Rosslyn Key Bridge,** 1900 N. Fort Myer Dr., Arlington, VA (☎ **703/807-2000**), 1 block to Crystal City Metro stop.

 ## Days Inn Premier Convention Center Hotel
$. Downtown.

When your activities include the Convention Center, Chinatown, Ford's Theatre, the FBI, and other sightseeing, you won't find a better location. The neighborhood is commercial and not too pretty, but convenience is the name of the game here. A super summertime perk is the rooftop swimming pool. Families fill up in Savannah's, open for a breakfast buffet (large enough that you can skip lunch, maybe), lunch, and dinner. Meeting rooms and a coin-operated laundry are on site.

1201 K St. NW (at 12th St.). ☎ *800/ 562-3350 or 202/842-1020. Fax 202/ 898-0154. Web site: www.daysinn.com.* **Metro:** *Metro Center, right (north) at 12th St., 3 blocks to K St.* **Parking:** *$14.* **Rack rates:** *$59–$165 double. Children under 18 stay free in parents' room, and be sure to ask for the "Family Plan" during the winter months. Ask about corporate rate and September Days (for seniors) programs for discounts. AE, CB, DC, DISC, JCB, MC, V.*

Don't Leave Home Without This: Credit Card Abbreviations

AE	American Express
CB	Carte Blanche
DC	Diners Club
DISC	Discover Card
ER	EnRoute
JCB	Japan Credit Bank
MC	MasterCard
V	Visa

Hear Ye! Hear Ye!

The "free continental breakfast" offered by some hotels may not be the pancakes, eggs, and bacon you're used to at home. Often it consists of juice, a muffin or bagel, and hot beverage. Although this may be adequate morning fare, it may not be a savings, and there are plenty of breakfast places throughout D.C. When all is said and done, even a light complimentary breakfast is a convenience, allowing you to catch a few extra z's.

Four Seasons
$$$$$. Georgetown.

Sumptuous surroundings and impeccable service are hallmarks of the Four Seasons, located on the edge of Georgetown. Many rooms and public areas overlook Rock Creek Park (and traffic) and the C&O Canal. Furnishings include antique reproductions, desks, down-filled bedding, and armchairs comfortable enough to snooze in. Free HBO, VCRs, and CD players are standard. The round-the-clock concierge service is to die for, whether you want a tuxedo or a toothbrush. Fido is welcomed with a bone and water served on a silver tray. In the Garden Terrace, deals are sealed and love affairs begin over high tea or cocktails. There's an indoor pool, health club (Vichy shower, hydrotherapy, aerobics studio, quiet rooms, whirlpool, steam, and sauna), and phones coming out the kazoo (who makes all these calls?). John Travolta, Sheryl Crow, Nicholas Cage, and Tom Hanks have tumbled into the triple-sheeted beds. VICs (very important children) under 16 stay free and are spoiled with natural sodas, snacks, mini–candy bars, balloons, games, and magazines. At check-in, kids receive a personal note from the hotel manager, plush kid-sized terrycloth bathrobes, and colorful pillow covers. Older children can entertain themselves with the free Sony Playstation, Super Nintendo, Sega Genesis, board games, video games, and coloring books provided by the hotel free of charge. A special children's menu is offered in the Garden Terrace and at "Tea Time for Tots." If you can afford the price, go for it! You get what you pay for.

2800 Pennsylvania Ave. NW (at 28th St.).
☎ ***800/332-3442*** *or 202/342-0444. Fax 202/944-2076. Web site: www.fourseasons. com.* **Metro:** *Foggy Bottom station, up the*

Best Hotels for Celebrity Gawking

Four Seasons	$$$$$
Jefferson	$$$$$
Loews L'Enfant Plaza	$$$$
Swissôtel Washington	$$$$$
Willard Inter-Continental	$$$$

*escalator, take a left at 23rd St., left at the traffic circle, left onto Pennsylvania Ave., and continue 4 blocks to hotel. **Parking:** $24 (ask if your package includes parking). **Rack rates:** $355 and up. Ask about weekend rates and special packages. AE, DC, ER, JCB, MC, V.*

Kids George Washington University Inn
$$. Foggy Bottom.

Formerly the Inn at Foggy Bottom, this hotel is just 2 blocks from George Washington University and not far from the Kennedy Center for the Performing Arts. The hotel's commodious 95 rooms (including 31 one-bedroom suites) have been redecorated to give you a Williamsburg feel with elegant furnishings. Each room has a minirefrigerator, microwave, coffee-maker, iron and ironing board. Fully equipped kitchenettes are also available. Enjoy the quaint Foggy Bottom neighborhood, secure underground valet parking, and complimentary passes to the campus fitness facilities. Expect personalized and courteous service. There's a coin-operated laundry facility if you run out of socks.

*824 New Hampshire Ave. (between H and I sts.). ☎ **800/426-4455** or 202/337-6620. Fax 202/298-7499. Web site: www.gwuinn.com. **Metro:** Foggy Bottom/GWU, exit the station and make a U-turn, to New Hampshire Ave., and left. The inn is on the right. **Parking:** $14. **Rack rates:** $105–$155. AE, DC, MC, V.*

Kids Grand Hyatt Washington at Washington Center
$$$$$. Downtown.

With an underground tunnel that leads directly to the Metro Center Metro Station, the world is your oyster at the Grand Hyatt. It's a piece of cake to get wherever you're going from here. The large and well-appointed rooms and suites are set around the 12-floor glass-enclosed atrium. With the Convention Center located across the street, conventioneers abound when there's a meeting in town—they're particularly abundant on weekdays. Other amenities include a heated indoor pool (kids under 16 must be accompanied by an adult), steam room, sauna, health club with Jacuzzi that's free on weekends, exercise/aerobics room, and massage room. There's also shuffleboard and minibasketball. Baby-sitting can be arranged through the concierge.

*1000 H St. NW (at 11th St.). ☎ **800/233-1234** or 202/582-1234. Fax 202/637-4781. Web site: www.hyatt.com. **Metro:** Metro Center, Washington Center/Grand Hyatt exit, then walk through the tunnel and up the escalator to the hotel. **Parking:** $12. **Rack rates:** From $259 double. Children under 18 stay free in their parents' room; there are special family weekend rates, or children can have their own room at half price and other benefits. AE, CB, DC, DISC, MC, V.*

 Holiday Inn on the Hill
$$. Capitol Hill.

This Holiday Inn with a primo location—only 2 blocks from the Capitol—offers recently renovated, large, and comfortable rooms. If large isn't big enough for you, request an adjoining parlor that features a Murphy bed. A rooftop pool is open for summer enjoyment and a great view of the area. Service is key, and a huge percentage of the employees are long-term, indicating their satisfaction is your satisfaction, or vice versa. In the evenings (especially in summer), there are often programs for children.

415 New Jersey Ave. NW (between D and E sts.). ☎ *800/638-1116 or 202/638-1616. Fax 202/638-0707.* **Metro:** *Union Station, cross 1st St. and Massachusetts Ave. to E St., turn right. Walk down E St. 2 blocks, turn left onto New Jersey Ave., and hotel is on left-hand side.* **Parking:** *$11.* **Rack rates:** *$120–$160. Children 18 and under stay free in parents' room. Ask for seasonal packages and weekend rates. AE, DC, DISC, MC, V.*

Hotel George
$$$. Capitol Hill.

Bring in da' George, bring in da' funk. After major reconstructive surgery, the erstwhile Bellevue Hotel reopened in 1998 as the Hotel George. Ever wonder what George Washington would look like if he were around today? Look no further. Posters of a modern-day George hang in the hip, spacious, and well-appointed rooms. Award-winning chef Jeff Buben wields the whisk in the French bistro restaurant, Bis. Cigar smoking is de rigueur in the billiard room. A short walk from Union Station and the Capitol, George is a top choice for executives and lobbyists with business on the Hill and for families.

15 E St. NW (unit block of E St.). ☎ *800/576-8331 or 202/347-4200. Fax 202/347-4213. Web site: www.hotelgeorge.com.* **Metro:** *Union Station, walk 1 block west on Massachusetts Ave., left (south) at N. Capitol St. (post office), 1 block to right at E St. and hotel (in first block).* **Parking:** *$18.* **Rack rates:** *$185–$220 double. Children under 14 stay free. AE, CB, DC, DISC, MC, V.*

Hotel Harrington
$. Downtown.

The Harrington is your basic group hotel prized for its convenience (to Metro, the FBI, Ford's Theatre, the Shops at National Place, and the Pavilion at the Old Post Office) and affordability. Planet Hollywood is within easy orbiting distance. Family suites consist of two rooms (one with a queen bed, the other with two twins) and two baths. A good deal, and you won't be tripping over each other. Cribs and refrigerators are free, and a self-service laundry is on the premises (if you miss doing laundry). There are plenty of dining options in and around the hotel.

11th and E sts. NW. ☎ *800/424-8532 or 202/628-8140. Fax 202/347-3924. Web site: www.hotel-harrington.com.* **Metro:** *Metro Center, 11th St. exit to the corner of G St., walk 2 blocks to E St. and the hotel.* **Parking:** *$6.50.* **Rack rates:** *From $79. AE, DC, DISC, MC, V.*

Hotel Sofitel
$$$. Dupont Circle.

Smack dab in the middle of Embassy Row, you'd expect this 144-room (including 38 suites) hotel to have a European flavor, and it does. Guest rooms feature elegant appointments, and a multilingual concierge is on hand to assist you. There's 24-hour room service and, of course, an evening turn-down (with chocolate and a rose). Rooms have telephones with computer- and fax-access lines. A health facility and sports complex is across the street to help you work off the fine cuisine from Le Trocadero restaurant. (The house recommends the salmon with an herb crust or the portabello mushroom sandwich, followed by the chocolate ganache or the apple tart. Burp.)

Best Service for Fido

| Four Seasons | $$$$$ |
| Loews L'Enfant Plaza | $$$$ |

1914 Connecticut Ave. NW (at 19th St.). ☎ *800/424-2464 or 202/797-2000. Fax 202/462-0944. Web site: www.sofitel.com.* **Metro:** *Dupont Circle, north exit. Walk up Connecticut Ave. 3 blocks to the hotel on the left.* **Parking:** *$15.* **Rack rates:** *$149–$209 double. AE, DC, DISC, MC, V.*

Hotel Tabard Inn
$. Dupont Circle.

Rest your tootsies in this Dupont Circle inn, whose namesake appears in Chaucer's *Canterbury Tales*. The hotel's 40 rooms, some with shared baths, are furnished with Victorian and American Empire antiques. A real down-home touch. The Tabard Inn restaurant is open for complimentary breakfast as well as lunch and dinner (not complimentary, but quite good).

1739 N St. NW, (between 17th and 18th sts. ☎ *202/785-1277. Fax: 202/ 785-6173.* **Metro:** *Dupont Circle. Leave the station via the south exit, onto Connecticut Ave., turn left on N St., and walk about 3 blocks to the hotel.* **Parking:** *limited street parking and two garages on the block.* **Rack rates:** *$80–$130 double. MC, V.*

Hotel Washington
$$. Downtown.

Start on top at the outdoor Sky Terrace rooftop bar for a view of the July 4th fireworks, the under-renovation Washington Monument, and the White

House lawn. At the oldest continuously operating hotel in the city, you can select a room with a view and maybe catch sight of how many pizzas are being delivered on a crisis night at the White House. The rooms are furnished with antique reproductions. Bathrooms are heavy on marble and have a telephone. The hotel is convenient to the National, Shakespeare, and Warner theaters, Smithsonian, and many other attractions. There's a fitness center if the spirit moves you.

515 15th St. NW (at Pennsylvania Ave.). ☎ ***800/424-9540*** *or 202/638-5900. Fax 202/638-1594. Web site: www.hotelwashington.com.* **Metro:** *Metro Center, leave 12th and F sts. exit, walk up F St. 3 blocks to 15th St. The hotel is on the corner.* **Parking:** *$20.* **Rack rates:** *$100–$145 double. AE, DC, MC, V.*

 ## Hyatt Regency Washington
$$$$. Capitol Hill.

Just about as close as you can get to Congress without running for office, the Hyatt Regency is favored by conventioneers, lobbyists, and tourists. The 834

Best Luxury Choice

Four Seasons	$$$$$
Jefferson Hotel	$$$$$

rooms and 31 suites surround the 5-story atrium lobby. Request a south-side-facing room—these have a view of the Capitol. Another 2-story glass atrium covers the pool (with snack bar). A health club is available for a fee. Children have special menus in the restaurant and for room service. The Capitol View Club offers a bird's-eye view of the Capitol and so-so food the last time we tried it.

400 New Jersey Ave. NW (at E St.). ☎ ***800/233-1234*** *or 202/737-1234. Fax 202/737-5773. Web site: www.hyatt.com.* **Metro:** *Union Station, walk down E St. 3 blocks, and the hotel is on the left.* **Parking:** *$19.* **Rack rates:** *$235–$240 double. The Camp Hyatt program offers a second room at half price, or children under 18 stay free in their parents' room. AE, DC, DISC, MC, V.*

Jefferson Hotel
$$$$$. Downtown.

This charming hotel with 68 rooms and 32 suites has classic charm with a lobby topped by balconies. The gracious rooms are filled with antiques and reproductions as well as original art. Although on a busy intersection, the windows are double-glazed to keep in the quiet. The staff is noted for remembering previous guests by name, and your laundry is hand-ironed and delivered in wicker baskets (just like home. Not). It's a member of the Small Luxury Hotels, meaning its standards are sky high. There's an indoor pool and a fitness center with a sauna and Jacuzzi.

1200 16th St. NW (at M St.). ☎ ***800/ 368-5966*** *or 202/347-2200. Fax 202/ 785-1505. Web site: www.slh.com.* **Metro:** *Farragut North, leave via Connecticut and L sts. Follow L St. to 16th St. and turn left for 1 block to M St. The hotel's on the left side.* **Parking:** *$20.* **Rack rates:** *$300 double. AE, DC, MC, V.*

Hotels with the Best Views

Hotel Washington	$$
J. W. Marriott Hotel	$$$
Loews L'Enfant Plaza	$$$$
Omni Shoreham	$$$$$

 J. W. Marriott Hotel
$$$. Downtown.

With one of the best downtown addresses, the 772-room (34 suites) J. W. is conveniently located within the same building as the Shops at National Place (boutiques and eateries) and the National Press Club. Sights, restaurants, and theaters are ever so close. Rooms are spacious and come with the expected electronic communications connections required these days. If you want to go one better, request a "Room with a View" overlooking Pennsylvania Avenue or the Washington Monument for an extra $10. Try the health club and the indoor pool, while the kids visit the video arcade. Four restaurants offer a range of menus and prices. Lots of conferences and convention meetings are held here, so you'll see lots of suits in the lobby.

1331 Pennsylvania Ave. NW (at 13th St.). ☎ ***800/228-9290*** *or 202/393-2000. Fax 202/626-6991. Web site: www.Marriotthotels.com.* **Metro:** *Metro Center, take the 13th and F sts. exit, and at the top of the escalator take a left at F St. toward the Shops at National Place. Enter the shopping mall and go down one level, turn right at Boston Seafood (we are not making this up). Keep walking straight ahead to the hotel.* **Parking:** *$16.* **Rack rates:** *$169–$244 double. Children under 18 stay free in their parents' room. Ask for seasonal weekend rates and make sure you're a member of the Marriott Awards programs. AE, CB, DC, DISC, ER, JCB, MC, V.*

 Lincoln Suites
$$. Downtown.

This charming little all-suite property, just 2 blocks from the Connecticut Avenue business corridor, features studio suites, each richly decorated, with either a fully equipped kitchen or wet bar with a microwave and refrigerator. The King Suites offer all the comforts of a "home office" and include a desk, second phone, and computer jack. There are 99 studio suites and 30 employees, so the service is very personal. Would you believe cookies

Best Hotels Near the Mall

J. W. Marriott Hotel	$$$
Loews L'Enfant Plaza	$$$$

and milk every evening from 6 to 8pm? Julius, at the front desk, will be your guardian angel and tell you everything you want to know about the Washington Monument (he used to be a National Park Service ranger). Guests partake of full privileges at Bally Total Fitness Center nearby. On weekends a complimentary continental breakfast is served in the lobby.

1823 L St. NW (between 18th and 19th sts.). ☎ ***800/424-2970*** *or 202/ 223-4320. Fax 202/223-8546. Web site: www.lincolnhotels.com.* **Metro:** *Farragut North or Farragut West, exit onto 18th St., turn left and go 2 blocks, then left onto L St. for half a block.* **Parking:** *$16 on weekdays; discounted weekends.* **Rack rates:** *$129–$149 double. Children under 16 stay free in parents' room. AE, CB, DC, DISC, MC, V.*

Kids Loews L'Enfant Plaza
$$$$. Downtown.

Here's a location, location, location hotel, for sure. It's right on top of the L'Enfant Plaza Metro station, a 2-block walk to the Air and Space Museum, and only a slightly longer walk to other Smithsonian museums. In the other direction is the Maine Avenue waterfront. There's a beautiful outdoor pool (covered in the winter) with a snack bar and inedible but pretty potted plants. The superbly appointed suites and guest rooms are on the top 4 floors of an office building. Rooms on the 14th and 15th floors have balconies. Consider a room near the pool if you have kids in tow, or take your choice of views: presidential monuments or Potomac riverfront. Children eat free from the children's menu when accompanied by a paying adult between 5:30 and 7:30pm. The hotel also has a game-lending library, tours, and supervised recreational programs. Gift shop, express check-in, and business-class rooms with three phones (one in the bathroom, of course) and all the electronics any executive could imagine. There's a health club on the 11th floor. Not only are pets welcome but there's an annual "Doggy Ball" with proceeds going to the ASPCA.

480 L'Enfant Plaza, 7th and D sts. SW. ☎ ***800/23-LOEWS*** *or 202/484-1000. Fax 202/646-4456. Web site: www.loewshotels.com.* **Metro:** *L'Enfant Plaza station, exit at 9th and D sts. exit, and that puts you into the underground shopping area with signs leading to the hotel.* **Parking:** *$16.* **Rack rates:** *$235 double. Children under 18 stay free in parents' room (and receive a gift). AE, DC, DISC, MC, V.*

Morrison–Clark Historic Inn
$$. Downtown.

Billed as a B&B, the Morrison–Clark crosses the line between cutesy bed-and-breakfast and sumptuous inn. Filled with antiques, wicker, and fresh flowers, the inn shines at pampering guests. This is a place to rest your psyche as well as your tired body. The maid visits, discreetly, twice a day, and overnight shoe shines are gratis. And the trellised balconies, fountained courtyard garden, and award-winning restaurant don't exactly hurt. The neighborhood

Best Hotels for Families

Days Inn Premier Convention Center Hotel	$
Four Seasons	$$$$$
Grand Hyatt Washington	$$$$$
Holiday Inn on the Hill	$$
Hotel Harrington	$
Hyatt Regency Washington	$$$$
J. W. Marriott Hotel	$$$
Lincoln Suites Hotel	$$
Loews L'Enfant Plaza	$$$$
Omni Shoreham	$$$$$
Red Roof Inn	$$
Renaissance Washington	$$$$

is iffy for a midnight stroll, but convenient to Metro Center, where you can hop a train on all five lines (but not at the same time). Weekend rates are sometimes as low as $100. This small and elegant old hostelry welcomes children, but they should be old enough to appreciate the value of the antiques. They break, *you* pay.

1015 L St. NW (at Massachusetts Ave. and 11th St. NW). ☎ *800/332-7898 or 202/898-1200.* **Metro:** *Metro Center. Exit right from the station, go up (north) 11th St. 3 blocks to Massachusetts and the inn.* **Parking:** *$12.* **Rack rates:** *$145–$205 double. AE, CB, DC, DISC, MC, V.*

 ## Omni Shoreham
$$$$$. Uptown.

Talk about a hotel with great views! If you like looking at trees rather than traffic, request a room on an upper floor facing southeast for a panorama of Rock Creek Park and beyond. Pearle Mesta used to hold court here, entertaining politicos and hoi-poloi. Now this place is jock heaven, with a fitness center, two outdoor pools, lighted tennis courts, shuffleboard, Ping-Pong, health club, 1.5-mile parcourse with 18 stations, and 10 miles of trails in Rock Creek Park (out the back door). When do guests have time to sightsee? A gazillion-dollar renovation should be complete by mid-1999. While the lobby undergoes a major face-lift, chintz fabric and mahogany furniture will lend elegance to the large (by any standard) rooms. Porcelain fixtures are making their

Best Location If You're into Nightlife

Four Seasons	$$$$$
Hotel Sofitel	$$$
Hotel Tabard Inn	$
Wyndham Bristol	$$$$

way into the bathrooms. Guests already have all the perks, including a bathroom telephone. (We go to the bathroom to get *away* from phones!) A new restaurant should be open by the time you read this. Forget the fitness equipment—you can walk to the zoo and talk to the animals.

2500 Calvert St. NW (at Connecticut Ave.). ☎ *800/THE-OMNI or 202/234-0700. Fax 202/332-1372. Web site: www.omnihotels.com.* **Metro:** *Woodley Park/Zoo, walk one-half block south on Connecticut Ave. to hotel (in front of you as you get off the escalator).* **Parking:** *$14.* **Rack rates:** *$250–$295 double. Children under 18 stay free in parents' room, and there's no charge for cribs. AE, CB, DC, DISC, ER, JCB, MC.*

Red Roof Inn
$$. Downtown.

This is not your ordinary Red Roof Inn that you see off the interstate. It's a 10-floor, 197-room downtown property on the edge of Chinatown. Also close to the Convention Center and the MCI Center, it's a good (and reasonable) pick for business travelers and families. King rooms have large desks with enhanced work space. *Beware:* You may have to drag the kids away from the in-room Nintendo (hourly charge). There's an exercise room and on-site restaurant, open from 6:30am to 10pm.

500 H St. NW (at 5th St.). ☎ *800/234-6423 or 202/289-5959. Fax 202/682-9152. Web site: www.redroof.com.* **Metro:** *Gallery Place/Chinatown, take the 7th St. exit to H St., and 2 blocks to 5th St.* **Parking:** *$8.50 (limited).* **Rack rates:** *$99–$119 double. AE, CB, DC, DISC, MC, V.*

Renaissance Washington, D.C. Hotel
$$$$. Downtown.

There's plenty of hustle and bustle weekdays at the 800-room Renaissance, which mainly serves the briefcases headed to the Convention Center across the street. The location is excellent for sightseeing and convenient to all five subway lines at Metro Center. There are, however, more stylish neighborhoods. Despite the fact that this is a chain hotel, the rooms are cozy. On weekends, families can save big time and enjoy all the extras on a shoestring. For a fee, you can use the health club with a lap pool, steam rooms, and whirlpool.

Best Hotels for a Romantic Escape

Four Seasons	$$$$$
Jefferson Hotel	$$$$$
Morrison–Clark Historic Inn	$$

999 9th St. NW (between K and I sts.). ☎ *800/228-9898 or 202/898-9000. Fax 202/789-4213. Web site: www.rennaissancehotels.com.* **Metro:** *Gallery Place, turn right out of the station from 9th St. Exit (onto 9th St.) and walk 2 blocks to* *the hotel.* **Parking:** *$15.* **Rack rates:** *from $209. Children 18 and under stay free in parents' room and eat free from the children's menu. AE, CB, DC, DISC, ER, JCB, MC, V.*

Swissôtel Washington: The Watergate Hotel
$$$$$. Foggy Bottom.

Few properties epitomize upscale Washington more than the Watergate Hotel. Located on the banks of the Potomac River, across from the Kennedy Center, the hotel has enjoyed a reputation for outstanding service (as well as scandal) for more than 30 years. The spacious rooms and suites (some overlooking the Potomac) are among the largest in the city, and many have balconies. The excellent health club (indoor pool, sauna, Jacuzzi, aerobic classes, Nautilus, and other beneficial equipment) can be crowded at times. Be good to yourself and schedule a massage or hair appointment in the salon (that's what Monica did just after the news broke about her affair with Bill Clinton). An umbrella is provided in each room. Nice touch. Concierge service is available from 7am to 11pm, and some rooms have kitchenettes. Complimentary limousine service is available from 7am to 10am Monday through Friday. Shopping options include Yves St. Laurent, Valentino, and Saks Jandel. Bring plenty of moolah.

Best Hotels That Will Treat You Like Royalty

Four Seasons	$$$$$
Hotel Sofitel	$$$
Jefferson Hotel	$$$$$
Morrison– Clark Historic Inn	$$
Willard Inter- Continental	$$$$

2650 Virginia Ave. NW. ☎ **800/424-2735** *or 202/965-2300. Fax 202/337-7915. Web site: www.watergatehotel.com.* **Metro:** *Foggy Bottom/GWU, turn right toward New Hampshire Ave., left onto New Hampshire Ave., right on Virginia Ave. to hotel.* **Parking:** *$20.* **Rack rates:** *$275–$290 double. AE, DC, MC, V.*

★Kids★ Washington International Hostel (WIH)
$. Downtown.

You won't find chocolates on your pillow here. And the only TV is in the recreation area. Whattaya expect for $21? (Kids pay $9.) Though strictly no-frills, the WIH is clean and comfortable, with dorm-style rooms in a historic building just 3 blocks from Metro Center (and all five subway lines). The rooms, segregated by gender, have 4 to 18 beds. The bathrooms are down the hall. Some four-person family rooms are available, but they're gobbled up fast, especially in spring and summer. Soap and towels are BYO, but linens, blankets, and pillows are provided. Take advantage of one of the walking tours, concerts, or movies, and let the savvy staff help you with your itinerary. A couple of grocery stores are within walking distance.

1009 11th St. NW (at K St.). ☎ *202/737-2333.* **Metro:** *Metro Center, walk north on 11th St. 3 blocks.* **Parking:** *Are you kidding?* **Rack rates:** *$21. MC, V.*

Willard Inter-Continental
$$$$. Downtown.
If you're looking for a special place to see or be seen, this is it. This historic landmark was closed for almost 15 years before the beaux-arts property underwent massive restoration. The Secret Service and State Department were called in to help design the secure "Heads of State" 6th-floor suites. Queen Anne reproductions fill more than 300 rooms and three dozen suites. Restaurants include the Willard Room, the intimate Round Robin bar, and Cafe Espresso. The Willard is 2 blocks from the White House, a block from National Theatre, and mere steps from the pulse of the nation. Ergonomic chairs and halide lighting are standard in business guest rooms.

1401 Pennsylvania Ave. NW (at 14th St.). ☎ *800/327-0200 or 202/628-9100. Fax 202/637-7326. Web site: www.interconti.com.* **Metro:** *Metro Center, F St. exit, left off escalator onto F St., walk less than 2 blocks to 14th St. and the hotel's rear entrance.* **Parking:** *$20.* **Rack rates:** *$229–$269 double. AE, DC, MC, V.*

Wyndham Bristol
$$$$. Foggy Bottom.
Designed for business guests with a taste for luxury, the 239 rooms (some suites) feature modem line, data ports, extended phone cords, voice mail, no long-distance access charge, excellent lighting, and large work areas. Furnishings are a blend of classic European and contemporary. The Wyndham even boasts of "real" hangers. Close to the Kennedy Center, it's a few blocks to Georgetown. There's an exercise room, and the lounge offers pretheater dinner or posttheater cocktails. Don't even think of trying to park on the street.

2430 Pennsylvania Ave. NW (at 23rd St.). ☎ *800/WYNDHAM or 202/ 955-6400. Fax 202/955-5765. Web site: www.wyndham.com.* **Metro:** *Foggy Bottom/GWU, use the south exit and turn left onto 23rd St., to Washington Circle, left on Pennsylvania Ave., go half a block, and you've arrived (look for the international flags hanging out front).* **Parking:** *$16.* **Rack rates:** *$189–$265 double. AE, DC, DISC, JCB, MC, V.*

Help! I Can't Make Up My Mind!
Some of you may be waiting for a presidential invitation to stay in the Lincoln Bedroom. It might be a good idea to make a hotel reservation in the interim. You can always cancel.

Decisive types know unequivocally that they want to roll out of bed onto the National Mall, or stay in a more residential neighborhood where they can soak up the local culture (or lack thereof). Theater lovers may opt to bed down near the Kennedy Center or downtown theater district. For those *few* of you who cannot make up your minds, I offer a chart on the next page. If you read through the reviews and said, at least once, "Hmm, that sounds appealing," I hope you put a checkmark or thumbprint next to it.

Your next assignment is to note your preferences on the chart. Then look over your selections and rank them. That way, if your number 1 choice is unavailable, you can move on to number 2. And, as we said before, if a White House invitation finds its way into your mailbox, you can always change your mind.

Hotel Preferences Worksheet

Hotel	Location	Price per night

Advantages	Disadvantages	Your Ranking (1–10)

Part 3

Learning Your Way Around Washington, D.C.

Planning your way around this planned city shouldn't be very difficult. Because Washington is a planned city and didn't develop spontaneously over time like other big cities, you'll find that the streets are (for the most part) neatly laid out in a logical way. Notice I say for the most part. **Beware:** *Numerous broad avenues, named for states, cut through the logic like a stiletto, confounding visitors and long-time residents alike—and it gets especially confusing when you try to get behind the wheel.*

But don't worry. In this part of the book, I'll personally guide you through the Washington area—from finding the best way to get from the airport or train station to your hotel, to exploring the city's diverse neighborhoods—stick with me, and I'll show you the way. To make your trip even easier, I'll explain the comprehensive and efficient transportation system, which is noteworthy for its proximity to most major attractions and for its user-friendly personality.

Getting Your Bearings

In This Chapter

➤ Point A to point B (from the airport or train station to your bed)

➤ Key to the city: learning the lay of the land

➤ How to get unlost

Navigating Washington's streets, especially in the main tourist areas, is duck soup. Because the major attractions are in proximity, walking is the best mode of transportation. Most of the Smithsonian museums are on the National Mall, a 2-mile-long parcel sweeping from the Lincoln Memorial eastward to the U.S. Capitol. The White House, other presidential memorials, and numerous other attractions are within walking distance of, or a short Metro ride from, the Mall. Sites further afield are easily accessible by Metro.

From Air to There

When your plane touches down, you can be sure it won't be on the White House lawn. And you won't exit the terminal opposite the U.S. Capitol either. Washington is 67 square miles of former swampland with no airport within its federal boundaries. Don't panic! Three major airports serve the capital city. Two—**Ronald Reagan National** ("Reagan National") and **Washington–Dulles International** ("Dulles")—are in Virginia; the third—**Baltimore–Washington International** ("BWI")—is in Maryland. Amtrak trains from all over the United States chug into Union Station, conveniently located on Capitol Hill.

Ronald Reagan National Airport (Reagan National)

Of the three major airports serving Washington, Reagan National is closest, just across the Potomac River in Alexandria, Virginia. But proximity can be deceiving. Reagan National, which recently had a major face-lift, is always crowded, baggage handling can be slow, and it is not uncommon to wait in line for a half hour or more to enter a taxi. For airport information, call ☎ 703/419-8000.

Unlike at Dulles or BWI, there is a Metro station at Reagan National. However, you'll have to schlepp your baggage over the pedestrian bridges to the train. Still, Metro is the most efficient and cheapest way to reach downtown, a 15- to 20-minute ride away. The fare, at nonpeak times, is $1.10. Trains run from 5:30am to midnight weekdays, 8am to midnight weekends and holidays. For Metro information, call ☎ 202/637-7000.

Taxi fare from Reagan National to the White House is about $10. The trip can take anywhere from 10 minutes (at 3am) to a half hour or more during rush hour. This is a sick Washington joke since rush hour starts *before* 6am, due to staggered government hours, and lasts until at least 9:30am. During the afternoon, the roads are often clogged from 3:30 to 7pm or later.

Tourist Traps

Stories of price gouging by taxi drivers at Reagan National Airport are rampant. Avoid a rip-off by asking an attendant or airport employee what the fare should be. Negotiate the price with the driver before you get in and ask up front if there are any extras. If you suspect hanky-panky, write down the company and driver's name, and cab number (on the door). And get a receipt. Report any problems to ☎ 202/331-1671.

SuperShuttle vans whisk passengers door-to-door from the airport to downtown and beyond. Depending on your destination, expect to pay $6 to $10 per person. SuperShuttle booths are located outside each terminal; pick up the white courtesy phone to make a reservation, or call ☎ 800/258-3826.

At Reagan National, the major car-rental agencies—**Alamo** (☎ 800/327-9633), **Avis** (☎ 800/879-2847), **Hertz** (☎ 800/654-3131), **Budget** (☎ 800/527-0700), and **National** (☎ 800/227-7368)—maintain counters on site in the south parking lot structure in Terminal A. Complete the paperwork, then board a gray courtesy shuttle to the parking lot, where your car will be waiting. To reach the off-site locations of **Dollar** (☎ 800/800-4000), **Enterprise** (☎ 800/325-8007), and **Thrifty** (☎ 800/367-2277), take the white courtesy shuttle.

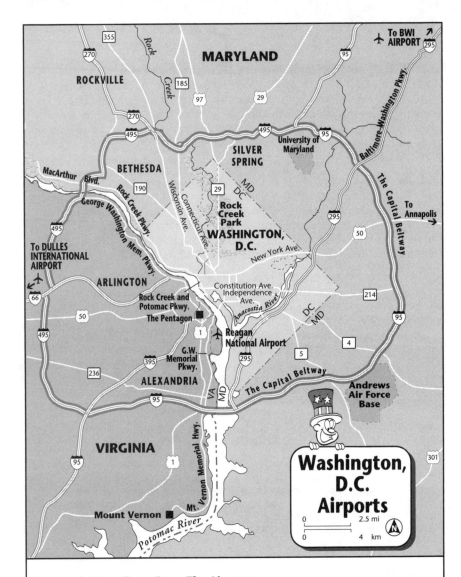

How To Get Into Town From The Airports

- **From Dulles International Airport:**
  Take the Dulles Airport access road (the only road out!) to I-66 east, through the Virginia suburbs and over the Theodore Roosevelt Bridge (still I-66), which will land you on Constitution Avenue and the western edge of the National Mall near the Lincoln Memorial.
- **From Baltimore Washington International Airport:**
  Take the airport access road to Highway 295 (Gladys Spellman Parkway; also known as the Baltimore-Washington Parkway) south to Route 50 west (New York Avenue).
- **From Reagan National Airport:**
  Take the George Washington Memorial Parkway north to I-395 north and continue over the Rochambeau Memorial Bridge (known as the 14th Street Bridge; and still I-395) into the District. Be sure you have specific directions to your hotel before you attempt this. It's tricky and still causes me palpitations.

Washington–Dulles International Airport (Dulles)

Dulles, a hub for domestic and international flights, is located in the boonies, actually Chantilly, Virginia, about 26 miles west of downtown D.C. Expansion, begun when Abe Lincoln was a teenager, is ongoing until at least 2010. At that time, the inconvenient mobile lounges that carry passengers to and from the midfield terminals—adding travel time—will be replaced by underground "people-movers." Ah, progress.

Hear Ye! Hear Ye!

Trying to figure out how to drive in from the airport to the downtown area? Flip to the map "Washington, D.C. Airports" on p. 80.

Expect a 40-minute ride between Dulles and downtown D.C. in non-rush-hour traffic; a month or more if you arrive or depart during rush hour (just kidding, but not by much). It's about a $45 cab ride to the White House.

The **Washington Flyer** operates buses between Dulles and the Airport Terminal Building at 1517 K St. NW. Fares are $16 one way, $26 round-trip. Kids 6 and under ride free. Departures are about every 30 minutes; you can pick up the bus outside the baggage claim area at curbside 1D. At the K Street terminal, you can pick up a free shuttle that stops at eight Washington hotels. Call ☎ **703/685-1400.**

If you're trying to pick up a rental car at Dulles, **Alamo, Avis, Budget, Dollar, Hertz,** and **National** are all located in the main terminal.

Baltimore–Washington International Airport (BWI)

Last, but first in efficiency and offering many bargain fares, is BWI. Despite its location outside of Baltimore, Maryland (25 miles northeast of Washington), and a 45-minute ride from D.C., this airport consistently runs more smoothly than the other two and recently underwent major renovation. For airport information, call ☎ **410/859-7111.**

Balancing the Budget

Expect to pay the following for an airport taxi to Washington, D.C.

➤ Reagan National $10
➤ Dulles $45
➤ BWI $40

Cab fare from BWI to Washington is about $40. The **Airport Connection (☎ 800/ 284-6066)** operates door-to-door van service (with 24 hours' notice) for an average fare of $24 per person. Another option is to take the courtesy shuttle to the BWI Rail Station, 5 minutes from the airport, for **Marc (☎ 800/325-RAIL)** and **Amtrak (☎ 800/USA-RAIL)** trains to Union Station in D.C. The Marc trains operate on **weekdays only.** The fare from the BWI rail station to Union Station is $14 each way, $28 round-trip on Amtrak; $5 one way and $8.75 round-trip on Marc.

You'll find **Alamo, Avis, Budget, Dollar, Hertz, National,** and **Thrifty** on the lower level between baggage claim areas 3 and 4.

On the Right Track: Arriving by Train

Amtrak offers service to Washington from Boston, New York, and several points in between and beyond. Passengers land at historic Union Station, conveniently located on Capitol Hill. Taxis are abundant and the fare shouldn't run more than $5 to most hotels. There's also a Metro station here, as well as shops, restaurants, and movies. For Amtrak information, call ☎ **800/USA-RAIL.**

How to Get There from Here—and Back Again

A good map, like the one inside the back cover, comes in handy about now. The District of Columbia is diamond-shaped and divided into quadrants: NE, NW, SE, and SW. Theoretically, the same address could appear in four different places, so it's important to pay attention to the NW, NE, SW, or SE designation when looking for an address. The U.S. Capitol is the city's center. North Capitol Street and South Capitol Street run north and south, respectively, from the Capitol. East Capitol Street divides the city north and south. West of the Capitol, you'll find the National Mall with most of the Smithsonian museums. Constitution Avenue and Independence Avenue mark the north and south sides of the Mall. Pennsylvania Avenue runs northwest between the Capitol and White House.

Lettered streets run alphabetically east and west. After W Street, one-syllable names (also alphabetical) come into play. Numbered streets run north and south. The major arteries—Pennsylvania, Constitution, Independence, Massachusetts, Connecticut, and Wisconsin avenues—slice through the lettered and numbered streets. What can I say? Thank Pierre L'Enfant, who placed circles at strategic intersections to fend off marauders. If you're lost or confused, ask someone on the street. After 35 years, I'm still asking directions.

The most frequently visited tourist areas are in the northwest and southwest quadrants and accessible on foot and via Metro. Apart from the Mall, familiarize yourself with the different neighborhoods and the sights in each.

Hear Ye! Hear Ye!

There is a method to the madness of lettered and numbered streets in D.C. To find an address on a lettered street, look at the first two digits. For example, 1750 K St. NW is between 17th and 18th streets in the northwest section of the city. On a numbered street, use your fingers (and toes when necessary). Look at the first digit and start counting from A. For example, the 8 in 815 10th St. NE equals H, the 8th letter of the alphabet. So the address is at H and 10th streets in the northeast quadrant. It's easy once you get the hang of it. Even though there's no B Street, count B as the second letter of the alphabet. There's no J Street either, so K becomes the 10th letter. I am not making this up. Good luck.

Washington, D.C. Neighborhoods

Adams–Morgan

Centered around 18th Street and Columbia Road NW, this upbeat, diverse neighborhood north of Dupont Circle and east of Rock Creek Park is a draw for its international cuisine, shops, and nightlife. Parking is impossible and the Dupont Circle Metro station is a 20-minute hike, but that doesn't keep the crowds away. Be street smart here. The neighborhood is iffy.

Capitol Hill

The Hill is home to the U.S. Capitol, Supreme Court building, Library of Congress, and Union Station. Politicos, lobbyists, and yuppies live in Victorian houses on residential streets and frequent the many restaurants and watering holes when not wheeling and dealing. The Hill extends east from the Capitol to the D.C. Armory. The north and south boundaries are H Street NE and the Southwest Freeway.

Downtown

Chinatown, the theater district, MCI Center, government office buildings, the White House, and the Connecticut Avenue and K Street business corridor (with shopping and many restaurants) rub shoulders in this large area, whose perimeter is 7th Street NW to the east; 22nd Street NW to the west; P Street NW and Pennsylvania Avenue NW, to the north and south, respectively. A heavy concentration of hotels and restaurants and proximity to the major sights make this a highly desirable neighborhood for visitors.

Dupont Circle

Dupont Circle is to D.C. what Greenwich Village is to Manhattan. All-night bookstores, movie houses, good restaurants, galleries, and a welcoming attitude to other-than-mainstream types give the neighborhood its unbuttoned, laid-back character. The area is north of downtown and fans out from Dupont Circle along Connecticut, Massachusetts, and New Hampshire avenues NW.

Foggy Bottom

A bustling port in bygone days, Foggy Bottom is one of the city's most charming areas. Lying just below Georgetown, Foggy Bottom occupies the West End of the city between the White House and the Potomac River. Within its borders are the Kennedy Center, Watergate, George Washington University, and State Department. Inviting doll-sized row houses nestle on quiet tree-lined streets made for walking.

Georgetown

First settled in colonial times before the District of Columbia existed, this historic neighborhood was once a bustling tobacco port. Remnants of a quieter, gentler era live on in the many beautifully restored homes off the main drag. Along the major arteries of Wisconsin Avenue and M Street, however,

83

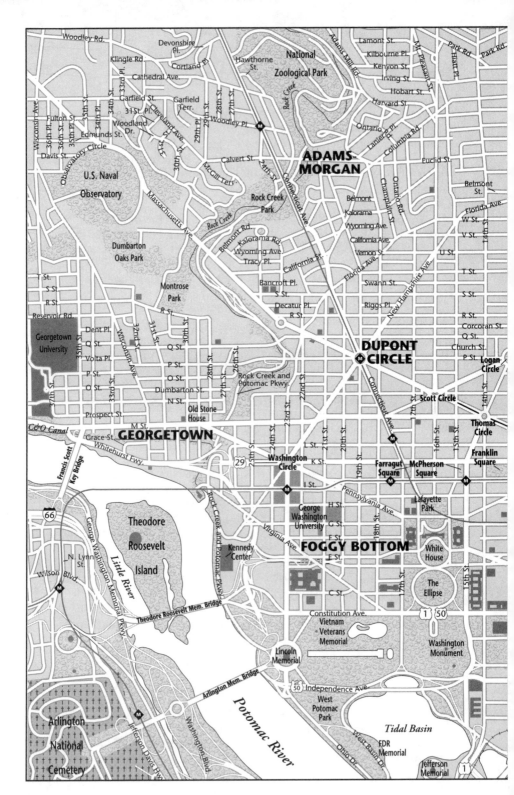

Washington, D. C. Neighborhoods

0 .25 mi
0 .4 km

Kenyon St.
Irving St.
Columbia Rd.
Harvard St.
Girard St.
Fairmont St.
Euclid St.

Trinity College

Michigan Ave.

McMillan Reservoir

Howard University

Channing St.
Bryant St.
Adams St.

13th St.
Barry Pl.

9th St.
8th St.

12th St.
11th St.
10th St.

2nd St.

Florida Ave.

North Capitol St.

French St.

Rhode Island Ave.

DOWNTOWN

7th St.
6th St.
5th St.
4th St.
3rd St.
1st St.

Brentwood Park

Gallaudet University

13th St.
12th St.
11th St.
10th St.
9th St.
8th St.

N St.

M St.

New Jersey Ave.

New York Ave.

Florida Ave.

L St.

K St.
I St.
H St.
G St.
F St.
E St.

1st St.

Mt. Vernon Square

New York Ave.

Massachusetts Ave.

Union Station

2nd St.
3rd St.
4th St.

Convention Center

CHINATOWN

3rd St.
2nd St.
1st St.

North Capitol St.

Pennsylvania Ave.

D St.

C St.

Louisiana Ave.

Delaware Ave.

Maryland Ave.

Constitution Ave.

NATIONAL   MALL

Madison Dr.

Jefferson Dr.

Independence Ave.

NW   NE
U.S.
Capitol
SW   SE

A St.
East Capitol St.
A St.

Stanton Square

Canal St.

South Capitol St.

New Jersey Ave.

CAPITOL HILL

Seward Square

North Carolina Ave.

C St.

South Carolina Ave.

D St.

395

Pennsylvania

85

D.C. Dirt

In 1910, President Taft appointed a Commission of Fine Arts to create monuments and fountains in the capital city. So, in 1912, when the Japanese presented the famous cherry trees to the United States, Mrs. Taft had the power to decide that they should be planted in the Tidal Basin, where they've been ever since.

the tone is anything but sedate and genteel. The many boutiques, restaurants, pubs, and music clubs attract area teens, out-of-town visitors, and other fun-seekers. Georgetown University, the prerevolutionary Old Stone House, Dumbarton Oaks, the riverfront, and the C&O Canal all contribute to Georgetown's enduring cache.

The Mall
The 300-foot-wide National Mall is the epicenter of sightseeing action. Most of the Smithsonian Institution museums and major art galleries are here. In this area, you can also visit the Washington Monument, Lincoln Memorial, and Vietnam Veterans Memorial. Many other attractions are within a short walk or Metro ride. In good weather, the tree-lined rectangle, extending for 2 miles from the Lincoln Memorial east to the Capitol, fills with in-line skaters, bikers, kite-fliers, and picnickers. Also enjoying the parklike space are tourists planning their next move and jogging congressional staffers.

Hear Ye! Hear Ye!

The greatest concentration of cherry trees is around the Tidal Basin (site of the Jefferson and FDR memorials) in the area known as West Potomac Park. To reach the Tidal Basin from the Smithsonian Metro, walk west on Independence Avenue 2 blocks and go left (south) on Raoul Wallenberg Place (15th Street SW), past the U.S. Holocaust Museum to the basin.

Upper Northwest
You probably won't find this marked on a map, since it's part geographical and part state of mind. The far northwest section of the city approaching the Maryland line is largely residential, punctuated by strip shopping centers, malls, restaurants, and family-filled vans. In the Woodley Park neighborhood is the National Zoo, reason enough to venture out of the main tourist zones. A couple of Washington's larger hotels (the Sheraton Washington and Omni Shoreham) are here, along with many restaurants that feed conventioneers and the local population.

Hear Ye! Hear Ye!

Listen to this. From the weather, to the news, or information about what's happening in D.C., the radio says it all. Instead of aimlessly flipping through the radio dial, tune in to the following: **88.5 FM** (National Public Radio); **90.9 FM** (Classical & NPR News); **94.7 FM** (Classic Rock); **98.7 FM** (Country); **100.3 FM** (Oldies); **101.1 FM** (Rock); **104.1 FM** (Top 40); **105.9 FM** (Smooth Jazz); **106.7 FM** (Talk & Sports); **730 AM** (CNN News); **980 AM** (Sports).

Street Smart: Where to Get Information After You've Arrived

There are several key places to gather information after you arrive in Washington. Start at the information desks in the airports and Union Station. When you check into your hotel, if you don't see reams of visitor information in the lobby, ask for the closest information booth.

➤ **White House Visitor Center,** 1450 Pennsylvania Ave. NW (between 14th and 15th streets), in the Department of Commerce Building; open 7:30am to 4pm daily, closed Thanksgiving, December 25, and January 1 (☎ **202/208-1631**). **Metro:** Metro Center or Federal Triangle, which is also a distribution center for White House passes.

➤ **Smithsonian Information Center,** 1000 Jefferson Dr. SW (on the Mall); open 9am to 5:30pm daily, closed December 25 (☎ **202/ 357-2700**). **Metro:** Smithsonian. The "Castle" is the place to go for information on the Smithsonian and other attractions. A 20-minute video gives an overview of the museums and schematics of the Mall, which helps visitors get their bearings. An electronic map locates scores of attractions, as well as Metro and Tourmobile stops (see chapter 12 for information about the Tourmobile). Interactive videos provide more information on sights and transportation, and monitors display daily events. If this is not enough, the volunteer staff will answer questions and help you plan your itinerary.

Hear Ye! Hear Ye!

From the Easter Egg Roll to Garden Tours, there's usually some special event going on at the White House that's open to the public. To find out what's happening when you're in town, call the 24-hour **White House information hot line** at ☎ **202/ 456-7041.** If you're planning on taking a tour of the White House, call this number to make sure that it's not closed for a State event.

For information about current events, look for the publications listed in chapter 4. Many are distributed free at newsstands, restaurants, and bookstores.

Chapter 8

Getting Around D.C.

In This Chapter

➤ Using mass transit

➤ Taking taxis

➤ Getting around on foot

Washington, D.C., has an extensive public transportation system. **Metrorail** (our subway, known as Metro) travels over 100 miles of track to more than 75 stations on five lines—Red, Blue, Orange, Yellow, and Green. **Metrobus** makes almost 16,000 stops on a 1,500-square-mile route extending through D.C., Virginia, and Maryland. You'll probably be using Metrorail exclusively, as stations are within a few blocks of almost all the sightseeing attractions, restaurants, and hotels recommended in this book. (We planned it that way!) For Metrorail and Metrobus transit information, call ☎ **202/637-7000.**

Goin' Underground—Using Metro

Forget painful memories you may carry from other cities of grinding wheels, graffiti, and stifling cars with slashed seats. Washington's Metro cars are air-conditioned, the seats are upholstered, and the tracks are rubber-cushioned. The stations are clean and well lit, and service is usually frequent and prompt.

Fares, based on distance traveled, cost considerably less during nonpeak hours (9:30am to 3pm and 8pm to midnight weekdays; all day Saturday, Sunday, and holidays). At these times the minimum fare is $1.10.

Metro stations are easy to find. Just look for the brown pole topped by the letter M and station name. There *should be* a colored stripe beneath the M to indicate the line or lines that stop there.

Check the **Metro map** at the front of this guide and the "Metro Stops" map in this chapter to familiarize yourself with the routes and to help understand where the trains stop. Metro runs on a **schedule,** theoretically at least. Trains are more frequent at peak (5:30 to 9:30am, 3 to 8pm) than nonpeak times. I've never waited more than 15 minutes, and that was late at night. Just go to the platform, wait with everyone else, and glance at your watch every 15 seconds or so. You'll probably be pleasantly surprised.

Hear Ye! Hear Ye!

When the sign on the Metro says NO EATING OR DRINKING ALLOWED, you best take heed. Conductors are known to throw eating passengers off the train or worse—stick them with a hefty fine. Now that's dedication to keeping Metro clean!

A computerized **fare card** will be your ticket to ride. You'll find it in a vending machine near the station entrance. But first you have to feed the machine, which eats nickels, dimes, quarters, and bills from $1 to $20. The machines return up to $4.95 in change—*coins only.* If you're planning on purchasing a $1.10 fare card, I strongly suggest paying with something smaller than a $10 or $20 bill, or you may have trouble walking.

If you plan on taking Metro several times during your visit, it makes sense to put more value on the fare card, rather than purchasing a new one each time you enter the system.

A **10% discount** is given on fare cards of $20 or more. Up to two children under 5 can ride free with a paying passenger. Seniors 65 and older and disabled persons ride for a reduced fare, but they must have valid proof.

After you insert your card in the entrance gate, it is stamped and returned. **Don't be a doofus** and walk off without it (as many of us have). You have to reinsert it in the exit gate at your destination, where the card is returned if there's value left. If you've underestimated the fare, you can add what's necessary at the Addfare machine.

Hints for Smooth Riding on Metro

➤ **In the stations,** consult the wall-mounted map and list of Metro stops (be sure you're choosing the closest one) and fare information.

➤ **Remember** when you enter the system to grab the card when it's returned to you. Tuck it away for reinsertion at your destination.

➤ **If you're rushing,** it's easy to get on the wrong train or one traveling in the opposite direction. Take a minute and check the station stops listed on the pole near the tracks.

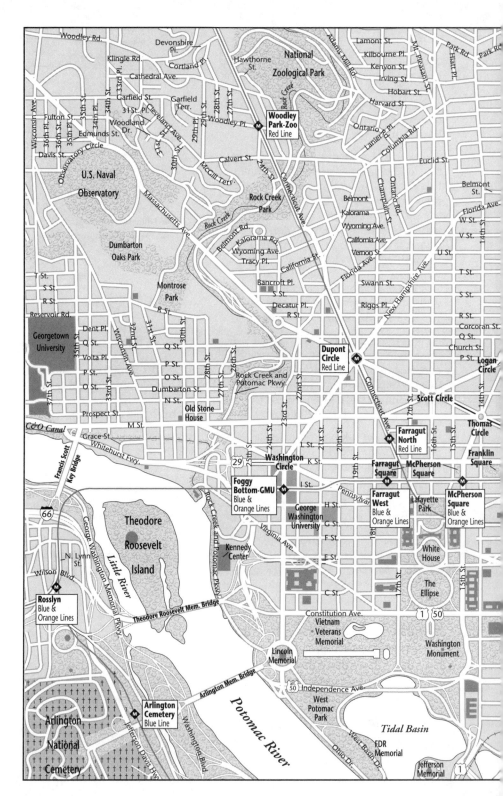

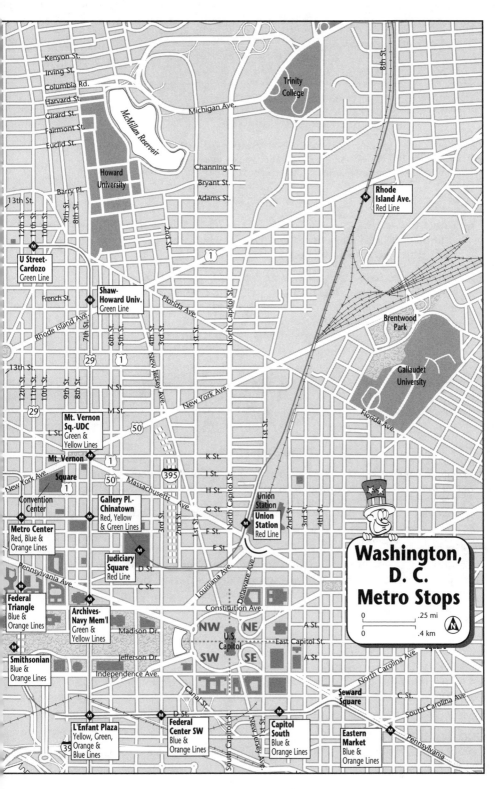

Kenyon St.
Irving St.
Columbia Rd.
Harvard St.
Girard St.
Fairmont St
Euclid St.

McMillan Reservoir

Michigan Ave.

Trinity College

8th St.

13th St.

Howard University

Barry Pl.

Channing St.
Bryant St.
Adams St.

Rhode Island Ave.
Red Line

U Street-
Cardozo
Green Line

13th St.
12th St.
11th St.
10th St.
9th St.
8th St.

French St.

Shaw-
Howard Univ.
Green Line

Florida Ave.

North Capitol St.

Brentwood Park

Rhode Island Ave.

13th St.
12th St.
11th St.
10th St.
9th St.
8th St.

7th St.

6th St.
5th St.
4th St.
3rd St.
1st St.

New Jersey Ave.

Gallaudet University

N St.
M St.

New York Ave.

Florida Ave.

Mt. Vernon
Sq.-UDC
Green &
Yellow Lines

L St.

Mt. Vernon

New York Ave.

Square

Convention Center

Massachusetts Ave.

K St.
I St.
H St.
G St.
F St.
E St.

1st St.

Union Station

Union
Station
Red Line

2nd St.
3rd St.
4th St.

Metro Center
Red, Blue &
Orange Lines

Gallery Pl.-
Chinatown
Red, Yellow
& Green Lines

3rd St.
2nd St.
1st St.

Judiciary
Square
Red Line

D St.
C St.

Louisiana Ave.

Delaware Ave.

Washington,
D. C.
Metro Stops

0   .25 mi
0   .4 km

Pennsylvania Ave.

Federal
Triangle
Blue &
Orange Lines

Archives-
Navy Mem'l
Green &
Yellow Lines

Madison Dr.

Constitution Ave.

NW **NE**

U.S.
Capitol

A St.
East Capitol St.

SW **SE**

Jefferson Dr.

A St.

Smithsonian
Blue &
Orange Lines

Independence Ave.

North Carolina Ave.

Canal St.

Seward
Square

C St.

South Carolina Ave.

D St.

L'Enfant Plaza
Yellow, Green,
Orange &
Blue Lines

Federal
Center SW
Blue &
Orange Lines

South Capitol St.

New Jersey Ave.

Capitol
South
Blue &
Orange Lines

Eastern
Market
Blue &
Orange Lines

Pennsylvania

Hear Ye! Hear Ye!

If you're in town for a special event call the **Metro's Events Hot Line** at ☎ **202/783-1070.** This service is updated weekly and provides round-the-clock information on how to use Metro to get to whatever special event you want to see.

➤ **Don't eat, drink, or smoke on Metro or in the station.** All are strictly prohibited and punishable by a fine. My unsuspecting son learned the hard way and ate a $25 banana one day.

➤ **If you're riding the subway and plan to continue via Metrobus to your destination,** pick up a **transfer** at the station *where you enter the system, not your destination station.* Transfer machines are on the mezzanines of most stations, before you descend to the tracks. A transfer is good for a discount on bus fares in D.C. and Virginia. (There are no bus-to-subway transfers.)

Time Savers

Walking is usually faster than taking a bus. Because traffic moves slower than a slug in the sun in most downtown areas, you'll see a lot more by hoofing it, as well as reach your destination more quickly.

Busing It

Understanding the Metrorail system is simple. Metrobus is another matter entirely. Red, white, and blue signs with route numbers mark bus stops. The killer is that the signs don't tell you where the buses go. For routing information, call ☎ **202/637-7000,** Monday through Friday from 6am to 10:30pm, weekends and holidays from 8am to 10:30pm. Bus fare is $1.10; transfers cost 10¢. Carry *exact change,* as the drivers don't make it. Most buses run daily around the clock. Service is frequent weekdays, especially during peak hours, less so on evenings and weekends. Up to two children under 5 ride free with a paying passenger. Reduced fares are available for seniors (☎ **202/ 962-7000**) and persons with disabilities (☎ **202/962-1245**).

Taxi Information

About 9,000 cabs ply Washington's streets, and it's usually easy to hail one, especially on the major arteries, or in front of a hotel or large office building.

Time Savers

If you don't want to risk being late for a meeting, dinner reservation, or theater event, try calling Diamond Cab (☎ **202/387-6200**), Yellow Cab (☎ **202/544-1212**), or Capitol Cab (☎ **202/546-2400**).

Although there is talk of changing D.C.'s whacko zone system to meters, talk is cheap—especially in this town. Here's how the nutsy zone system works.

If you travel from Point A to Point B within the same zone, the fare is $4 (refer to the map, "Taxicab Zones," on p. 94 to see which zones you will be traveling through). Since most attractions are in Zone 1, a D.C. cab ride is a good deal, at least theoretically. If you travel into a second zone, the fare is $5.50, $6.90 for a third zone, and so on up to $12.50 if you ride to zone 8. It's highly unlikely that you'll be traveling more than one or two zones, however. You should note that because zone lines go down the middle of some streets, your fare could jump to the next level, depending on which side of the street you enter or exit the cab. Tipping is your call, but the going rate is 10% to 15% of the fare. To find out fares within the District, call ☎ **202/645-6018.**

Sounds simple, right? Well, it's not. Here's how fares can add up:

➤ There's a rush-hour surcharge of $1 between 7 and 9:30am and 4 and 6:30pm.

➤ There's a $1.50 charge for each additional passenger.

➤ If you want to stop en route, add an extra $1 to the fare.

➤ Surcharges are added for large pieces of luggage; it's 50¢ for regular-sized luggage, $2 for something as big as a trunk.

➤ There's a $1.50 charge for calling a taxi.

Tourist Traps

Peculiar to Washington, and a major pain in the butt if you're in a hurry, is the practice that allows drivers to pick up as many passengers as they can cram into the cab. For this inconvenience, you'll pay the same fare as you would for *not* sharing the cab with strangers.

The zone system does not apply if you're traveling to a destination outside D.C. (like an airport or your Aunt Elsie's in the suburbs). In such cases, the fare is based on distance covered, and it's $2 just to step into a cab, 70¢ for

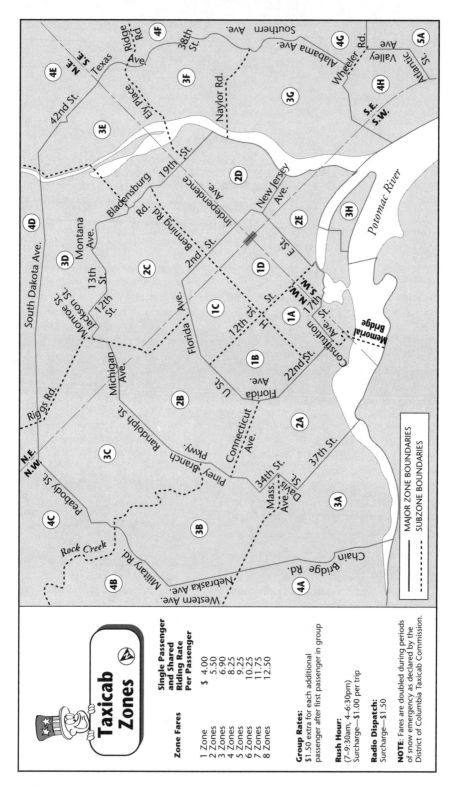

Taxicab Zones

Zone Fares

	Single Passenger and Shared Riding Rate Per Passenger
1 Zone	$ 4.00
2 Zones	5.50
3 Zones	6.90
4 Zones	8.25
5 Zones	9.25
6 Zones	10.25
7 Zones	11.75
8 Zones	12.50

Group Rates:
$1.50 extra for each additional passenger after first passenger in group

Rush Hour:
(7–9:30am, 4–6:30pm)
Surcharge—$1.00 per trip

Radio Dispatch:
Surcharge—$1.50

NOTE: Fares are doubled during periods of snow emergency as declared by the District of Columbia Taxicab Commission.

——— MAJOR ZONE BOUNDARIES
- - - - SUBZONE BOUNDARIES

each additional half mile. Call ☎ **202/ 331-1671** for information on fares between Washington and Maryland or Virginia.

It's been years since I've taken a cab in D.C., probably because I'm mathphobic and have difficulty figuring the fares. My advice: Unless you're burdened with luggage, it's raining cats and dogs, or you're headed for someplace not easily accessible (like Adams–Morgan), take Metro. You won't need a calculator to tally the fare.

Hear Ye! Hear Ye!

If you have a complaint, jot down the driver's name and the cab number, then call the Taxicab Complaint Office (☎ **202/727-5401**).

Car Talk

About half of D.C.'s visitors arrive by car. If they'd spoken to me first, the number would be a lot smaller. If you're driving to D.C., you have my sympathy. Traffic is molasses thick (especially on weekdays), parking spaces are at a premium, and parking lots and garages charge, well, whatever the traffic will bear. If you plan to garage your car during your stay, be prepared to pay up to $20 per day. (When you make a hotel reservation, be sure to ask about the parking fee.) Adding to an already difficult situation, many downtown streets end abruptly, then continue several blocks away. And the streets that were one way last week may be the other way this week. Also, many D.C. residents come from other states and countries where they learned to obey different traffic laws, or none at all. For these reasons (and more I don't have space for), few in their right mind enjoy driving here. If you must drive to Washington, I urge you to secure your wheels in a garage or lot and, during your visit, use Metro and your lower appendages.

Take a Walk on the Wild Side

The best way to get around the District is on your own two feet. You don't need a fare card, you don't have to wait to be picked up, and you can go wherever you want, whenever you want.

D.C. Dirt

In September 1998, Washington hosted bike couriers from around the world in the 6th annual Cycle Messenger World Championships. More than 500 spandex-clad messengers participated in the 4-day event on downtown streets that tested their mettle with the pedal.

Balancing the Budget

Purchase a One-Day Rail pass if you'll be taking Metro several times in a single day. For $5 you can ride as often as you like, from early morning 'til midnight, when the Metro closes down. Passes are sold at Metro stations. Call ☎ **202/ 637-7000** for more information.

In Washington, as in any big city, you have to be on your toes. Be alert to your surroundings. Hang on to your purse, best worn diagonally across your chest, and carry your wallet in an inside pocket. Keep your eyes peeled for bike messengers, in-line skaters, and drivers who don't know how to drive (unfortunately, there are a lot of these).

Most D.C. neighborhoods, but especially the Mall, Foggy Bottom, Georgetown, Dupont Circle, and Adams–Morgan, are tailor-made for strolling. Other good ambling areas are the Tidal Basin, Georgetown waterfront and C&O Canal, Theodore Roosevelt Island, and the National Zoo. (See chapter 16 for some suggested itineraries.)

Part 4

Washington, D.C.'s Best Restaurants

You may find this hard to believe, but Washingtonians do not live on scandal alone. Between the latest cover-up in the White House and discussions of who's bribing whom, we still need to eat. And with almost 3,500 restaurants to choose from, dining out might surpass philandering or "influencing" others as the activity of choice in Washington. What better place to make an illegal campaign contribution than a dimly lit Ethiopian restaurant?

Besides big government in Washington, there's clearly a big business in food. To help you battle this caloric jungle and sift through the groaning board of choices, I'll let you know where to dine and why. Once armed, you can savor my small, subjective hors d'oeuvrerie of the city's best dining establishments. The last step is yours to devour. Get out there and feed your face!

In chapter 10, I tell you the best bets for lunch and dinner. But that only scratches the surface, so in chapter 11, I share some tips for serious noshing.

Chapter 9

The Scoop on the D.C. Dining Scene

In This Chapter

➤ What's hot in the D.C. dining world

➤ The best dining neighborhoods

➤ The price of dining in D.C.

The restaurant scene in Washington is so diverse that it can please everyone from picky foreign ambassadors, to major campaign donors from China, lobbyists from New York, and senators from Nebraska. You'll find everything from down-home grits and gravy to exquisite continental fare. But in Washington, the proof is *not* necessarily in the pudding. Ambience, location, and presentation can make or break a restaurant. When blended, these factors spell the difference between a good restaurant and a dump. In addition to this book and restaurant guides, the best recommendations come from people you know who live in the area and those you meet during your visit.

What's Cookin' in Washington

The *Starr Report* may be the spiciest thing to come out of Washington in years, but fusion (and we're not talking physics here) is still riding the crest of popularity. More and more chefs are "fusing" cuisines from around the world and lacing their creations with Asian ingredients. You know, hamburgers with lemongrass, ravioli with water chestnuts, and the like. The truth is many otherwise ho-hum dishes are enhanced by the addition of exotic flavorings. Also big is Mediterranean cuisine. Covering more than the sea, Mediterranean takes in a big piece of real estate—Italy, southern France, Spain, Greece, and North Africa. Washingtonians love their red meat too. Tossing cholesterol to the wind, they eat their way through steak houses and smoke cigars for dessert.

Not that long ago, there was a noticeable shortage of seafood restaurants. Now, it seems, you'll find one on every street corner. Menus feature fresh and farm-raised fish and shellfish. For a taste of local fare, I urge you to try crab cakes, lump crabmeat cocktail, or something else made with *fresh,* not frozen, crabmeat from Maryland blue crabs, harvested in summer from the nearby Chesapeake Bay.

Blessedly, D.C.'s romance with Italian and Oriental fare has evolved from one-night-stand status to long-term commitment. Most Washingtonians love them both, with all their idiosyncrasies, unconditionally.

Chapter 10 tells you which restaurants serve up the best of all these trendy cuisines.

Wraps—as in "wrap it up" or "that's a wrap"—have become a big food fad. What was sandwiched in a bagel or pita a few short years ago now fills a tortilla. The result is a cold, messy, eggroll-like sandwich. (I still prefer my corned beef on rye.) We'll wrap this up, along with other light-bite suggestions, in chapter 11.

Beating the Lunch Bunch Crunch

Washington is a big lunch town. More deals are closed over omelets and Caesar salads than in conference rooms or halls of Congress. What does this mean for you? If you want to lunch in a popular dining establishment on a weekday, make a reservation or arrive before noon or after 2pm. Or add your name to the waiting list and take a walk. If you're in a hurry, eat in a coffee shop or deli with fast turnaround, or grab something from a street vendor to tide you over. Please note that many restaurants catering to the downtown business crowd are closed for lunch on weekends.

Location! Location! Location!

Like dark suits, restaurants and eateries are everywhere you turn in D.C. Some neighborhoods, however, boast a greater concentration. As a rule of thumb, the more popular an area is for nightlife, the more restaurants you'll find. Check out the following during your stay.

Adams–Morgan

The restaurant action is focused on several blocks near the crossroads of 18th Street and Columbia Road NW in this lively area. It's one of the best neighborhoods for variety seekers where you can eat anything from Ethiopian food with your fingers at **Meskerem,** 2434 18th St. NW, to pork chops and gravied mashed potatoes at **Felix,** 2406 18th St. NW. Adams–Morgan is also prime for browsing, nightlife, and people-watching, so allow time before or after your meal. Take a taxi, as parking is nonexistent and it's an uphill hike from the Dupont Circle Metro station. Smart walkers do not stray from the main drags.

Capitol Hill

When hunger strikes on the Hill, you can slurp Senate bean soup in the **Senate Dining Room** (☎ 202/224-3121), or comb the many restaurants and Food Court at **Union Station—B. Smith's,** 50 Massachusetts Ave. NE, is a standout for traditional Southern fare. Slip into one of the cafes or bistros on Massachusetts Avenue NE, like **Cafe Berlin,** 322 Massachusetts Ave. NE, near Union Station. Pubs and burger joints abound for those in search of a quick fix and pint of ale. Delightful **La Colline,** 400 N. Capitol St. NW, is a favorite of Senate staffers for its French food and convenience to the Capitol. Union Station is the most convenient Metro stop to most Hill restaurants. I don't advise walking the streets after dark. When in doubt, hail a cab.

Downtown

This is a big geographical area, so I'll break it down for easier digestion. **Chinatown** sprouts around 7th and H streets NW with oodles of noodle factories and excellent Asian restaurants like **Full Kee,** 509 H St. NW. The Convention Center and MCI Center are nearby. Below Chinatown, along the so-called **7th Street Arts Corridor,** you'll find Brazilian, Spanish, continental, and American fare. **Jaleo,** 480 7th St. NW, started the local tapas craze and features flamenco dancers some evenings. Feeding the **theater district** audiences around 13th Street and Pennsylvania Avenue NW are eateries specializing in Southwestern, American, and brew pub fare. Seasonal dishes shine at D.C.'s oldest saloon, the **Old Ebbitt Grill,** 675 15th St. NW (between F and G streets), which packs 'em in day and night. One of the city's largest concentrations of pricey and sought-after restaurants is along **Connecticut Avenue,** between H and M streets, and on **K Street** west of Connecticut (for as far as the eye can see). Despite a lot of competition, the **Prime Rib,** 2020 K St. NW, is still *the* place for roast beef. Seafood lovers are hooked on the fins and scales at **Legal Sea Foods,** 2020 K St. NW.

Dupont Circle

The myriad choices in this unzipped area, fanning out from the Dupont Circle roundabout, reflect the diverse, multicultural local population. Pizzas from the oak-burning oven at **Pizzeria Paradiso,** 2029 P St. NW, are tops. But that's just the cream of the cappuccino. Italian, seafood, Mediterranean, and organic American fare are well represented in Dupont Circle. **Afterwords,** 1517 Connecticut Ave. NW (between Q Street and Dupont Circle), a cafe/restaurant within Kramerbooks, is open around the clock on weekends. Count nose rings or browse the galleries and bookstores before or after dining in this colorful neighborhood that never sleeps.

Foggy Bottom

The pickin's are slimmer in the city's West End, but one of my favorites, **Kinkead's,** 2000 Pennsylvania Ave. NW (actually on I Street between 20th and 21st streets), holds court a few blocks from the White House. Award-winning chef/owner Bob Kinkead turns out some of the best seafood dishes in the city. Or anywhere else for that matter. Who needs choices when you have Kinkead's?

Georgetown

At last count there were more restaurants than T-shirt shops in Georgetown, which is saying something. Sink your teeth into the area's best hamburger and super ribs at **Houston's,** 1065 Wisconsin Ave. NW (between K and M streets). Pig out on desserts at **Patisserie Cafe Didier,** 3206 Grace St. NW (between M and K streets), or flip a coin for help in deciding among the myriad choices, including bistro French, Ethiopian Italian, Indian, Mexican, seafood, Southern, and plain-old American. If I've left anything out, rest assured, you'll find it in Georgetown. You'd have to be a masochist to try to park on the street. For a garage or lot spot, get here early. The Foggy Bottom Metro station is a healthy 20-minute walk away. It's fine on a nice day; otherwise, jump on a bus at Pennsylvania Avenue, headed to M Street and Georgetown, or cab it.

Lunch for Mall Crawlers

If you're visiting the Mall museums at lunchtime, you're a captive audience. And don't you think the museums are aware of this? If you're on a roll, you probably won't want to break up the day and lose a couple of hours lunching in a restaurant 8 blocks away. For a quick bite you can grab a hot dog or soft pretzel and a drink from a street vendor and it'll set you back less than $3.

If you can spare a half hour, fall into one of the museum restaurants, cafes, or cafeterias. The food is hardly gourmet fare and it's pricey for what you get, but it fills the void and will free you to resume museum-hopping in a short time. The lines peak between noon and 1pm, so impatient Type A's are advised to arrive earlier or later. Some of the museum eateries are a cut above, not because the food is sensational, but because the surroundings are more pleasing and less institutional. If you stick to the basics, you can eat for $6 or less. See chapter 11 for detailed descriptions of the Mall's best eateries.

Balancing the Budget

Many D.C. restaurants offer lunch specials that cost up to twice as much at dinner. If we can believe the nutritionists, it's healthier to eat a big meal mid-day than in the evening. You can be good to your body (face it, the only one you'll ever have) and save money by dining at lunch and grazing at dinner.

The Price Is Right

You don't have to be a rocket scientist to know that the price of a meal depends on what you order. If you select the most expensive items in a tony restaurant and consume three or four courses, you're going to run up a bill equaling the national debt. If you stick to a main course or order an appetizer and salad, you'll have money left over for dessert later on.

In the chapter 10 listings you'll find two price indicators: a dollar symbol to give you an idea of what a complete meal will cost, and the price range of the entrees on the menu. These two price elements should help you decide if the restaurant suits your budget (see chapter 2). One dollar sign ($) means dirt cheap; five dollar signs ($$$$$—the max) means extravagant. Prices include appetizer, entree, dessert, one drink, taxes, and tip (per person).

All the listings are for good (often *very* good or excellent) restaurants where you'll get a satisfying meal. I'm not steering you to any gross places just because they're cheap. Nor did I list any overpriced places where you'll blow a week's salary on an artistic arrangement of julienned veggies. My selections are based on good quality food for a fair price. In other words, I'm talking value here. The difference between categories has more to do with extras, such as location, ambience, decor, service, and (gag) trendiness. Yadda, yadda, yadda.

➤ **$ (Dirt Cheap):** These are popular places that have been around for a while. You can expect plain food in simple surroundings. Plan on spending between $10 and $15 per person.

➤ **$$ (Inexpensive):** These are finds. They're cheaper than might be expected because they're located a little out of the way and/or lack crystal chandeliers and linen nappery. Expect to pay $15 to $25 for a meal.

➤ **$$$ (Medium):** These are good bets for a fine dinner that doesn't blow the budget out of the water. Expect nice decor, good service, and better-than-good food. A meal in one of these places will set you back $25 to $35.

➤ **$$$$ (Expensive):** These are among the top D.C. restaurants: tops for food, chefs, service, and decor. You don't get somethin' for nothin' in this life, so be prepared to fork over about $35 to $50 per person.

➤ **$$$$$ (Very Expensive):** These are the big kahunas of Washington restaurants, where the well heeled, well connected, and well reimbursed sup. A senior senator, media executive, lobbyist, real estate tycoon, or CIA operative may be at the next table. Maybe. The odds are 50–50 that your dining companions will be a suburban couple celebrating their 25th anniversary or conventioneers on an expense account who are three

Balancing the Budget

Many restaurants within walking distance of the theaters offer pretheater, fixed-price menus that include an appetizer or salad, entree, dessert, and beverage (nonalcoholic). These menus are usually in effect from 4:30 or 5pm to 6 or 6:30pm. You can make out like a bandit and spend considerably less than you would ordering à la carte later in the evening. If you have tickets for a show at the Kennedy Center, **Aquarelle,** Watergate Hotel, 2650 Virginia Ave. NW (at New Hampshire Ave.), has a pretheater menu; **701,** 701 Pennsylvania Ave. NW at 7th Street, near the Shakespeare Theatre also offers pretheater specials.

sheets to the wind. They have all come because the restaurants are well known, usually for their chefs, atmosphere, and high-rolling clientele.

To Dress or Not to Dress? That Is the Question

Washington is a conservative town, and you'll find many diners (especially weeknights) attired in business clothes, probably because they've come from work. With the exception of the fancier spots, there's no need to drag out the dark suit. In the finest establishments, men should wear a jacket and tie (which they can later remove if other gentlemen diners are tie-less) and don't forget the pants. If a jacket is required, I've noted it in the restaurant description. Women have more leeway and can get by in the top places with dressy slacks, a skirt, or a simple dress. In all other restaurants, dress codes are relaxed, so you might as well be comfortable. Jeans are acceptable in dirt cheap, inexpensive, and medium-priced places. The bottom line is that restaurants will gladly accept your plastic and greenbacks, even if you look like a slob.

Mind If I Smoke?

Follow this if you can. Smoking is allowed in the bar areas of D.C. restaurants. Otherwise, the individual restaurant decides whether to have a smoking section. The bottom line, if you're a smoker or the sight of a match makes you ill, ask.

Paying Your Taxes & Figuring Out Your Tip

The tax on food in Washington, D.C., is 10%. This makes it easy to compute the tip on your bill. Since 15% is considered an average tip for good service, multiply the tax amount times 1.5 for the amount to tip. Since servers receive little in wages, they rely on tips for their bread and butter (and to pay the rent); don't leave less than 15% unless the service is horrendous. Waiters and waitresses get blamed for much of what goes wrong in a restaurant, when the kitchen is really at fault. If the service is acceptable but you're dissatisfied with the food, explain your complaint to the manager. Why punish the wait staff for another's sins? If service is stupendous (and you'll know it when it happens), show your appreciation by tipping more generously.

Reservation, Sir?

When I say that a reservation is recommended, I mean for dinner and at the top restaurants for lunch. Otherwise, in many instances, you'll be seated promptly. At popular restaurants that don't accept reservations, however, be prepared to wait. At lunch, to avoid a long line (especially weekdays in heavy business areas downtown and weekends in tourist districts like Georgetown and Adams–Morgan) it's wise to arrive by noon or after 1:30 or 2pm. At dinner, plan on arriving before 7pm without a reservation. If you're catching a theater performance, be seated by 6pm, as most curtains go up at 7:30 or 8pm. And choose a restaurant near the theater. If service is slow, it's easier to sprint a couple of blocks than to hail a cab or cool your heels in a Metro station. For Friday and Saturday dinner, make reservations at any place accepting them, preferably several days in advance.

Washington, D.C. Restaurants from A to Z

In This Chapter

➤ Restaurant indexes by location, price, and cuisine

➤ Full reviews of all the best restaurants in town

➤ The best places for families, romantic couples, and more

Others may say, "It's the economy," but it may be more appropriate to say, "It's the food, stupid." This chapter will make sure that you don't feel stupid when it comes to finding the perfect place to eat. It starts with indexes you can use for figuring out the best bets for your particular tastes and needs. The restaurants are indexed by location so that you can find a place near the attractions you're visiting, by price so that you can budget, and by cuisine so that you can satisfy your individual cravings. I've also provided specialized listings for romantic duos, night-owl noshers, and theatergoers.

From there I proceed to my picks of the best restaurants, listed alphabetically for easy referral. Each restaurant name is followed by its price range, location, and the type of cuisine featured.

Price Categories

To rehash the price codes described in the last chapter, remember that prices include an appetizer, entree, dessert, one drink, taxes, and tip. If you usually skip an appetizer and/or dessert, adjust the price accordingly.

$ = Under $15
$$ = $15–$25
$$$ = $25–$35
$$$$ = $35–$50
$$$$$ = Over $50

These icons will give you a general idea of how much a place will cost. Don't rely on them solely, as some restaurants offer prix-fixe meals or other deals that will affect the icon rankings.

Quick Picks: Washington, D.C. Restaurants at a Glance
Restaurant Index by Location

Adams–Morgan

Felix $$$

I Matti $$$

Meskerem $$

Capitol Hill

B. Smith's $$$$

Cafe Berlin $$

La Colline $$$$

Market Lunch $

Downtown

Aroma $$

A. V. Ristorante $$

Cafe Atlantico $$$

Capitol City Brewing Company $$

Coco Loco $$$

Dean and Deluca Cafe $

Full Kee $$

Georgia Brown's $$$

Ginza's $$

Hunan Chinatown $$

Il Radicchio $$

Jaleo $$

Legal Sea Foods $$$$

Le Rivage $$$

Les Halles $$$

Luigino $$$

Luna Grill & Diner $

Marrakesh $$$

Morrison–Clark Inn $$$

Morton's $$$$

Mykonos $$

Occidental Grill $$$$

Old Ebbitt Grill $$

Oodles Noodles $

Pan Asian Noodles and Grill $$

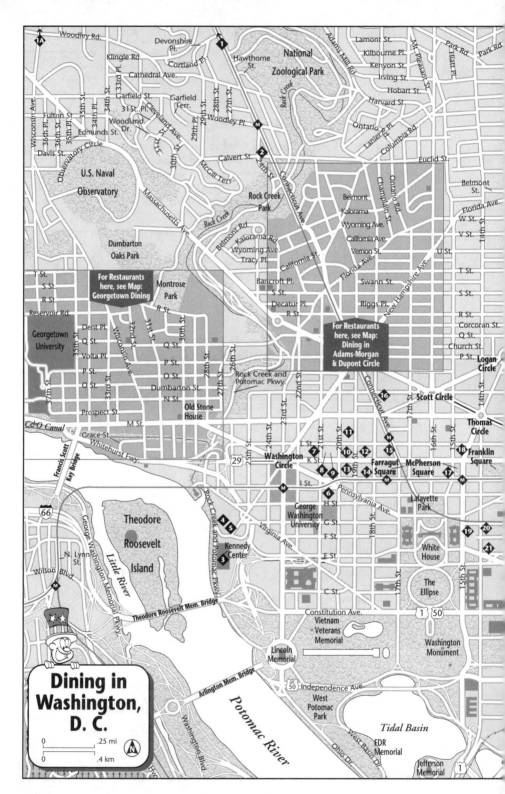

Dining in Washington, D. C.

0   .25 mi
0   .4 km

For Restaurants here, see Map: Georgetown Dining

For Restaurants here, see Map: Dining in Adams-Morgan & Dupont Circle

A.V. Ristorante 27
Aquarelle 4
Aroma 13
B. Smith's 36
Cafe Atlantico 31
Cafe Berlin 37
Capitol City Brewing Company 23
Cheesecake Factory 1A
Clyde's of Chevy Chase 1A
Coco Loco 28
Cup'A Cup'A 5
Full Kee 30
Georgia Brown's 17
Ginza's 7
Greenwood at Cleveland Park 1
Hunan Chinatown 29
Jaleo 32
Kinkead's 6
La Colline 35
Le Rivage 34
Legal Sea Foods 8
Les Halles 22
Luigino 24
Luna Grill & Diner 16
Market Lunch 38
Marrakesh 26
Morrison-Clark Inn 25
Morton's of
  Chicago (Downtown) 15
Mykonos 12
New Heights 2
Occidental Grill 21
Old Ebbitt Grill 19
Oodles Noodles 11
Pan Asian Noodles and
  Grill (Downtown) 18
Prime Rib 9
Red Sage 20
Roof Terrace Restaurant,
  Kennedy Center 3
701 33
Sholl's Colonial Cafeteria 10
Taberna Del Alabardero 14

**See individual maps for
restaurants in Adams-Morgan
and Dupont Circle; and
in Georgetown.**

107

Prime Rib $$$$$

Red Sage $$–$$$$

701 $$$$

Sholl's Colonial Cafeteria $

Taberna del Alabardero $$$$

Dupont Circle

BeDuCi $$$

Brickskeller $

Galileo $$$$

Il Radicchio $$

Obelisk $$$$

Pan Asian Noodles and Grill $$

Pesce $$$

Pizzeria Paradiso $$

Foggy Bottom

Aquarelle $$$$$

Cup'A Cup'A $

Kinkead's $$$$

Roof Terrace Restaurant, Kennedy Center $$$$

Georgetown

Austin Grill (Glover Park) $$

Bistro Français $$$

Cafe Milano $$

Chadwick's $$

Clyde's $$

Dean and Deluca Cafe $

Enriqueta's $$

Hibiscus Cafe $$$

Houston's $$

Il Radicchio $$

Morton's $$$$

Music City Roadhouse $$

Patisserie–Cafe Didier $

Rockland's (Glover Park) $

Uptown

Chadwick's $$

Cheesecake Factory $$

Clyde's $$

Greenwood $$$$

New Heights $$$$

Restaurant Index by Price

$$$$$

Aquarelle (Foggy Bottom)

Prime Rib (Downtown)

$$$$

B. Smith's (Capitol Hill)

Galileo (Dupont Citcle)

Greenwood (Uptown)

Kinkead's (Foggy Bottom)

La Colline (Capitol Hill)

Legal Sea Foods (Downtown)

Morton's (Downtown, Georgetown)

New Heights (Uptown)

Obelisk (Dupont Circle)

Occidental Grill (Downtown)

Red Sage/Dining Room (Downtown)

Roof Terrace Restaurant, Kennedy Center (Foggy Bottom)

701 (Downtown)

Taberna del Alabardero (Downtown)

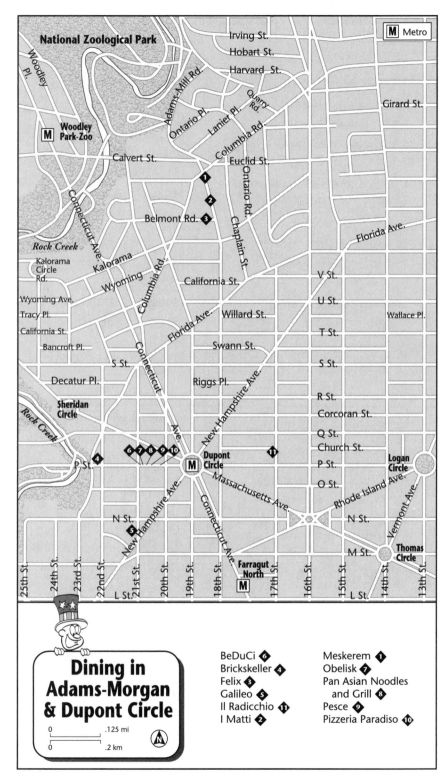

National Zoological Park

Irving St.
Hobart St.
Harvard St.

Girard St.

M Metro

Woodley Pl.

M Woodley Park-Zoo

Adams-Mill Rd.

Ontario Pl.

Lanier Pl.

Quarry Rd.

Columbia Rd.

Calvert St.

Euclid St.

Ontario Rd.

1

2

Belmont Rd. **3**

Chaplain St.

Florida Ave.

Rock Creek

Kalorama Circle Rd.

Kalorama

Connecticut Ave.

Wyoming

Columbia Rd.

California St.

V St.

U St.

Wyoming Ave.
Tracy Pl.
California St.

Florida Ave.

Willard St.

T St.

Wallace Pl.

Bancroft Pl.

S St.

Swann St.

S St.

Decatur Pl.

Connecticut

Riggs Pl.

New Hampshire Ave.

R St.

Sheridan Circle

Corcoran St.

Rock Creek

Ave.

Q St.

Church St.

11

Logan Circle

P St.

4

6 **7** **8** **9** **10**

Dupont Circle **M**

P St.

O St.

Massachusetts Ave.

Rhode Island Ave.

Vermont Ave.

N St.

New Hampshire Ave.

5

Connecticut Ave.

N St.

Thomas Circle

M St.

25th St.
24th St.
23rd St.
22nd St.
21st St.
20th St.
19th St.
18th St.
17th St.
16th St.
15th St.
14th St.
13th St.

L St.

Farragut North **M**

L St.

Dining in Adams-Morgan & Dupont Circle

0   .125 mi
0   .2 km

BeDuCi **6**
Brickskeller **4**
Felix **3**
Galileo **5**
Il Radicchio **11**
I Matti **2**

Meskerem **1**
Obelisk **7**
Pan Asian Noodles and Grill **8**
Pesce **9**
Pizzeria Paradiso **10**

$$$

BeDuCi (Dupont Circle)

Bistro Français (Georgetown)

Cafe Atlantico (Downtown)

Coco Loco (Downtown)

Felix (Adams–Morgan)

Georgia Brown's (Downtown)

Hibiscus Cafe (Georgetown)

I Matti (Adams–Morgan)

Le Rivage (Downtown)

Les Halles (Downtown)

Luigino (Downtown)

Marrakesh (Downtown)

Morrison–Clark Inn (Downtown)

Pesce (Dupont Circle)

$$

Aroma (Downtown)

Austin Grill (Glover Park, north of Georgetown)

A. V. Ristorante (Downtown)

Cafe Berlin (Capitol Hill)

Cafe Milano (Georgetown)

Capitol City Brewing Company (Downtown)

Chadwick's (Georgetown, Uptown, Old Town, Alexandria)

Cheesecake Factory (Uptown)

Clyde's (Georgetown, Uptown)

Enriqueta's (Georgetown)

Full Kee (Downtown)

Ginza's (Downtown)

Houston's (Georgetown)

Hunan Chinatown (Downtown)

Il Radicchio (Downtown, Dupont Circle, Georgetown)

Jaleo (Downtown)

Meskerem (Adams–Morgan)

Music City Roadhouse (Georgetown)

Mykonos (Downtown)

Old Ebbitt Grill (Downtown)

Pan Asian Noodles and Grill (Downtown, Dupont Circle)

Pizzeria Paradiso (Dupont Circle)

Red Sage/Chili Bar (Downtown)

$

Aroma (Downtown)

Brickskeller (Dupont Circle)

Cup'A Cup'A (Foggy Bottom)

Dean and Deluca Cafe (Downtown, Georgetown)

Luna Grill & Diner (Downtown)

Market Lunch (Capitol Hill)

Oodles Noodles (Downtown)

Patisserie–Cafe Didier (Georgetown)

Rockland's (Glover Park, north of Georgetown)

Sholl's Colonial Cafeteria (Downtown)

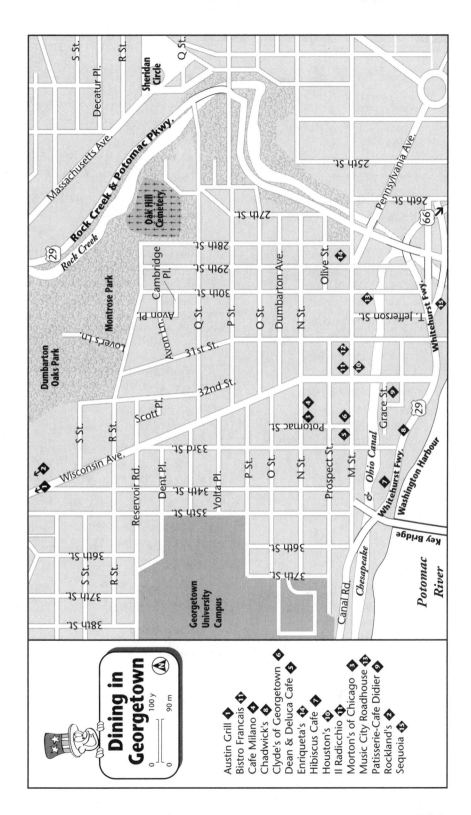

Dining in Georgetown

N

0 ——— 100 y
0 ——— 90 m

Austin Grill **1**
Bistro Francais **11**
Cafe Milano **4**
Chadwick's **8**
Clyde's of Georgetown **6**
Dean & Deluca Cafe **5**
Enriqueta's **14**
Hibiscus Cafe **7**
Houston's **10**
Il Radicchio **11**
Morton's of Chicago **3**
Music City Roadhouse **13**
Patisserie-Cafe Didier **9**
Rockland's **2**
Sequoia **15**

111

Restaurant Index by Cuisine

American

Aquarelle (Foggy Bottom, $$$$$)

Austin Grill (Glover Park, north of Georgetown, $$)

Brickskeller (Dupont Circle, $)

B. Smith's (Capitol Hill, $$$$)

Capitol City Brewing Company (Downtown, $$)

Chadwick's (Georgetown, Uptown, Old Town, Alexandria, $$)

Cheesecake Factory (Uptown, $$)

Clyde's (Georgetown, Uptown, $$)

Cuppa, Cuppa (Foggy Bottom, $)

Dean and Deluca Cafe (Downtown, Georgetown, $)

Felix (Adams–Morgan, $$$)

Georgia Brown's (Downtown, $$$)

Greenwood (Uptown, $$$$)

Houston's (Georgetown, $$)

Kinkead's (Foggy Bottom, $$$$)

Legal Sea Foods (Downtown, $$$$)

Luna Grill & Diner (Downtown, $)

Market Lunch (Capitol Hill, $)

Morrison–Clark Inn (Downtown, $$$)

Morton's (Downtown, Georgetown, $$$$)

Music City Roadhouse (Georgetown, $$)

New Heights (Uptown, $$$$)

Occidental Grill (Downtown, $$$$)

Old Ebbitt Grill (Downtown, $$)

Pesce (Dupont Circle, $$$)

Prime Rib (Downtown, $$$$$)

Red Sage (Downtown, $$–$$$$)

Rockland's (Glover Park, north of Georgetown, $)

Roof Terrace Restaurant, Kennedy Center (Foggy Bottom, $$$$)

701 (Downtown, $$$$)

Sholl's Colonial Cafeteria (Downtown, $)

Asian

Oodles Noodles (Downtown, $)

Pan Asian Noodles and Grill (Downtown, Dupont Circle, $$)

Barbecue

Market Lunch (Capitol Hill, $)

Rockland's (Glover Park, north of Georgetown, $)

Brazilian

Coco Loco (Downtown, $$$)

Caribbean

Cafe Atlantico (Downtown, $$$)

Hibiscus Cafe (Georgetown, $$$)

Chinese

Full Kee (Downtown, $$)

Hunan Chinatown (Downtown, $$)

Ethiopian

Meskerem (Adams–
Morgan, $$)

French

Bistro Français
(Georgetown, $$$)

La Colline (Capitol Hill, $$$$)

Le Rivage (Downtown, $$$)

Les Halles (Downtown, $$$)

Patisserie–Cafe Didier
(Georgetown, $)

German

Cafe Berlin (Capitol Hill, $$)

Greek

Mykonos (Downtown, $$)

Hamburgers

Chadwick's (Georgetown,
Uptown, Old Town,
Alexandria, $$)

Clyde's (Georgetown,
Uptown, $$)

Houston's (Georgetown, $$)

Old Ebbitt Grill
(Downtown, $$)

Indian

Aroma (Downtown, $$)

International

New Heights (Uptown, $$$$)

701 (Downtown, $$$$)

Italian

A. V. Ristorante
(Downtown, $$)

Cafe Milano (Georgetown, $$)

Galileo (Dupont Circle, $$$$)

Il Radicchio (Downtown,
Dupont Circle, Georgetown, $$)

I Matti (Adams–Morgan, $$$)

Luigino (Downtown, $$$)

Obelisk (Dupont Circle, $$$$)

Pizzeria Paradiso (Dupont
Circle, $$)

Japanese

Ginza's (Downtown, $$)

Latin American

Cafe Atlantico
(Downtown, $$$)

Mediterranean

BeDuCi (Dupont Circle, $$$)

Mexican

Coco Loco (Downtown, $$$)

Enriqueta's (Georgetown, $$)

Moroccan

Marrakesh (Downtown, $$$)

Pizza ($ symbol reflects price
of meal with pizza entree)

A. V. Ristorante (Downtown, $)

I Matti (Adams–Morgan, $$)

Luigino (Downtown, $$)

Pizzeria Paradiso (Dupont
Circle, $$)

Seafood

Greenwood (Uptown, $$$$)

Kinkead's (Foggy Bottom, $$$$)

Legal Sea Foods (Downtown,
$$$$)

Market Lunch (Capitol Hill, $)

Pesce (Dupont Circle, $$$)

Southern

B. Smith's (Capitol Hill, $$$$)

Georgia Brown's
(Downtown, $$$)

113

Morrison–Clark Inn
(Downtown, $$$)

Music City Roadhouse
(Georgetown, $$)

Southwestern

Austin Grill (Glover Park,
north of Georgetown, $$)

Houston's (Georgetown, $$)

Red Sage (Downtown, Chili
Bar $$, Dining Room $$$$)

Spanish

Jaleo (Downtown, $$)

Taberna del Alabardero
(Downtown, $$$$)

Steak House

Les Halles (Downtown, $$$)

Morton's (Downtown,
Georgetown, $$$$)

Prime Rib (Downtown, $$$$$)

Thai

Pan Asian Noodles and Grill
(Downtown, Dupont
Circle, $$)

My Favorite Washington, D.C. Restaurants

Aquarelle

$$$$$. Foggy Bottom. AMERICAN.

Get your foie gras or pheasant fix at this sophisticated Watergate restaurant featuring French-kissed New American cuisine. Request a window table for a scenic water view of the Potomac. The $38 pretheater menu attracts diners who are attending performances at the Kennedy Center, which is across the street. Grilled meats and fish shine; the fruit tarts are sublime.

Watergate Hotel, 2650 Virginia Ave. NW (at New Hampshire Ave.). ☎ *202/ 298-4455. Reservations recommended.* **Metro:** *Foggy Bottom, then walk west 1½ blocks on I St. to left at New Hampshire Ave. Walk 2 blocks and cross Virginia Ave. to Watergate.* **Main courses:** *$19–$27. AE, DISC, MC, V.* **Open:** *Daily 11:30am–2:30pm, 5:30–7pm pretheater menu, 7–10:30pm.*

Best Places for Whispering Sweet Nothings

Aquarelle (Foggy Bottom, $$$$$)
Greenwood (Uptown, $$$$)
La Colline (Capitol Hill, $$$$)
Le Rivage (Downtown, $$$)
Morrison–Clark Inn (Downtown, $$$)
701 (Downtown, $$$$)

Aroma
$$. Downtown. INDIAN.

The lace curtains and formally attired wait staff are somewhat misleading at this cozy and casual eatery perfumed by aromatic curries. Don't expect a magic carpet ride, but it's a good refueling spot when you're caught in the business district centered around Connecticut Avenue and K Street. Tandoori chicken is the standout of the main dishes, flavorful and tender as baby food. Put the kabosh on the kebabs, which tend to be ho-hum and dry.

1919 I St. NW (between 19th and 20th sts.). ☎ *202/833-4700. Reservations recommended for lunch.* **Metro:** *Farragut West, then walk west on I St. 2 blocks.* **Main courses:** *$7–$16. AE, DISC, MC, V.* **Open:** *Mon–Fri 11:30am–2:30pm, Sat–Sun noon–2:30pm; daily 5:30–10:30pm.*

Kids Austin Grill
$$. Glover Park (north of Georgetown). AMERICAN/ SOUTHWESTERN.

Lay off the crispy corn chips and flavorful salsas if you want to save room for crabmeat quesadillas, carne asada, and grilled fish. Tried-and-true tacos, burritos, and enchiladas are always available. The generous margaritas, country-western ambience, and reasonable prices attract families and Generation X'ers. If you want to converse, go elsewhere. The toe-tapping music can be deafening, but a margarita or long neck reduces the noise to a pleasant buzz.

2404 Wisconsin Ave. NW (a 15-minute walk north on Wisconsin Ave. from Georgetown, or take a taxi. ☎ *202/337-8080. Reservations not accepted.* **Metro:** *Tenleytown, then no. 32, 34, or 36 bus south on Wisconsin Ave.* **Main courses:** *$6–$15. DC, DISC, MC, V.* **Open:** *Mon–Fri 11:30am–11pm, Sat 3pm–midnight, Sun 3–10:30pm.*

Kids A. V. Ristorante
$$. Downtown. ITALIAN/PIZZA.

The godfather of D.C. Italian restaurants sits on a not-too-pretty block close to the Convention Center. The truck-driver portions of bold-sauced pasta are best shared, maybe as an accompaniment to a simply dressed fish or veal dish. White pizza (without cheese for purists and calorie counters) is a must, and the thin-crusted New York–style pizza is better than most. Opera resonates from the jukebox, dressing up the down-and-dirty decor at this Washington institution. In winter, a dimly lit table near the back room fireplace is perfect for stolen kisses between bites of Linguine Puttanesca or Spaghetti Caruso.

607 New York Ave. NW (between 6th and 7th sts.). ☎ *202/737-0550. Reservations required for 12 or more.* **Metro:** *Mt. Vernon Square–UDC, then walk south on 7th St. 2 blocks to left at New York Ave.* **Main courses:** *$7–$15. AE, CB, DC, DISC, MC, V.* **Open:** *Mon–Fri 11am–11pm, Sat 5pm–midnight.*

Best Restaurants for the Suit Set

Galileo (Dupont Circle, $$$$)
Georgia Brown's (Downtown, $$$)
Kinkead's (Foggy Bottom, $$$$)
La Colline (Capitol Hill, $$$$)
Legal Sea Foods (Downtown, $$$$)
Morton's (Downtown, $$$$)
Old Ebbitt Grill (Downtown, $$)
Prime Rib (Downtown, $$$$$)

BeDuCi
$$$. Dupont Circle. MEDITERRANEAN.
Charming is the operative word at BeDuCi ("Below Dupont Circle"; get it?).
With its sunny porch, sidewalk tables, and art-enhanced interior rooms, this
Dupont Circle eatery could get by on looks alone. But it's not just another
pretty face. The kitchen turns out pastas, paellas, and vegetarian dishes
(sometimes encased in phyllo) that are inspired and colorful. More impor-
tant, they taste good. The fudge-frosted brownies may not have
Mediterranean origins, but who's going to complain?

2100 P St. NW (at 21st St.). ☎ *202/223-3824. Reservations recommended.*
Metro: *Dupont Circle, then walk west on P St. 2 blocks.* ***Main courses:***
$13–$21. AE, DC, DISC, MC, V. ***Open:*** *Mon–Fri 11:30am–2:30pm; Mon–Sat
5:30–10:30pm, Sun 5:30–9:30pm.*

Bistro Français
$$$. Georgetown. FRENCH.
Its tables joined like Siamese twins, Bistro Français is a little touch of Paris on
the *rive gauche* of busy M Street. After hanging up their toques, local French
chefs gather under the hanging ferns until the wee small hours to talk shop
and unwind over onion soup au gratin, pâtés, and pastry. Inventive daily
specials enhance a menu with predictable bistro fare such as coq au vin and
minute steak. Make tracks to the succulent rotisserie chicken, flavored with
fresh tarragon.

3128 M St. NW (between 31st and 32nd sts.). ☎ *202/338-3830. Reservations recommended.* ***Metro:*** *Foggy Bottom, but it's a trek, so take a taxi.* ***Main courses:***
$16–$22. AE, MC, V. ***Open:*** *Sun–Thurs 11am–3am, Fri–Sat 11am–4am.*

Kids Brickskeller
$. Dupont Circle. AMERICAN.
It's déjà vu all over again at the Brickskeller, which has been popular since I
was a college student (*!#+$! years ago). At Washington's version of Cheers,

the frat house setting, juicy burgers, french fries, and brew menu (more than 700 at last count) are a nostalgia trip; a reminder of long-gone days—and nights. The decor runs to stale smoke, darts, and walls obscured by empties. The staff knows its brewskis and will help you decipher the myriad choices. Or, if you're in it for the long haul, you can start with the A's and drink your way through the alphabet.

1523 22nd St. NW (between P and Q sts.). ☎ *202/293-1885. Reservations accepted for 6 or more.* **Metro:** *Dupont Circle, then walk west on P Street 3 blocks.* **Main courses:** *$7–$16. AE, DISC, MC, V.* **Hours:** *Mon–Thurs 11:30am–2am, Fri 11:30am–3am, Sat 6pm–3am, Sun 6pm–2am.*

B. Smith's
$$$$. Capitol Hill. SOUTHERN.
I've rolled downstairs to Metro more than once after food orgies at B. Smith's. This vast, vaulted-ceilinged Union Station restaurant raises Southern cooking to heavenly heights. The red beans and rice appetizer is a meal in itself, but why stop there? Fish is done to perfection, sauced or naked, at times bedded on crunchy julienned vegetables. By dessert you'll be begging the waiter to "shut mah mouth." The ribs, fried catfish, and cheesecake with pecans and cherries would restore Blanche DuBois's sanity. A jazz combo plays most evenings after 8pm.

50 Massachusetts Ave. NE (Union Station). ☎ *202/289-6188. Reservations recommended.* **Metro:** *Union Station, then take escalator to main floor.* **Main courses:** *$13–$22. AE, CB, DC, DISC, MC, V.* **Open:** *Mon–Fri 11:30am–4pm; Sun–Thurs 5–11pm, Fri–Sat 5pm–midnight; Sun brunch 11:30am–4pm.*

Cafe Atlantico
$$$. Downtown. CARIBBEAN/LATIN AMERICAN.
The rainbow-bright food echoes the colorful panels and tiles of Cafe Atlantico's stacked dining rooms, convenient to the 7th Street art galleries, Shakespeare Theatre, and FBI. The ceviche, empañadas, mixed grill, and jerk chicken elicit *"muy buenos"* from diners. *Asopao,* a creamy Puerto Rican seafood stew, wins kudos, as does the chocolate bread pudding topped with glazed banana slices. *Deliciosa!*

405 8th St. NW (between D and E sts.). ☎ *202/393-0812. Reservations accepted until 7:30pm.* **Metro:** *Archives/Navy Memorial, then walk north on 7th St. 2 blocks to left at D St., and right at 8th St.* **Main courses:** *$12–$19. AE, DC, MC, V.* **Open:** *Mon–Fri 11:30am–2:30pm; Mon–Thurs 5:30–11pm, Fri–Sat 5:30pm–midnight, Sun 5:30–10pm.*

Cafe Berlin
$$. Capitol Hill. GERMAN.
Standing in the shadow of the Capitol, this intimate town house restaurant reeks with *gemütlichkeit.* In good weather, the outdoor tables fill with congressional staffers and locals. Life is short, so you may want to eat dessert

first (strudel, black forest cake, and the like) before moving on to sauerbraten, paprikash, or Wiener schnitzel (veal). At lunch the soup-and-sandwich special is a bargain, as are the entrees (two to three times as much at dinner). When visiting the Hill, you could do *wurst*—a lot *wurst*—than breaking pumpernickel bread at Cafe Berlin.

322 Massachusetts Ave. NE (between 3rd and 4th sts.). ☎ ***202/543-7656.*** *Reservations recommended.* **Metro:** *Union Station, then walk east 3 blocks on Massachusetts Ave.* **Main courses:** *$8–$17. AE, CB, DC, MC, V.* **Open:** *Mon–Thurs 11:30am–10pm, Fri–Sat 11:30am–11pm; Sun 4–10pm.*

Cafe Milano
$$. Georgetown. ITALIAN.
Even if you don't consider yourself chic, you can join the beautiful people at this trendy Georgetown spot. Jet-setters and miniskirts hobnob downstairs, where things heat up between 11pm and 1am. For quiet and privacy, sit upstairs and enjoy a delectable salad (the insalata giardino sports chunks of tomatoes, potatoes, red onion, cucumber, and celery in a balsamic vinegar dressing) or antipasto, with bread and a glass of Pinot Grigio. The pastas, pizzas, and grilled fare are adequate but nothing to write home about. Try the patio for lunch.

3251 Prospect St. (off Wisconsin Ave. between M and N sts.). ☎ ***202/333-6183.*** *Reservations recommended.* **Metro:** *Foggy Bottom, then a long walk—walk north on 23rd St. 1 block to Pennsylvania Ave. Walk halfway around Washington Circle and continue west on Pennsylvania Ave. 3 blocks, where it merges with M St. Walk west on M St. 3 blocks. Take a right at Wisconsin Ave. NW, go 1 block, and then take a left at Prospect St. If you're not up for walking, take a no. 30, 32, 34, 35, or 36 bus from Pennsylvania Ave. to Wisconsin Ave., get off at M St., walk north 1 block on Wisconsin Ave., and turn left at Prospect St. Or take a taxi.* **Main courses:** *$7–$15. AE, MC, V.* **Open:** *Mon–Sat 11:30am–2:30pm and 5:30–11pm (restaurant only; bar closes at 1am), Sun noon–11pm.*

Best Dining Rooms with a View

Le Rivage (Downtown, $$$)
Roof Terrace Restaurant,
  Kennedy Center
  (Foggy Bottom, $$$$)

Kids ★ **Capitol City Brewing Company**
$$. Downtown. AMERICAN.
It's busy, big, and boisterous, but the hamburgers and seasoned fries are bodacious in this bar-scene brew pub. Besides the crowd dining here before a show at the National, Shakespeare, or Warner theaters, Capitol City also attracts business types (the Convention Center is within spitting distance), tourists, and singles.
Dunk a complimentary soft pretzel in the horseradish-mustard dip while waiting to order and wash it down with one of the in-house microbrews (I like the amber). It could be a while. If you're in a hurry, belly up to the bar.

1100 New York Ave. NW (corner of H and 11th sts.). ☎ *202/628-2222. Reservations not accepted.* **Metro:** *Metro Center, then walk east 1 block on G St., left at 11th St., and walk 1 block.* **Main courses:** *$9–$23. AE, DC, DISC, MC, V.* **Open:** *Sun–Thurs 11am–11pm, Fri–Sat 11am–midnight.*

Kids Chadwick's
$$. Uptown. AMERICAN.

Like an old friend, Chadwick's is welcoming, warm, and dependable. Long a favorite with families and diners seeking decent pub fare and efficient service at reasonable prices, Chadwick's still cuts the mustard with all of the above. This restaurant is particularly convenient for those shopping at Mazza Gallerie or Chevy Chase Pavilion. The paper-topped tables and crayons keep everyone amused until the grub arrives. The burgers, sandwiches, and salads are ample and well prepared. Brunch here is satisfying—and reasonable. You'll also find Chadwick's in Georgetown at 3205 K St. NW (☎ **202/333-2565**); and in Old Town at 203 S. Strand St., Alexandria, VA (☎ **703/836-4442**).

5247 Wisconsin Ave. NW. ☎ *202/362-8040. Reservations recommended.* **Metro:** *Friendship Heights, then walk south on Wisconsin Ave. 2 blocks.* **Main courses:** *$9–$17. AE, DC, DISC, MC, V.* **Open:** *Mon–Thurs 11:30am–midnight, Fri–Sat 11:30am–1am; Sun 4pm–midnight.*

Kids Cheesecake Factory
$$. Uptown. AMERICAN.

Personally, I don't have the patience to stand in line at the Cheesecake Factory, but I'm in the minority judging by the crowds. Arrive early at this hugely popular eatery—before noon for lunch; before 6pm for dinner—for the Godzilla-sized salads (any species with chicken is a safe bet). Heartier appetites can choose a chicken or pasta dish or one of the Dagwood-style sandwiches from the extensive menu. The spicy Thai chicken on linguine entree is killer! You may want to box half for later consumption so that you'll have room for the cheesecake. More than 30 permutations are offered, but I like my cheesecake pure, without chips, nuts, fruit, or overpowering flavorings. The choices (and calories) are yours.

5345 Wisconsin Ave. NW (in the Chevy Chase Pavilion). ☎ *202/364-0500. Reservations not accepted (be prepared for very long lines).* **Metro:** *Friendship Heights, then walk south on Wisconsin Ave. 1 block to Chevy Chase Pavilion.* **Main courses:** *$9–$20. AE, DC, DISC, MC, V.* **Open:** *Mon–Thurs 11:30am–11:30pm, Fri–Sat 11:30am–12:30am, Sun 10am–11pm.*

Kids Clyde's
$$. Uptown. AMERICAN/HAMBURGERS.

There's plenty to look at besides the menu and your dining companions in this cavernous restaurant. For starters, a model train circles overhead. The raceway and flight-related memorabilia may have you believing you're in Indianapolis or an annex of the Air and Space Museum. Service is attentive

119

and friendly. Based on several visits, here are a few observations: The kitchen is kinder to fish than to meat. Most dinner entrees are overpriced. Sandwiches, salads, and omelets are safe: tasty, filling, and more reasonable. When in doubt, order a hamburger and dessert. Pizza and more casual fare is served downstairs at the huge bar (reminiscent of the cantina in *Star Wars*). Also visit the original Clyde's in Georgetown (the granddaddy of D.C. saloons, where "Afternoon Delight" was penned) at 3236 M St. NW (☎ **202/333-9180**).

76 Wisconsin Circle (just across the D.C. border in Chevy Chase, Maryland). ☎ 301/951-9600. Reservations recommended. **Metro:** *Friendship Heights, then walk north 1 block on Wisconsin Ave.* **Main courses:** *$10–$17. AE, DC, DISC, MC, V.* **Open:** *Mon–Thurs 11am–11:30pm, Fri–Sat 11am–12:30am; Sun 4:30–11:30pm.*

Coco Loco
$$$. Downtown. BRAZILIAN/MEXICAN.
Begin with a caipirinha cocktail (lime flavored and potent) at this frenetic and friendly hot spot with tropical decor near the Shakespeare Theatre and 7th Street galleries. Then, if you can still focus, check out the Mexican tapas menu, with an overwhelming selection of tempting vegetable, seafood, and meat delectables. If you're able to make up your mind before the kitchen closes, you can create a satisfying and affordable meal from two or more of the choices. Larger appetites applaud the *churrascaria*, a Brazilian all-you-can-eat feast that begins with a self-serve cold buffet of salads and vegetables, followed by skewered meats (chicken, chorizo sausage, pork ribs, beef) and bowls of coconut rice and roasted potatoes. Brazilian dancers stir things up some evenings. Request a window table in the front room if you want to escape the noisy goings-on at the bar.

810 7th St. NW (between H and I sts.). ☎ 202/289-2626. **Main courses:** *$10–$27 (tapas much less). AE, CB, DC, MC, V. Reservations recommended.* **Metro:** *Gallery Place, then walk north on H St. 2 blocks.* **Open:** *Mon–Fri 11:30am–2:30pm; Mon–Thurs 5:30–10pm, Fri–Sat 5:30–11pm.*

D.C. Dirt

In October 1998, Harrison Ford and other cast and crew members of *Random Hearts* wrapped up filming at Coco Loco, where they downed 49 caipirinha cocktails with dinner. Sure hope they didn't drive back to their hotels. You'll rest easier knowing they paid the $4,200 tab in cold hard cash. Wonder if that included the tip. . . .

Cup'A Cup'A
$. Foggy Bottom. AMERICAN.

Perfect for a quick bite before a Kennedy Center performance, Cup'A Cup'A is a pleasant self-serve cafe in the Watergate, across the street from the performing arts center. Colorful photographs, wicker furnishings, and soothing music raise Cup'A Cup'A a notch above the typical plain Jane cafe. The salads, sandwiches, soups, wraps, personal pizzas, and pastry are tasty and inexpensive. From a patio table you can watch the musicians and dancers pass by on their way to the Ken Cen. Wine by the glass and domestic and imported beers are available. A coffee bar features a lengthy list of espresso and cappuccino variations. There are other locations at 1911 K St. NW, ☎ **202/466-3678;** 1900 G St. NW, ☎ **202/466-6570;** The Shops at National Place, 529 14th St. NW, ☎ **202/466-2663;** 1350 Connecticut Ave. NW, ☎ **202/466-6571.**

600 New Hampshire Ave. at Rock Creek Parkway. ☎ *202/466-3677. Reservations not accepted.* **Metro:** *Foggy Bottom, then take free shuttle bus to Kennedy Center, walk down hill, and cross New Hampshire Ave.* **Main courses:** *$3.25–$7. AE, MC, V.* **Open:** *Sun 10am–7pm, Mon–Thurs 7:30am–8pm, Fri–Sat 7:30am–11pm.*

Dean and Deluca Cafe
Kids
$. Georgetown. AMERICAN.

Shoppers, tourists, and students from nearby Georgetown U. enjoy people-watching with their salads and sandwiches (like grilled veggies on a baguette or focaccia)—washed down with designer water, yuppie coffee, or fresh-squeezed juice—at this offshoot of the New York food emporium with a 'tude. The lines are slow at peak times, but once settled at an outdoor table on a sunny day, the wait is quickly forgotten. When you're done eating, take a few minutes to browse through the groceries and housewares. (Note: The Georgetown store on M Street is the nicest and largest with groceries and housewares sections.) The two downtown locations are at 1299 Pennsylvania Ave. NW in the Warner Theatre Building, ☎ **202/628-8155,** and 1919 Pennsylvania Ave. NW (3 blocks from the White House), ☎ **202/296-4327.**

3276 M St. NW (between 32nd and 33rd sts.). ☎ *202/342-2500. Reservations not accepted.* **Metro:** *Foggy Bottom, then walk north on 23rd St. and left at Pennsylvania Ave., which merges with M St., and continue west on M St. 8 blocks.* **Main courses:** *$6–$8. AE, MC, V.* **Open:** *Sun–Thurs 9am–8pm, Fri–Sat 9am–9pm.*

Enriqueta's
$$. Georgetown. MEXICAN.

A Georgetown landmark for *muchos años,* this Mexican spot serves authentic fare in a colorful, closet-sized space where the tables are closer than relatives in a *barrio* tenement. No matter. Diners come here to eat, not to linger. Sure, you can get tacos and enchiladas at Enriqueta's, but to truly test the kitchen, try a regional fish specialty or the flavorful chicken mole (the tomato and beef-based sauce is flavored with onions, chiles, and Mexican chocolate). Aficionados gather at lunch where good value leaves dinero in their wallets for dinner. Some think the uncomfortable chairs are designed to promote fast turnaround.

2811 M St. NW (between 28th and 29th sts.). ☎ *202/338-7772. Reservations accepted for 5 or more.* **Metro:** *Foggy Bottom, then walk north on 23rd St. to left at Pennsylvania Ave. Continue west on M St. for 5 blocks.* **Main courses:** *$9–$13. AE, MC, V.* **Open:** *Mon–Sat 11:30am–2:30pm; Sun–Thurs 5–10pm, Fri–Sat 5–11pm.*

D.C. Dirt

In the early days of his administration, President Clinton liked to stop at McDonald's, 1299 New York Ave. NW, for coffee and to press flesh during predawn jogs around the White House and West Potomac Park. The spontaneous klatches drove his secret service detail nearly to drink (something stronger than coffee). Because of the security risk and other factors exhausted ad nauseum by the media, the leader of the free world has confined his coffee drinking to the 1600 Pennsylvania Avenue dog house where he's had other fish to fry. He seldom frequents local restaurants (or if he does, his presence is hush-hush).

Felix
$$$. Adams–Morgan. AMERICAN.

Martinis are the beverage of choice at the first-floor bar. But the ambience is more of a blend of South Beach, Soho, and a Big 10 campus. Couples get acquainted in dimly lit corners and locals reconnect in a fantasy cityscape setting. The cuisine is predominantly American, but touched by Italy, France, and Asia. Hence, seafood ravioli, peppered foie gras, and charred tuna sashimi. Me? I'll have a vodka martini (shaken not stirred), a double order of the smoked salmon/potato pancake appetizer, and a strawberry mousse parfait.

2406 18th St. NW (at Belmont Rd.). ☎ *202/48-FELIX. Reservations recommended.* **Metro:** *Uh-uh. Take a cab.* **Main courses:** *$14–$23. AE, CB, DC, DISC, MC, V.* **Open:** *Sun–Thurs 5:30–10:30pm, Fri–Sat 5:30–11pm; bar open Sun–Thurs until 2am, Fri–Sat until 3am.*

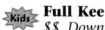

Full Kee
$$. Downtown. CHINESE.

Like a fortune cookie promising true love or a large inheritance, Full Kee brings a smile to diners' lips. Consistency is the hallmark of its food and service. Quite simply, this Chinatown bastion rarely, if ever, disappoints. And it's open until 3am Friday and Saturday, in case you can't sleep or want to rub shoulders with D.C.'s top chefs who eat here after closing their kitchens. Aside from excellent Cantonese fare, Full Kee is known for its dumpling soup, fresh fish, and seafood. It is also known for its bare-bones decor and BYO liquor policy.

509 H St. NW. ☎ *202/371-2233. Reservations accepted for 6 or more.* **Metro:** *Gallery Place/Chinatown, then walk north 1 block on 7th St., right at H St., and continue 2 blocks.* **Main courses:** *$9–$15. No credit cards; cash only.* **Open:** *Mon–Thurs and Sun 11am–1am, Fri–Sat 11am–3am.*

Galileo
$$$$. Dupont Circle. ITALIAN.

With its whitewashed walls, Galileo resembles a grotto one might find in northern Italy. The restaurant is handsome and dignified without being pretentious or stuffy—diners in jeans or suits are equally welcome. But if you're looking for a cheap spaghetti garden, and quantity rather than quality, move on. Some think the prices are inflated. Others say the food and service are inconsistent. Most say the quality is excellent. They're all right. In fact, Washingtonians use Galileo as the standard when measuring the quality of other Italian restaurants. Award-winning Chef Roberto Donna uses only the freshest, seasonal ingredients in dishes reflecting the best of his birthplace, Italy's Piedmont region. Think risotto, grilled portobello mushrooms, roasted fish and meat. Think light (except for the bread and dessert). Think delicious. And don't think about the cost.

1110 21st St. NW (between L and M sts.). ☎ *202/293-7191. Reservations recommended.* **Metro:** *Farragut North, then walk west on L St. 4 blocks to right at 21st St. and north 1 block.* **Main courses:** *$17–$30. AE, CB, DC, DISC, MC, V.* **Open:** *Mon–Fri 11:30am–2pm; Mon–Thurs 5:30–10pm, Fri–Sat 5:30–10:30pm, Sun 5–10pm.*

Georgia Brown's
$$$. Downtown. AMERICAN/SOUTHERN.

Diversity—in the clientele, wait staff, and kitchen—is alive and well in this southern belle of a restaurant overlooking McPherson Square, a short walk from the White House. Pace yourself. It's easier said than done once the biscuits and corn bread arrive with whipped butter (here enhanced with honey and peach morsels). The menu celebrates the Low Country cooking of the Carolinas and coastal Georgia. Remember the mouthwatering dining room scene in *Midnight in the Garden of Good and Evil*? That's sweet Georgia Brown's. We're talkin' shrimp, black-eyed peas, grits, and greens, suga'. Just like yo mammy *tried* to make.

950 15th St. NW (between I and K sts.). ☎ *202/393-4499. Reservations recommended.* **Metro:** *McPherson Square, then walk west on I St. 1 block and right at 15th St. 1 block.* **Main courses:** *$15–$20. AE, CB, DC, DISC, MC, V.* **Open:** *Mon–Thurs 11:30am–11:30pm, Fri 11:30am–midnight, Sat 5:30pm–midnight, Sun 11:30am–11pm.*

123

Ginza's

$$. Downtown. JAPANESE.

I'm not into sushi (*if* I were going to eat something small and pretty that did-n't fill me up, I'd choose flowers), but the tempura, beef or chicken teriyaki, and other hot entrees on the extensive menu are delish. My more gastronomi-cally adventurous sources tell me Ginza's has the best raw fish in D.C. Hey, whatever floats your boat. The setting may be lackluster and service some-times ho-hum, but you can eat well for less than $30. A fixed-price dinner is a steal at $19.95. If you're not sure what to order, ask the Japanese businessmen at the next table.

1009 21st St. NW (between K and L sts.). ☎ **202/833-1244.** *Reservations recom-mended.* **Metro:** *Farragut North, walk west on L St. 3½ blocks, and left at 21st St. a half block.* **Main courses:** *$10.95–$23.95. AE, MC, V.* **Open:** *Mon–Fri 11:45am–2:30pm and 5–10pm; Sat 5–10pm.*

Greenwood

$$$$. Uptown (near the zoo). AMERICAN/SEAFOOD.

Chef Carole Greenwood turns out creative, eclectic dishes that change sea-sonally in this sophisticated yuppie outpost near the National Zoo. The mood is upbeat and romantic; quiet enough for hushed conversation. The menu is served in a cookbook cover, just one of the touches that make Greenwood's hard not to love. This is a place where young couples exchange meaningful looks while dipping forkfuls of bread and fruit into fondue. The seared tuna steak and tuna burger (don't knock it if you haven't tried it) are out of sight, as are the desserts.

3529 Connecticut Ave. NW (at Porter St.). ☎ **202/833-6572.** *Reservations recom-mended.* **Metro:** *Cleveland Place, then walk north half a block.* **Main courses:** *$14–$26. AE, MC, V.* **Open:** *Tues–Sun 6–11pm.*

Hibiscus Cafe

$$$. Georgetown. CARIBBEAN.

Tucked into a corner of Georgetown under the Whitehurst Freeway, this two-level dining room brightened with neon art serves some of the best Caribbean cookin' for miles around. The appetizer platter is a meal in itself, with sea-food fritters, jerk-seasoned buffalo wings, fried calamari, pineapple chutney, and other goodies. Tops among the entrees are the tangy, but not too spicy, Caribbean-sauced fish and pasta dishes. Waits, in keeping with the "don't worry, be happy" attitude of the islands, are common, so make a reservation.

3401 K St. NW (at 34th St.). ☎ **202/965-7170.** *Reservations recommended.* **Metro:** *Foggy Bottom is far away, but if you insist on walking—walk north on 23rd St. 1 block to Pennsylvania Ave., then walk halfway around Washington Circle and continue west on Pennsylvania Ave. 3 blocks, where it merges with M St. Walk west on M St. 7 blocks to 34th St., take a left on 34th St., and walk 1 block to K St., right to the restaurant. If your feet hurt, walk north on 23rd St. to Pennsylvania Ave. and take a no. 30, 32, 34, 35, or 36 bus to Wisconsin Ave., get off at M St., walk west 3 blocks on M St., left at 34th St., go 1 block to K St., and* *right to restaurant. Or take a taxi.* **Main courses:** *$17–$27. AE, DC, MC, V.* **Open:** *Tues–Sat 6pm–midnight, Sun 5–10pm.*

Kids Houston's.
$$. Georgetown. AMERICAN.

Houston's is still the one, serving—without a doubt—the best hamburger in D.C. It's big, it's juicy, it's delicious. When I'm on the wagon (off red meat) and counting calories, I tear into one of Houston's monster salads, like the Club, with chunks of fried chicken, real bacon bits, eggs, and avocado atop a tureen-sized bowl of mixed greens. Who'm I kidding? Houston's is closed weekdays for lunch. Arrive here Saturday or Sunday by noon or between 3 and 6pm. Weeknights, get here by 5:30pm. Even then, you may have to wait. If so, put your name on the list and take a walk. To Nepal. Oh yes, the ribs are very good too.

1065 Wisconsin Ave. NW (between K and M sts.). ☎ **202/338-7760.** *Reservations not accepted.* **Metro:** *Foggy Bottom is a hike—walk north on 23rd St. 1 block to Pennsylvania Ave. Walk halfway around Washington Circle and continue west on Pennsylvania Ave. 3 blocks, where it merges with M St. Walk west on M St. 3 blocks to Wisconsin Ave. Take a left at Wisconsin Ave. and walk half a block to the restaurant. If you're not a walker, crawl north on 23rd St. to Pennsylvania Ave. and take a no. 30, 32, 34, 35, or 36 bus to Wisconsin Ave. and M St., then walk south on Wisconsin Ave. half a block to the restaurant. Or take a taxi.* **Main courses:** *$9–$25. AE, MC, V.* **Open:** *Mon–Thurs 5–11pm, Fri 5pm–midnight, Sat noon–midnight, Sun noon–11pm.*

Hunan Chinatown
$$. Downtown. CHINESE.

Hunan Chinatown is something of an oxymoron: a handsome Chinese restaurant. You can actually speak softly and be heard across the table in this Chinatown standby. No clanging pots or cursing from the kitchen. Sit back and enjoy a leisurely meal in a mirrored dining room with cushy chairs and soft lighting. The food is not trendsetting, but it's more than adequate. Try the dumplings and tea-smoked duck.

624 H St. NW (between 6th and 7th sts.). ☎ **202/783-5858.** *Reservations recommended for 6 or more.* **Metro:** *Gallery Place/Georgetown, then walk north on 7th St. 1 block to right at H St.* **Main courses:** *$9–$25. AE, DISC, MC, V.* **Open:** *Sun–Thurs 11am–10pm, Fri–Sat 11am–11pm.*

Kids Il Radicchio
$$. Dupont Circle. ITALIAN.

Have it your way (pizza or pasta, that is). Start with a basic pie and order toppings from the long list, or a bottomless bowl of pasta and choose from a wide variety of sauces. Your bill will reflect your choices. The prices are modest, service is efficient, and the colorful murals are amusing. Another of Chef Roberto Donna's successful undertakings (along with Galileo and I Matti), this is glorified Italian fast food that's authentic and good. Sometimes very

125

Most Convenient Pretheater Dining

Kennedy Center (Foggy Bottom)
Aquarelle ($$$$$ à la carte; $$$$ pretheater menu)
Cup'A Cup'A ($)
Roof Terrace Restaurant, Kennedy Center ($$$$)

Warner, National, and Ford theaters (Downtown)
Capitol City Brewing Company ($$)
Old Ebbitt Grill ($$)
Red Sage ($$ Chili Bar; $$$$ Dining Room)

Shakespeare Theatre (Downtown)
Cafe Atlantico ($$$)
Coco Loco ($$$)
Jaleo ($$)
701 ($$$$ à la carte; $$$ pretheater menu)

good. Another branch is in Georgetown at 1211 Wisconsin Ave. NW (between M and N streets; ☎ 202/337-2627). A third is on Capitol Hill at 223 Pennsylvania Ave. SE (between 2nd and 3rd streets SE, behind the Capitol), ☎ 202/547-5114.

1509 17th St. NW (between P and Q sts.). ☎ *202/986-2627. Reservations not accepted.* **Metro:** *Dupont Circle, then walk east on P St. 2 blocks and turn left at 17th St. 1 block.* **Main courses:** *$8–$16. AE, CB, DC, MC, V.* **Open:** *Mon–Thurs 11:30am–11pm, Fri–Sat 11:30am–midnight; Sun 5–11pm.*

I Matti
$$$. Adams–Morgan. ITALIAN/PIZZA.
Still packin' 'em in after several successful years, I Matti serves better-than-average Italian fare—everything from pizza to dreamy polenta (a meal in itself, but available as a side order) to chicken and rabbit sausage stew—at moderate prices. This is no-nonsense cooking served in unpretentious surroundings, where the mood is pleasant and upbeat. Try the fish or home-made pasta after emptying the bread basket.

2436 18th St. NW (between Belmont and Columbia rds.). ☎ *202/462-8844. Reservations recommended.* **Metro:** *Take a taxi.* **Main courses:** *$13–$18. AE, DC, MC, V.* **Open:** *Mon–Sat noon–2:30pm; Sun–Thurs 5:30–10pm, Fri–Sat 5:30–10:30pm.*

Jaleo
$$. Downtown. SPANISH.
Loosely translated, *jaleo* means "revelry," or "racket." Both are abundant at this popular and lively tapas bar and restaurant. Sip sangría and enjoy

flamenco music while mulling over the possibilities, but don't dilly-dally if you have tickets to the Shakespeare Theatre next door. One could eat here nightly for a week and not scratch the surface of tasty tidbits offered. A few recommendations: anything dressed in aioli (garlic mayo) or containing chorizo sausage or shrimp, potatoes (any way), and the grilled chicken with capers and olives. From there, you're on your own.

420 7th St. NW (between D and E sts.). ☎ *202/628-7949. Reservations recommended.* **Metro:** *Gallery Place/Chinatown, then walk south on 7th St. 3 blocks.* **Main courses:** *$15–$25 (tapas much less!). AE, DC, DISC, MC, V.* **Open:** *Sun–Mon 11:30am–10pm, Tues–Thurs 11:30am–11:30pm, Fri–Sat 11:30am–midnight.*

Kinkead's
$$$$. Foggy Bottom. AMERICAN/SEAFOOD.
Award-winning chef Bob Kinkead wields his Midas touch on all things seaborn. The meat is nothing to sneeze at, but seafood stars at one of the best all-around restaurants in the nation's capital. Grilled squid, the creamy clam chowder, and fried clams (served with fried lemons) are outrageously delicious. The bread and desserts are also noteworthy. The crème brûlée is to die for. I prefer the bar area (with piano music) or courtyard, where you can design a four-star meal from the appetizers, over the sprawling (and more formal) upstairs dining room.

2000 Pennsylvania Ave. NW (at I St. between 20th and 21st sts.). ☎ *202/296-7700. Reservations recommended.* **Metro:** *Foggy Bottom, then walk east on I St. 2 blocks.* **Main courses:** *$18–$25. AE, CB, DC, DISC, MC, V.* **Open:** *Mon–Sat 11:30am–2:30pm; Sun–Thurs 5:30–10pm, Fri–Sat 5:30–10:30pm; Sun brunch 11:30am–2:30pm.*

La Colline
$$$$. Capitol Hill. FRENCH.
High-backed leather booths and a dignified air invite conversation and leisurely dining at this standard bearer of classic French cuisine, frequented by Hill staffers. The kitchen bows to current trends too, in dishes such as shrimp with curry sauce and ravioli filled with lobster and shiitake mushrooms. Fresh lemon juice and chopped nuts anoint sautéed soft-shell crabs. Be sure to leave room for one of the confections on the rolling dessert cart (flaky-crusted apple pie, perhaps). Sit near the Hill staffers (briefcases and neat hair) who breakfast here weekdays and you may gum some juicy gossip with your sunny-side uppers.

400 N. Capitol St. NW (at D St.). ☎ *202/737-0400. Reservations recommended.* **Metro:** *Union Station. Walk west 1 block on Massachusetts Ave., left at N. Capitol St., and continue 3 blocks.* **Main courses:** *$15–$20. AE, CB, DC, MC, V.* **Open:** *Mon–Fri 7–9am and 11:30am–3pm; Mon–Sat 6–10pm.*

Legal Sea Foods

$$$$. Downtown. AMERICAN/SEAFOOD.

Choose a piece of fish and have it broiled, grilled, baked, stuffed with crab-meat and baked, or Cajun style (rubbed with hot spices and grilled). Lobster lovers hunker down with their favorite crustacean and, aside from the K Street traffic and clothed tables, pretend they're in New England. A branch of the Boston-area chain, Legal buys fish while it's still squirming at the dock and handles our finned friends with T.L.C. Try the fried onion strings, fried clams, and clam chowder at this wood-paneled, softly lit fish house.

2020 K St. NW (between 20th and 21st sts.). ☎ *202/496-1111. Reservations recommended.* **Metro:** *Farragut West, then walk north on 18th St. 2 blocks, turn left at K St., and continue 3 blocks.* **Main courses:** *$14–$25. AE, DC, DISC, MC, V.* **Open:** *Mon–Thurs 11am–10:30pm, Fri 11am–11pm; Sat 4–11pm, Sun 4–10pm.*

Best Spots for Eavesdropping

Cafe Milano
  (Georgetown, $$)
Kinkead's
  (Foggy Bottom, $$$$)
La Colline
  (Capitol Hill, $$$$)
Old Ebbitt Grill
  (Downtown, $$)
Prime Rib
  (Downtown, $$$$$)

Le Rivage

$$$. Downtown. FRENCH.

Le Rivage, which enjoys one of D.C.'s most scenic waterfront settings, is both gracious and underappreciated. Unlike many of the nearby seafood houses, Le Rivage serves fish that is *fresh,* not frozen. The crab bisque, mussels in white wine, and seafood au gratin are exemplary. Fans recommend the daily specials, given a modern spin with exotic spices and seasonings. Those in search of hearty fare are directed to dishes with duck or beef. Desserts, from sorbet to tarts, are made in-house. The location is perfect for diners going to the nearby Arena Stage afterward.

1000 Water St. SW (between Maine Ave. and 9th St.). ☎ *202/488-8111. Reservations recommended.* **Metro:** *L'Enfant Plaza, 9th St. exit, then walk south 4 blocks to waterfront.* **Main courses:** *$14.50–$20. AE, CB, DC, DISC, MC, V.* **Open:** *Mon–Fri 11:30am–2:30pm; Mon–Thurs 5:30–10:30pm, Fri–Sat 5:30–11pm, Sun 5–9pm.*

Les Halles

$$$. Downtown. FRENCH/STEAK HOUSE.

This steak-and-potatoes brasserie on revitalized Pennsylvania Avenue, near the Warner and National theaters, is comfy and inviting. A large, partially covered sidewalk patio is made for people-watching. Regulars stick to the restaurant's signature offering: steak, pommes frites, and salade. Deviants dig the cassoulet, blood sausage, and rotisserie lamb.

1201 Pennsylvania Ave. NW (at 12th St.). ☎ *202/347-6848. Reservations recommended.* **Metro:** *Metro Center, then walk south 3 blocks on 12th St. and hang* *a right at Pennsylvania Ave.* **Main courses:** *$16–$24. AE, DC, DISC, MC, V.* **Open:** *Daily 11:30am–midnight.*

Luigino
$$$. Downtown. ITALIAN/PIZZA.

When was the last time you ate ravioli in a bus station? Never? Then slip into the slick art deco dining room in the former Greyhound terminal. Aside from the inevitable pizza, pasta, fish, veal, and chicken one would expect, you'll find goat stew, chicken sausage, and other more adventurous fare on an extensive list of Italian- and French-inspired daily specials. The place bustles at lunch with conventioneers doin' biz at the Convention Center. Things are less hectic at dinner and the service is, understandably, more reliable.

1100 New York Ave. NW (at 11th St.). ☎ *202/371-0595. Reservations recommended.* **Metro:** *Metro Center, then walk north on 12th St., and hang a right at New York Ave.* **Main courses:** *$12.50–$24.50. AE, DC, MC, V.* **Open:** *Mon–Fri 11:30am–2:30pm; Mon–Thurs 5:30–10:30pm, Fri–Sat 5:30–11:30pm, Sun 5–10pm.*

Kids Luna Grill & Diner
$. Downtown. AMERICAN.

Hurrah, a diner in the heart of downtown where you can get bacon and eggs all day. This is no greasy spoon, but you won't find foie gras or balsamic vinegar either. You will find turkey, meat loaf, and other comfort foods, like grilled cheese, cheesesteak with fried onions and mushrooms, and outstanding french fries. For a tasty treat, try the fried sweet potatoes or lumpy mashed potatoes drowning in gravy with your grilled or roasted chicken. Whimsical lunar ceramics look down on customers, most of whom are neatly groomed and well heeled.

1301 Connecticut Ave. NW (at N St.). ☎ *202/835-2280. Reservations not accepted.* **Metro:** *Dupont Circle, then walk south on Connecticut Ave. 2 blocks.* **Main courses:** *$7–$15. AE, CB, DC, DISC, MC, V.* **Open:** *Mon–Sat 7:30am–10pm, Fri–Sat 7:30am–11pm, Sun 7:30am–3pm.*

Kids Market Lunch
$. Capitol Hill. AMERICAN/BARBECUE/SEAFOOD.

When hunger strikes while browsing through the Eastern Market, with its colorful food, produce, and antiques/junk stands, stop for a great breakfast of blueberry pancakes or ham and eggs with grits on the side. The crab cake sandwich (made with shredded or lump crabmeat), smoky Carolina-style barbecue, fried fish and shrimp are the big draws at lunch. You may have to wait in line to place your order. Seating is first-come at one of the counters or tables. After a hearty meal, resume strolling through the red brick building designed by Adolph Cluss (also responsible for the Smithsonian Arts and Industries Building on the Mall).

225 7th St. SE (between C and D sts.). ☎ *202/547-8444. Reservations not accepted.* **Metro:** *Eastern Market, then walk north 1 block on 8th St.* **Main courses:** *$4–$11. No credit cards; cash only.* **Open:** *Tues–Sat 7:30am–3pm.*

129

Best Restaurants for Kids

A. V. Ristorante (Downtown, $$)
Austin Grill (Glover Park, north of Georgetown, $$)
Brickskeller (Dupont Circle, $)
Capitol City Brewing Company (Downtown, $$)
Chadwick's (Georgetown, Uptown, $$)
Cheesecake Factory (Uptown, $$)
Clyde's (Georgetown, Uptown, $$)
Dean and Deluca Cafe (Downtown, Georgetown, $)
Full Kee (Downtown, $$)
Houston's (Georgetown, $$)
Il Radicchio (Downtown, Dupont Circle, Georgetown, $$)
Market Lunch (Capitol Hill, $)
Meskerem (Adams–Morgan, $$)
Music City Roadhouse (Georgetown, $$)
Old Ebbitt Grill (Downtown, $$)
Oodles Noodles (Downtown, $)
Patisserie–Cafe Didier (Georgetown, $)
Pizzeria Paradiso (Dupont Circle, $$)
Rockland's (Glover Park, north of Georgetown, $)
Sholl's Colonial Cafeteria (Downtown, $)

Marrakesh

$$$. Downtown. MOROCCAN.

I always feel like I'm in a grade-B Ali Baba flick at Marrakesh. It's touristy and kitschy, but it's also lots of fun. Where else can you eat a seven-course meal with your hands and not have your mother smack you? Diners slump against pillows and begin the food fest with salads (eaten with bread scoopers), progressing through little filled phyllo pillows, chicken, lamb, couscous, fruit, nutty turnovers, and tea. (Better pack the antacid so that you don't throw up on the belly dancer). The wine pours freely and, be advised, that's how you can run up a hefty bill.

617 New York Ave. NW (between 6th and 7th sts.). ☎ *202/393-9393.*
Reservations recommended. **Metro:** *Mt. Vernon Square–UDC, then walk south on 7th St. 2 blocks and left at New York Ave.* **Main courses:** *$24 fixed-price dinner. No credit cards; cash and personal checks.* **Open:** *daily 6–11pm.*

Kids Meskerem

$$. Adams–Morgan. ETHIOPIAN.

Ethiopian food has been hot in Washington for many years, and we're not just talking about seasoning. Diners sip honey wine or a full-bodied Ethiopian beer (both produced in exotic northern Virginia) to put out the fiery stews (chicken, beef, lamb, shrimp, or vegetable) flavored with red pepper paste. Items listed as *watt* are hot and spicy. Sensitive stomachs can order the stews mild (*alitchas*). Dining is communal style at basket-weave tables, and *injera* (spongy pancakelike bread) takes the place of forks and spoons. An Ethiopian band plays Friday and Saturday evenings (late!).

2434 18th St. NW (at Columbia Rd.). ☎ *202/462-4100. Reservations recommended.* **Metro:** *Take a taxi.* **Main courses:** *$8–$12. AE, DC, MC, V.* **Open:** *Sun–Thurs noon–midnight, Fri–Sat noon–1pm.*

Morrison–Clark Inn

$$$. Downtown. AMERICAN/SOUTHERN.

The lace-curtained dining room of this Victorian-style inn is genteel in manner. The kitchen is anything but shy and retiring, however. The menu changes seasonally and features hearty (but ungreasy) takes on Carolina Low Country fare, such as rabbit loin stuffed with pecan cornbread and Virginia ham coupled with scalloped oysters. The garlic grits are reason enough for Yankees to turn coats and join the Rebel side. Desserts are outstanding. The chocolate caramel tart is lathered in praline whipped cream. A bite of the chocolate–peanut butter mousse cake, and one wonders why the South lost the war.

1015 L St. NW (between 11th St. and Massachusetts Ave.). ☎ *202/898-1200. Reservations recommended.* **Metro:** *Metro Center, then walk north 4 blocks on 12th St. and turn right at L St. Better yet, since this isn't a showplace neighborhood, take a cab.* **Main courses:** *$19–$22. AE, DISC, MC, V.* **Open:** *Mon–Fri 11am–2pm; Mon–Thurs 6–9:30pm, Fri–Sat 6–10pm, Sun 6–9pm; Sun brunch 11am–2pm.*

Morton's

$$$$. Downtown. AMERICAN/STEAK HOUSE.

You'll have to break out the jacket and tie to enter the pearly gates of beef-lovers' heaven. With its cigar-and-martini attitude and clubby setting, Morton's might be dismissed as cold and calculating. Though other cow palaces have come and gone, Morton's consistently serves great steak. Have your favorite prime cut black-and-blue (seared outside; purple inside), rare, or medium. Order it well done and they may hang you in the meat locker. Anti-steakers tear into the giant lobsters and flavorful veal chops. Keep things simple and order the crispy hashed browns, large enough for two or three to share. The desserts are forgettable. You won't have room anyway. Morton's is also in Georgetown at 3251 Prospect St. NW (☎ **202/342-6258**) and 8075 Leesburg Pike (opposite Bloomingdale's in Tysons Corner), Vienna, Virginia (☎ **703/883-0800**).

1050 Connecticut Ave. NW (at L St.). ☎ *202/955-5997. Reservations recommended.* **Metro:** *Farragut North, then up the escalator.* **Main courses:** *$20–$30. AE, MC, V.* **Open:** *Mon–Fri 11:30am–2:30pm; Mon–Sat 5:30–11pm, Sun 5–10pm.*

Music City Roadhouse

Kids

$$. Georgetown. AMERICAN/SOUTHERN.

There's no extra charge for refills on side dishes at this family-style, down-home establishment with a fixed-price menu and rollicking music. It's best to fast for a day or two before embarking on a food expedition here. In good weather, tables are set up along the C&O Canal. Diners start by choosing three meats and/or fish (fried or barbecued chicken, pot roast, ribs, fried catfish, broiled trout). Go-withs include gravied mashed potatoes, sweet potatoes, coleslaw, black-eyed peas, greens, cornbread, and biscuits. Are you sick yet? Celebrate the Lord's day at the rousing Sunday gospel brunch.

1050 30th St. NW (between M and K sts.). ☎ *202/337-4444. Reservations recommended.* **Metro:** *Foggy Bottom, then walk north on 23rd St. to Pennsylvania Ave., turn left, and continue 4 blocks, left at M St. for 2 blocks, left at 30th Street. Or take a taxi. Main courses: $13 (family-style meal). AE, DC, DISC, MC, V.* **Open:** *Tues–Sat 4:30–10pm; Sun 10:30am–2pm, 3–11pm; Tues–Sat 10pm–1am (late-night fare $4–$7.50).*

Mykonos

$$. Downtown. GREEK.

Mykonos delivers traditional Greek cuisine in a sunny setting further brightened by friendly service. Check out the specials for clues to the kitchen's strong suits. When in doubt, order the crunchy taverna salad topped with chicken, or any lamb-based dish. At lunch you can build a tasty and satisfying meal from the appetizers. The cucumber and yogurt *tzatziki*, slathered on the crusty bread, is addictive at this temple to Aegean fare in the Connecticut Avenue/K Street business district.

1835 K St. NW (between 18th and 19th sts.). ☎ *202/331-0370. Reservations recommended.* **Metro:** *Farragut West, then walk west 1 block on I St., right at 18th St. 1 block, and left at K St.* **Main courses:** *$10–$17. AE, CB, DC, DISC, MC, V.* **Open:** *Mon–Fri 11:30am–3:30pm; Mon–Sat 5:30–10pm.*

New Heights

$$$$. Uptown. AMERICAN/INTERNATIONAL.

The elegant, art-filled space overlooking Rock Creek Park, near the National Zoo, attracts adventurous diners. Numerous Washington chefs cut their eye teeth in New Heights's kitchen, and the restaurant is known for pushing the culinary envelope (sometimes into the next galaxy). Discerning diners keep the chef in line when he strays into outerspace. The food frequently flirts with excellence, but if the idea of soft-shell crabs with fried plantains makes you queasy, K.I.S.S. (keep it simple, stupid) and stick with unembellished fish or meat.

2317 Calvert St. NW (at Connecticut Ave.). ☎ *202/234-4110. Reservations recommended.* **Metro:** *Woodley Park/Zoo, then walk south 1 block on Connecticut Ave. and right at Calvert St.* **Main courses:** *$17–$26. AE, DC, DISC, MC, V.* **Open:** *Sun–Thurs 5:30–10pm, Fri–Sat 5:30–11pm; Sun brunch 11am–2:30pm.*

Obelisk
$$$$. Dupont Circle. ITALIAN.

Less is more at Obelisk. Pure, ungimmicky, northern Italian cooking shines at the tiny Dupont Circle trattoria. The walls are simply adorned, and a basket of fresh vegetables and crusty house-made bread form the centerpiece. The fixed-price menu features three—not 30—choices. The pasta is homemade, the wines are carefully selected, and the wait staff is knowledgeable and charming. Attention to detail is evident the moment you walk in the door. Better make reservations now, if you want to experience Obelisk, the *Zagat* survey's top Italian restaurant pick in 1998.

Best Spots for Night-Owl Noshers

Bistro Français
  (Georgetown, $$$)
Chadwick's
  (Georgetown, Uptown, $$)
Full Kee (Downtown, $$)
Meskerem
  (Adams–Morgan, $$)
Music City Roadhouse
  (Georgetown, $$)
Old Ebbitt Grill
  (Downtown, $$)

2029 P St. NW (between 20th and 21st sts.).
☎ *202/872-1180. Reservations recommended.* **Metro:** *Dupont Circle, then walk west 1 block on P St.* **Main courses:** *$45 fixed-price dinner. DC, MC, V.* **Open:** *Mon–Sat 6–10pm.*

Occidental Grill
$$$$. Downtown. AMERICAN.

Celebrity photographs, spacious booths, and polished dark wood give the Occidental Grill the unmistakable feel of a good-old-boys club. Politicians, tourists, suits, and pretheater diners rub elbows in this reincarnated historic restaurant. The food runs from sandwiches and other light fare to meat and potatoes. Grilled meats and fish take top honors. The business lunch bunch goes for the grilled swordfish sandwich, a variation on the club sandwich theme. Service is cordial and efficient.

1475 Pennsylvania Ave. NW (in the Willard complex, between 14th and 15th sts.). ☎ *202/783-1475. Reservations recommended.* **Metro:** *Federal Triangle, then walk north on 12th St. 2 blocks, and left at Pennsylvania Ave. 2 blocks.* **Main courses:** *$16–$29. AE, DC, MC, V.* **Open:** *Mon–Sat 11:30am–11pm, Sun noon–9:30pm.*

Kids Old Ebbitt Grill
$$. Downtown. AMERICAN/HAMBURGERS.

The Old Ebbitt, in the style of an old pub and part of the mightily successful Clyde's chain, is all things to all customers. Power brokers develop strategy plans over breakfast. Locals belly up to the bar before the long commute home to the 'burbs. Theatergoers grab a bite before curtain time. Tourists plan or rehash their sightseeing. Visitors to the White House eat breakfast as they wait until the timed tickets they picked up at the Visitor Center become valid. With a wide selection of upscale pub fare, entrees, and desserts, the

Ebbitt menu also includes seasonal specialties, such as local corn, vegetables, and berries in summer. I wish I had a nickel for every hamburger the kitchen turns out in a single week. There's a raw bar, and Sunday brunch is SRO. The reliable Old Ebbitt is a good bet from morning to night, *if* you have reservations.

675 15th St. NW (between F and G sts.). ☎ *202/347-4800. Reservations recommended.* **Metro:** *Metro Center, then walk west on G St. 3 blocks, left at 15th St.* **Main courses:** *$12–$19. AE, DC, DISC, MC, V.* **Open:** *Mon–Fri 7:30am–1am, Sat 8am–1am, Sun 9:30am–1am.*

Kids Oodles Noodles
$. Downtown. ASIAN.

Value reigns at Oodles Noodles. For little more than the price of a fast-food fix, you can fill up on dumplings, satays, and delicious and satisfying bowls of soup chock full of seafood, chicken, or vegetables, and, of course, oodles of noodles. Several varieties—from wiry ramen to soft udon—come spicy or mild, dry or wet, sauced or souped. The style is yours for the choosing: Chinese, Japanese, Indonesian, Malaysian, or Thai. Naturally, there is often a wait. But at these prices who's complaining?

1120 19th St. NW (between L and M sts.). ☎ *202/293-3138. Reservations recommended for 6 or more.* **Metro:** *Farragut North, then walk west on L St. 2 blocks and right on 19th St.* **Main courses:** *$7–$10. AE, DC, MC, V.* **Open:** *Mon–Fri 11:30am–3pm; Mon–Sat 5–10pm.*

Pan Asian Noodles and Grill
$$. Dupont Circle. ASIAN/THAI.

The drunken noodles, wide and sauced with spicy ground chicken, warm the innards on a chilly day at this cheery little restaurant brightened by lacquer and neon. The spring rolls, crisp nuggets, and grilled goodies on a skewer whet your appetite for a main course of noodles with a variety of Asian toppings and flavors. It's possible to dine here for under $10. A second location is near the McPherson Square Metro (and the White House) at 1018 Vermont Ave. NW (☎ **202/783-8899**).

2020 P St. NW (between 20th and 21st sts.). ☎ *202/872-8889. Reservations recommended.* **Metro:** *Dupont Circle, then walk west on P St. 1½ blocks.* **Main courses:** *$8–$13. AE, DC, DISC, MC, V.* **Open:** *Mon–Sat 11:30am–2:30pm; Sun–Thurs 5–10pm, Fri–Sat 5–11pm.*

Kids Patisserie–Cafe Didier
$. Georgetown. FRENCH.

This genteel Gallic gem is tucked away on a quiet Georgetown side street, seconds from bustling M Street, but worlds away in atmosphere. Come for a continental breakfast of croissants, Danish, or muffins and fresh-squeezed juice. Come for an onion soup, cold-cut, salad, soufflé, or quiche lunch. Come for a midafternoon mug of hot chocolate and madeleine or fruit tart.

Come to soothe your soul with classical music, soft tablecloths, and fresh flowers. The portions may be small, but the quality and ambience more than compensate.

3206 Grace St. (between M and K sts.). ☎ *202/342-9083. Reservations recommended for 6 or more.* **Metro:** *Foggy Bottom.* **Main courses:** *$7–$9. DC, DISC, MC, V.* **Open:** *Tues–Sat 8am–7pm, Sun 8am–5pm.*

Pesce
$$$. Dupont Circle. AMERICAN/SEAFOOD.
Pesce fits the mold of an ideal neighborhood restaurant. It's casual, noisy, and friendly. The menu is chalked on a blackboard. The food is beyond good and decently priced. This simple storefront bistro is known for fish (a.k.a. *pesce*). Have it grilled, baked, or sautéed; sauced, served simply with a squirt of lemon, or topping a plate of pasta. Lobsters and soft shells (crabs) are offered in season. Many consider Pesce D.C.'s best seafood restaurant.

2016 P St. NW (between 20th and 21st sts.). ☎ *202/466-3474. Reservations recommended.* **Metro:** *Dupont Circle, then walk west 1½ blocks on P St.* **Main courses:** *$14–$18. AE, DC, DISC, MC, V.* **Open:** *Mon–Fri 11:30am–2:30pm, Sat noon–2:30pm; Mon–Thurs 5:30–10pm, Fri–Sat 5:30–10:30pm, Sun 5–9:30pm.*

Kids Pizzeria Paradiso
$$. Dupont Circle. ITALIAN.
Now this is pizza! Baked in a wood-burning oven, the pies show the same attention as the food at Obelisk, also owned by Peter Pastan. Not everyone likes shelled mussels on their dough, but few can resist the fresh vegetables or Parma ham. There are also a few sandwiches and salads on the menu of this shoebox-sized parlor. It's usually crowded, so you may want to join the locals who carry their piece of paradise to the front stoop or nearby Dupont Circle park.

2029 P St. NW. ☎ *202/223-1245. Reservations not accepted.* **Metro:** *Dupont Circle, then walk west on P St. 2 blocks.* **Main courses:** *$7–$16.* **Credit cards:** *DC, MC, V.* **Open:** *Mon–Sat 11am–11:30pm, Sun noon–10pm.*

Prime Rib
$$$$$. Downtown. AMERICAN/STEAK HOUSE.
Where's the beef? It's here—in a black and gilt-trimmed supper club with leather chairs and piano music. The bar scene (and it is a scene) includes high rollers congratulating themselves over their latest deals and conquests, and nubile women looking to be conquered. Okay, the testosterone level would choke Schwartzenegger, but it's fun to play rich once in a while. And the thick cut of prime rib au jus with horseradish shavings knocks my socks off faster than Prince Charming's kiss. The crab imperial is widely applauded, but most have one thing in mind at the Prime Rib: "Where's the beef?" *Note:* This is jacket-and-tie territory, and prices are a whole lot less at lunch.

2020 K St. NW (between 20th and 21st sts.). ☎ *202/466-8811. Reservations recommended.* **Metro:** *Farragut West, then walk north to K St. and west 3 blocks.* **Main courses:** *$18–$40. AE, DC, MC, V.* **Open:** *Mon–Fri 11:30am–3pm; Mon–Thurs 5–11pm, Fri–Sat 5–11:30pm.*

Red Sage
$$ (Chili Bar); $$$$ (Dining Room). Downtown.
AMERICAN/SOUTHWESTERN.

Skip the formal, noisy, pretentious, overrated, and overpriced downstairs section of this restaurant. Who wants to get clipped for 50 bucks or more in a basement dining room? Now that we've swept that out of the way . . . You can enjoy a margarita, delicious burrito, quesadilla, or bowl of chili—this is a great place to share—and have a swell old time in the colorful ground-level cantina and walk away with change from $25. The location makes Red Sage a good choice near the White House and downtown theaters.

605 14th St. NW (between F and G sts.). ☎ *202/638-4444. Reservations recommended for Dining Room; not accepted for Chili Bar.* **Metro:** *Metro Center, then walk west on G St. 2 blocks and left at 14th St.* **Main courses:** *$19–$30 (Dining Room), boo hiss; $9–$13 (Chili Bar), yeah!* **Open:** *Restaurant: Mon–Fri 11:30am–2pm; Mon–Sat 5:30–10:30pm, Sun 5–10pm. Chili Bar: Sun–Thurs 11:30am–11:30pm; Fri–Sat 11:30–12:30am.*

Kids Rockland's
$. Glover Park, north of Georgetown. AMERICAN/
BARBECUE.

First off, seating is limited to stools and counters, and the decor is Early Carryout. But one bite into a barbecue sandwich and you'll be cushioned by clouds and listening to harp music. The smoky ribs are heavenly too, chewy but not ropey. Add grilled fish on a bun, homemade apple sauce, tasty side salads (try the Caesar—on a par with fancy-shmancy restaurants), corn pudding, and tart lemonade, and Rockland's is well worth a visit, even though it's off the beaten path (about a mile north of Georgetown) for most tourists.

2418 Wisconsin Ave. NW (at Calvert St.). ☎ *202/333-2558. Reservations not accepted.* **Metro:** *Tenleytown, then take no. 32, 34, or 36 bus south on Wisconsin Ave. Or walk (uphill) about a mile from Georgetown. Or take a cab.* **Main courses:** *$4–$10. AE.* **Open:** *Mon–Wed 11:30am–10pm, Thurs–Sat 11:30am–midnight.*

Roof Terrace Restaurant, Kennedy Center
$$$$. Foggy Bottom. AMERICAN.

The setting is gracious and grand, with crystal chandeliers and sweeping window walls overlooking the riverfront and beyond. To dine here is no bargain, but for Kennedy Center theatergoers, the convenience can't be beat. Servers are particularly attentive to ticket holders, ensuring time for a pit stop before the curtain rises. The traditional menu—mostly beef, fish, and chicken—changes seasonally. The appetizers are pricey and lackluster, so I'd stick with the salmon or another fish, or the special of the day, and dessert. An elaborate Sunday buffet brunch, served from 11:30am to 3pm, includes a glass of champagne, a mimosa, or fresh squeezed orange juice for $26. If you don't want to drop $50 for dinner in the dining room, try the Hors d'Oeuverie, open for drinks and light fare and with the same fabulous view (if you're fortunate enough to garner a window table). Make a reservation or arrive by 5:30pm Tuesday through Saturday—or forget about it! Down the hall is the self-service Encore Cafe, also with a rooftop view. A full dinner here will set you back $15 or less.

New Hampshire Ave. NW and Rock Creek Parkway. ☎ *202/416-8555. Reservations strongly recommended.* **Metro:** *Foggy Bottom, then free Kennedy Center shuttle bus.* **Main courses:** *$23–$30. AE, CB, DC, MC, V.* **Open:** *Mon–Sat 11:30am–2pm, Sun 11:30am–3pm; Tues–Sat 5:30–9pm.*

701
$$$$. Downtown. AMERICAN/INTERNATIONAL.

Piano music wafts from the bar area of this elegant dining room close to the FBI, National Gallery of Art, Archives, 7th Street galleries, and downtown theaters. Service is first class and the kitchen tries, quite successfully, to be all things to its customers. Many look no further than the vodka and caviar menu to build a minimeal before taking in a performance at the Shakespeare Theatre around the corner. But you don't have to be a ticket holder to enjoy the $22.50 pretheater menu, served from 5:30 to 7pm. The Caesar salad is one of the best anywhere. Those with the time and resources enjoy sophisticated cuisine.

701 Pennsylvania Ave. NW (at 7th St.). ☎ *202/393-0701. Reservations recommended.* **Metro:** *Archives–Navy Memorial, then walk east 1 block on Pennsylvania Ave.* **Main courses:** *$15–$23. AE, DC, MC, V.* **Open:** *Mon–Fri 11:30am–3pm; Mon–Sat 5:30–11pm, Sun 5–9:30pm.*

Sholl's Colonial Cafeteria
$. Downtown. AMERICAN.

An institution since 1928 (that's no misprint; the year before the *big* crash), Sholl's still excels at serving locals and busloads of tourists home-style food at cut-rate prices. We're talkin' plain food. Comfort food. Full breakfasts for under $6. Chopped steak platters. Turkey and stuffing. Fresh fruit pies. Rice pudding. The decor may be barebones, but the customers and servers provide plenty of visual interest.

1990 K St. NW (in the Esplanade Mall, between 19th and 20th sts.). ☎ *202/296-3065. Reservations not accepted.* **Metro:** *Farragut West, then walk west on K St. 2 blocks.* **Main courses:** *$2–$6. No credit cards; cash only.* **Open:** *Mon–Sat 7am–2:30pm, Sun 8am–3pm.*

Taberna del Alabardero
$$$$. Downtown. SPANISH.
Spain's King Juan Carlos and his family dine here when visiting Washington.
Why shouldn't you? You'll need a jacket and tie (a mantilla wouldn't hurt,
either) at this ornate restaurant that reminds me of my grandmother's with
its brocade drapes, velvet upholstery, and lace antimacassars. Enough about
decor. Try the lobster and seafood paella (for two) or the Basque-style crabmeat dish (which for a million dollars I couldn't spell). Tapas, priced
between $5 and $10, are served throughout the day. Start with a glass of
Spanish sherry. This Old World restaurant is one of four, but the *only* one
outside of España. And if you run into King Juan Carlos, tell him I said
"Hola!"

1776 I St. NW (entrance on 18th St.). ☎ *202/429-2200. Reservations recommended.* **Metro:** *Farragut West, then walk west on I St. half a block and turn right
at 18th St.* **Main courses:** *$16–$27.* **Open:** *Mon–Fri 11:30am–2:30pm;
Mon–Thurs 6–10pm, Sat 6–11pm. Tapas served throughout the day.*

Chapter 11

Light Bites & Munchies

In This Chapter

➤ How to get on the fast snack track

➤ Power breakfasts

➤ Sweet treats and afternoon tea

➤ Eating on the Mall

➤ Happy hours and other great snack deals

A few years back, for a few hundred thousand dollars (or maybe even less), President Clinton would personally welcome you at the White House for coffee and a light snack. The snack part stuck, and today, Washingtonians still like to nosh in the middle of the day. Fortunately, these days, a coffee and muffin won't cost you an election. In fact, snacking throughout the day can be more economical than surviving on the traditional three-meal plan. Besides, sightseeing burns calories by the truckload and requires tremendous stamina. That in mind, read on for the whole scoop on snacking sites. Couched another way, a snack by any other name—nosh, indulgence, nibble, yum-yum, munchie—will taste just as good.

Power Breakfasts

Washington's power brokers begin their days with eggs scrambled with cell phones, bulging briefcases, and laptops. If you wish to check out the breakfast scene, head for a hotel dining room near the White House or Capitol.

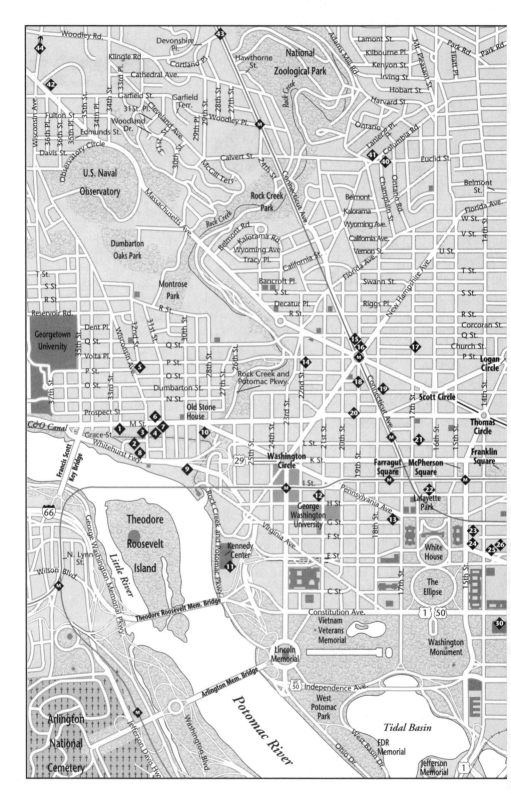

Where to Grab a Snack in Washington, D. C.

0 .25 mi
0 .4 km

Au Bon Pain **34**
Ben & Jerry's (Georgetown) **6**
Ben & Jerry's (Adams-Morgan) **40**
Brickskeller **14**
Buffalo Billiards **18**
Bullfeathers **39**
Cafe Berlin **38**
Chadwick's (Georgetown) **8**
Cheesecake Factory **44**
Chief Ike's Mambo Room **41**
Ching Ching Cha **3**
Concourse Buffet (National Gallery of Art) **32**
CyberSTOP Cafe **17**
Dean & Deluca (Downtown) **27**
Dean & Deluca (Georgetown) **1**
Flight Line Cafeteria (Air and Space Museum) **33**
Four Seasons **10**
Full Circle Cafe (Hirshhorn) **31**
Haagen Dazs (Union Station) **36**
Ha'Penny Lion **21**
Hay-Adams Hotel **22**
Hors D'Oeuverie (Kennedy Center) **11**
Kramerbooks & Afterwords Cafe **15**
Kron Chocolatier **44**
La Colline **35**
Luna Grill & Diner **19**
Mr. Smith's **7**
Old Ebbitt Grill **23**
Old Post Office Pavilion **28**
Palm Court Cafe (Museum of American History) **30**
Patent Pending (National Portrait Gallery/Museum of American Art) **29**
Patisserie-Cafe Didier **2**
Roof Terrace **11**
Rumor's **20**
Sequoia **9**
Shops at National Place Food Hall **26**
Sky Terrace (Hotel Washington) **24**
Starbuck's **13**
Thomas Sweet **5**
T.G.I. Friday's (Foggy Bottom) **12**
Union Station Food Hall **37**
Uptown Scoop **43**
Washington National Cathedral **42**
Willard Inter-Continental **25**
Wrap Works (Dupont Circle) **16**
Wrap Works (Georgetown) **4**

The handsome **Hay–Adams,** at 800 16th St. NW (at H Street; ☎ **202/638-6600**), and the **Willard Inter-Continental,** at 1475 Pennsylvania Ave. NW (between 14th and 15th streets; ☎ **202/783-1475**), which both have reputations for attracting wheeler-dealer types, are good places to start. At **La Colline,** 400 N. Capitol St. NW (☎ **202/737-0400**), a few blocks from the Capitol, lobbyists meet congressional reps and peddle influence while raising funds with their glasses of o.j.

Breakfast with No Hidden Agendas

If the power scene leaves you cold, but you need a hearty breakfast to jump-start your engine, try the **Old Ebbitt Grill** at 675 15th St. NW (between F and G streets; ☎ **202/347-4800**). Just a few blocks away from the White House Visitor Center, the Old Ebbitt Grill is a perfect place for breakfast if you're going on a tour of the White House. Wake up early, stand on line for tickets, and then while you wait until you can enter the White House, you can load up on some bacon and eggs.

At the **Luna Grill & Diner,** 1301 Connecticut Ave. NW (at N Street; ☎ **202/835-2280**), "breakie" is served all day. In Dupont Circle's **Kramerbooks & Afterwords Cafe,** 1517 Connecticut Ave. NW (between Q Street and Dupont Circle; ☎ **202/387-1462**), you can crack a book with your soft-boiled egg.

For a light breakfast—juice, coffee, and a croissant or brioche—try the authentically French **Patisserie–Cafe Didier** in Georgetown at 3206 Grace St. NW (☎ **202/342-9083**). Commercial, but not bad for a chocolate-filled croissant or bran muffin and a cup of java, are the branches of **Au Bon Pain** (about a dozen are sprinkled liberally throughout downtown, especially on Pennsylvania Avenue NW between 10th and 20th streets). Near the Mall, try Au Bon Pain in L'Enfant Plaza, 7th and D streets SW. Yes, of course, Washington has several Starbucks. But, at the risk of being stoned by the coffee-swilling masses who worship at this shrine, I make better coffee, and Starbucks's pastry is dull and overpriced.

D.C. Dirt

At the Starbucks closest to the White House, 1730 Pennsylvania Ave. NW (Metro: Farragut West), you may run into a staffer getting a caffeine fix to deal with one of Clinton's all-nighters. Then again, you may not. A friend who worked in the White House in the '80s, and wishes to remain anonymous, tells me that senior-level employees head for the White House mess for a cup of java, while underlings have coffee pots in their offices. You never know. Back in the good old days, George Stephanopoulos was spotted buying coffee here.

Tea for Two (or One)

If the American Revolution had been a battle of culinary delights, the British would have suffered an even worse defeat. However, had it been a battle of tea parties, the Americans wouldn't have stood a chance. The fact that even after the Battle of 1812, several Washington hotels still embrace the idea of high tea shows the popularity of the high tea tradition. Tea in this context is actually a mini-meal, with neat sandwiches (cut on the diagonal, no crusts), assorted sweets, and the requisite pot of fresh-brewed tea. Those who sip their cuppa late in the afternoon often skip dinner altogether and snack later in the evening. I like to take my white gloves and Vaselined patent leather pumps to the **Four Seasons,** 2800 Pennsylvania Ave. NW (☎ **202/ 342-0444**), whenever possible. The gracious Garden Terrace, with fresh flowers, cushy love seats, and a commanding view of Rock Creek Park, is a favored setting in which to enjoy finger sandwiches, tartlets, breads, biscuits, scones with double Devonshire cream, fresh-brewed tea, and a nip of sherry for medicinal purposes. A pianist plays Tuesday through Sunday, starting at 4pm. Tea is served Monday through Saturday 3 to 5pm, Sunday 3:30 to 5pm; $15.50 per adult and $9 per child; reservations suggested.

In recent years, Washingtonians have embraced the ancient Chinese tea ritual, as practiced in a former Georgetown bagelry near the C&O Canal. **Ching Ching Cha,** at 1063 Wisconsin Ave. NW (☎ **202/338-8288**), offers 33 teas from China and Taiwan, at $4 to $20 a serving (no charge for refills). The owner, a former hairstylist who lent her Chinese name, Ching Ching, to the tea parlor, has fashioned a serene setting enhanced by classical Chinese music. To get here, take Metro to the Foggy Bottom station. Walk north on 23rd Street to Pennsylvania Avenue, go halfway around Washington Circle, and continue west on Pennsylvania to its merger with M Street. Continue on M Street for 3 blocks to Wisconsin Avenue and left to Ching Ching Cha.

Tea in the **Washington National Cathedral,** Massachusetts and Wisconsin avenues NW (entrance on Wisconsin Avenue), is an event befitting the grand Gothic structure, which serves as the nation's Episcopal house of prayer. High tea in the Observation Gallery caps the Tuesday and Wednesday 1:30pm tours of the world's sixth-largest cathedral. In May and September, visitors have a choice of either a garden or cathedral tour. The tours finish on the seventh floor of the West Tower, whose arched windows take in a stunning view of the city and its monuments, and beyond to Sugarloaf Mountain in Maryland. Reservations are required (☎ **202/ 537-8993**). Tea costs $15 per person. During the school year, you can descend from the tower in time to enjoy evensong services performed at 4pm by the Youth Choir. To get here, take the Metro to Tenleytown, then walk for 20 minutes south on Wisconsin Avenue. Or take the Metro to Dupont Circle and hop on any N bus traveling up Massachusetts Avenue. Get off at Massachusetts and Wisconsin avenues.

D.C. Dirt

The Washington National Cathedral is the sixth-largest religious structure in the world.

Pick-Up Places

Visitors intent on cramming in as many sightseeing attractions as possible often don't want to squander precious time in restaurants. Delis, coffee shops, and assorted holes-in-the-wall (as well as many restaurants) gladly pack orders to go. On a nice day, nothing is finer than an alfresco lunch or snack in one of the District's parks or open spaces.

Dean and Deluca has two locations downtown: 1299 Pennsylvania Ave. NW (in the Warner Theater Building; ☎ 202/ 628-8155), and 1919 Pennsylvania Ave. NW (☎ 202/296-4327); and one in Georgetown at 3276 M St. NW (☎ 202/342-2500). Pick up gourmet sandwiches, exotic salads, scrumptious desserts, and designer water at these branches of the illustrious New York food emporium.

Park Your Fanny Here

If the weather's nice, pick up your food at Dean and Deluca and head to a wide-open space. From the 1299 Pennsylvania Avenue location, head for **Pershing Park** (Pennsylvania Avenue and 15th Street) or **Lafayette Square,** across from the White House. From the 1919 Pennsylvania Avenue D&D, mosey over to **Farragut Square,** Connecticut Avenue NW between I and K streets. In Georgetown, brown bag it behind the **Old Stone House,** 3051 M St. NW; along the C&O Canal, at the foot of Thomas Jefferson Street, and head in either direction; or Washington Harbour, 30th and K streets NW.

Wrap It Up

Washington's hurried office workers and visitors on a tight sightseeing schedule embrace wraps, the latest fast-food craze sweeping D.C. Similar in appearance to a burrito, a wrap is a meal encased in a tortilla and can be filled with chicken, beef, fish, veggies, or numerous combinations thereof. The concept is neat; eating one is not. Like an ice-cream cone with a hole in it, a wrap is often sloppy and unwieldy, so plenty of napkins is a necessity. Removing that designer tie or covering your Sunday best is highly recommended before digging in. Many coffee shops and carry-outs feature wraps among their standard sandwich fare. **WrapWorks,** with West Coast roots, has two locations: 1601 Connecticut Ave. NW at Q Street in the Dupont Circle neighborhood (Metro: Dupont Circle; ☎ 202/265-4200), and 1079 Wisconsin Ave. NW at M Street (Metro: Foggy Bottom–GWU; ☎ 202/333-0220), and further expansion is planned. Try the "Ken and Barbecue," a spinach tortilla wrapped around spicy chunks of chicken or beef, corn relish, black beans, and chipotle sauce (you'll see why you need napkins). WrapWorks is open Sunday through Thursday from 11am to 11pm and Friday and Saturday from 11am to midnight.

Sweet Surrenders

Sweet tooth crave a fix? Break into a 'brest (Parisian-style), napoleon, or any of the other exquisite pastries at **Patisserie–Cafe Didier** (see "Breakfast with No Hidden Agendas" above). The strudels, tortes, and pies taste like grandma's (maybe not yours or mine, but *someone's* grandmother) at **Cafe Berlin,** 322 Massachusetts Ave. NE, on Capitol Hill (☎ **202/543-7656**). The **Cheesecake Factory** in Friendship Heights, just south of the Maryland border at 5345 Wisconsin Ave. NW (☎ **202/364-0500**), hawks about 35 versions of the cholesterol-rich pie. Many find a slice too rich to consume in a single sitting. (I can't imagine.) Across the street in the Mazza Gallerie, **Kron Chocolatier** (☎ **202/966-4946**) sells all manner of world-class chocolate. I've emptied a pound box of champagne truffles on the up escalator. Try them along with the chocolate-dipped strawberries. Mention this book and maybe they'll toss you a bittersweet crumb.

Hear Ye! Hear Ye!

The **Hors d'Oeuverie Lounge** of the Roof Terrace Restaurant in the Kennedy Center (☎ **202/416-8555**) serves a dessert, champagne, and coffee Buffet, for $7, Thursday through Saturday evenings from 9pm until a half-hour after the last performance. Although the dessert choices change from time to time, past selections have included key lime pie, fruit tarts, apple cobbler, a decadent chocolate cake, and fresh berries with whipped cream. A standing ovation for the Kennedy Center! This production is a hit with theatergoers who ate a light supper or wish to digest the evening's performance along with a rich dessert.

I Scream, You Scream . . .

If there's a quicker way to get a sugar rush and rejoin the human race when spirits lag, I don't know it. The ice-cream craze drips on, and I doubt one can walk more than a D.C. block without passing a place to buy ice cream or frozen yogurt. Nearly every restaurant (including those in museums and galleries), deli, and carry-out sells it. Branches of the Vermont-based **Ben & Jerry's** are located in Georgetown at 3135 M St. NW (between 31st and 32nd streets; ☎ **202/965-2222**), and Adams–Morgan at 2503 Champlain St. NW (near 18th Street and Columbia Road; ☎ **202/667-6677**). The rich ice cream is made with natural ingredients. On Capitol Hill, and needing no introduction, you'll find **Häagen-Dazs** in the Union Station Food Court, 50 Massachusetts Ave. NE (☎ **202/789-0953**). **Thomas Sweet,** in Georgetown at 3214 P St. NW (at Wisconsin Avenue; ☎ **202/337-0616**), is an old-fashioned ice-cream parlor that dishes out its own brand to locals and many area restaurants. Stop at the **Uptown Scoop,** 3510 Connecticut Ave. NW (☎ **202/244-4465**), near the National Zoo, for a double-dip cone or sundae of excellent Lee's ice cream (made in Baltimore).

Fast & Cheap

Don't want to take the time for a sit-down meal when you're ricocheting between museums? Try any of the street vendors on the Mall for a hot dog before catching the next exhibit. Or nibble your way through the food stands in the **Old Post Office Pavilion,** at 11th Street and Pennsylvania Avenue NW, which is convenient to the National Archives, FBI, Ford's Theatre, and Museums of Natural and American History. A few blocks away is the **Food Hall in the Shops at National Place,** 1331 Pennsylvania Ave. NW (enter on Pennsylvania Avenue or F Street), which is a perfect pit stop for people visiting the White House, White House Visitor Information Center, National Aquarium in the Department of Commerce Building, or the National and Warner theatres.

When on Capitol Hill or shopping at Union Station, check out the immense **Food Court in Union Station,** where you'll find everything from hot dogs, hamburgers, and sandwiches to sushi and fresh-squeezed lemonade. This is not your average food court—you'll be pleasantly surprised by the high-quality "fast food" available here.

D.C. Dirt

Walls can't talk, but bartenders can. And in a Washington bar anything can happen. Jim Hewes, the bartender at the **Willard's Round Robin,** 1401 Pennsylvania Ave. (Metro: Metro Center), has seen a lot transpire in his tenure here. Like what, you ask? You'll have to get it from the horse's mouth. Hewes's schedule is always changing. Call ☎ **202/637-7348** to see when he's serving up some dirt.

Drink in the View

A pleasant way to decompress at day's end is to drink in Washington's photogenic features along with a cocktail. For a soothing experience, sip your poison of choice at the edge of the Potomac River. In Georgetown, the Oscar for scenic design and cast of characters goes to **Sequoia,** 3000 K St. NW (☎ **202/944-4200**), in the Washington Harbour complex (Metro: Foggy Bottom). On a mild night, the terrace of this glitzy, touristy restaurant provides a spectacular panorama and an endless supply of spontaneous customer-generated entertainment. In foul weather, all is fair indoors from a bar-level alcove.

While the **Roof Terrace** restaurant of the Kennedy Center, 2700 F St. NW (at New Hampshire Avenue and Rock Creek Parkway; ☎ **202/416-8555**), struggles year in and year out with negative kitchen reviews (and many chefs' opening and closing nights), it always serves up a stellar view of downtown Washington, the Potomac River, and suburban Virginia (on a clear night you can make out the eternal flame marking JFK's grave). Snare a window table in the bar area (by 5:30pm or you'll be competing with ticket holders). Or slip into the cafeteria down the hall and enjoy the vista with a

$4 mini-bottle of rinky-dink wine. Heck, you can drink in the scene without spending a cent by strolling the promenade that completely encircles the performing arts center.

Between May and October, the **Sky Terrace** of the Hotel Washington, 15th Street and Pennsylvania Avenue NW (☎ **202/638-5900**), is *the* inner-city place to feast on the view and feel the breeze stirred by planes descending into Reagan National Airport. The inconsequential food and steep drink prices pale in comparison with the romantic setting in the thick of things. And you can almost see into the East Wing of the White House.

Surf & Turf Cafes

Surf through cyberspace while you sip a cocktail or cappuccino at **Kramerbooks & Afterwords,** 1517 Connecticut Ave. NW (between Dupont Circle and Q Street; ☎ **202/387-1462**). Customers are invited to check their e-mail or browse the Internet at this busy bookstore/cafe, the first in the area. Use of the computer at the bar ("I'll have a hard drive on the rocks") is free. Take Metro to Dupont Circle, then walk north on Connecticut Avenue for 1 block. Kramerbooks is open Monday through Thursday from 7:30am to 1am. Friday the doors open at 8am and don't close until Monday at 1am. For more information, visit Kramerbooks's Web site at www.kramers.com.

Also in the Dupont Circle neighborhood is **cyberSTOP Cafe,** 1513 17th St. NW (between P and Q streets; ☎ **202/234-2470**). Take Metro to Dupont Circle, then walk east on P Street for 1 block, and turn left at 17th Street. Customers enjoy coffee and desserts along with the 300-megahertz computers that have direct Internet connection. Computer use is $5 per hour. cyberSTOP is open Sunday through Thursday from 7:30am to midnight, Friday and Saturday from 7:30am to 2am.

Eating on the Mall

You can't possibly take in the museums on the mall without taking in any food. You can always grab a hot dog or ice cream if you're on the run, but if you need a brain rest, head to one of the following museum restaurants or cafeterias.

➤ Between Memorial Day and Labor Day, the outdoor *Kids* **Full Circle Cafe** at the **Hirshhorn Museum,** Independence Avenue and 8th Street SW, has self-service hot and cold sandwiches, pizza, salads, desserts, and some kids' fare, like minipizzas and hot dogs.

➤ In the **National Air and Space Museum,** Independence Avenue and 7th Street SW, wing it to the *Kids* **Flight Line Cafeteria**—okay, it's cavernous, but it's bright. The soaring space with attractive tubular scaffolding has huge windows overlooking the Mall. The food is varied and attractively presented at buffet stations.

➤ Satisfy your sweet tooth in the 🌟**Kids** **Palm Court Cafe** in the **National Museum of American History,** Constitution Avenue and 14th Street NW. The authentically re-created Victorian ice-cream parlor also serves light fare. But who wants light fare when hot fudge is available?

➤ The so-so food tastes better when you're seated at a window fronting a cascade of water in the **Concourse Buffet** (another glorified cafeteria) of the National Gallery of Art, Constitution Avenue and 6th Street NW.

➤ In the courtyard between the National Museum of Art and the National Portrait Gallery, you can soothe your soul at the peaceful **Patent Pending Café,** on 8th and G streets. In this charming hideaway, you can sit at a table under the trees and take in the fountains and sculpture. Sandwiches range from $2.75 to $3.75; the salad bar is 34¢ per ounce. The cafe is open for breakfast from 10am to 1pm, lunch from 11am to 3pm, and snacks from 3 to 3:30pm.

Happy-Hour Specials

Sightseeing is hard. Finding cheap drink specials or a quick bite to eat after a long day of visiting the sights isn't. The largest glut of bars and restaurants with happy hours is in the business section of downtown known informally as Farragut, around the Farragut North and Farragut West Metro stations. Numerous watering holes serve the hordes of laboring office workers seeking instant relief from cubicle-induced claustrophobia. Depending on where you are when the clock strikes 5, ringing in the cocktail hour, you might try the following.

Adams–Morgan

The nearest Metro stations, Dupont Circle and Woodley Park/National Zoo, are a good 20-minute walk, done most safely during daylight hours. After dark, I recommend taking a taxi.

Chief Ike's Mambo Room

From 4 to 7pm, all drinks are $1 off at Ike's. While there are no free hors d'oeuvres, a light-fare menu, with reasonably priced sandwiches, burgers, and appetizers, is available.

1725 Columbia Rd. NW. ☎ *202/332-2211.* **Metro:** *Woodley Park/National Zoo, then walk south 1 block on Connecticut Ave., left at Calvert St., continue half a mile to right at Adams–Mill Rd., immediate left onto Columbia Rd., and continue 1 block to Ike's.*

Capitol Hill

Bullfeathers

Happy hour runs from 5 to 8pm for all those thirsty Hill people, drained dry by House and Senate machinations. Drink specials vary. Sometimes they're two for one; other days they're $1 off. No free food is offered, but you can fill up with a tasty burger or an order of super nachos for under $7.

410 1st St. SE (between D and E sts.). ☎ *202/543-5005.* **Metro:** *Capitol South, then walk south on 1st St. 2 blocks.*

Downtown

Ha'Penny Lion

The Ha'Penny is one of the most popular watering holes for a sundowner in all D.C. You'd better arrive early if you hope to squeeze through the door, especially on Friday when local businesspeople are TGIF'ing. Happy hour stretches well into the evening, from 5 to 9pm. Drink specials change daily, from $1.95 for domestic beers and $1.65 for a glass of house wine to double-sized drinks for the price of a regular one. Complimentary hot hors d'oeuvres are featured nightly. As 1998 wound down, it was tacos on Tuesday, chicken wings on Wednesday, pasta on Thursday. On Monday and Friday, try your luck with the chef's choice.

1101 17th St. NW (at L St.). ☎ *202/296-8075.* **Metro:** *Farragut North, walk south half a block on Connecticut Ave., turn left at L St., and go 1 block to 17th St.*

Rumor's

Happy hour is in effect from 4 to 7pm at Rumor's, which has been taking care of pub-crawling suits since 1977. Appetizer specials—fried calamari, potato skins, and chicken wings—are $1.95 per order. Domestic beers, as well as house-brand drinks and wine, are $2.50.

1900 M St. NW (at 19th St.). ☎ *202/466-7378.* **Metro:** *Farragut North, walk north on Connecticut Ave. 1 block, turn left at M St., and continue 1½ blocks to 19th St.*

Dupont Circle

Buffalo Billiards

At happy hour, from 4 to 8pm, a pint of Bud or Bud Light runs $2.50; micro-brews, wine, and rail drinks are $3. On Monday, quesadillas are half price. Other nights, you're on your own to order from the regular menu, where all items are under $10. Monday through Wednesday, a table of four can shoot pool for $14 per hour (at other times it's $18).

1330 19th St. NW. ☎ *202/331-7665.* **Metro:** *Dupont Circle, then walk south 1 block on 19th St.*

Foggy Bottom

TGI Friday's

Friday's happy hour, from 4 to 7pm, attracts an eclectic crowd of GW students, think tankers, state department employees, and White House staffers (when they're not burning the midnight oil). During happy hour, count on

149

$1 off all drinks. A beer or two are featured for $1.50. Every night a different hot appetizer is offered for $1 per serving. Among the favorites are nachos and Mexican pizza.

2100 Pennsylvania Ave. NW (at 21st St.). ☎ *202/872-4344. **Metro:** Foggy Bottom, then walk east on I St. 2 blocks, left at 21st St., and go 1 block.*

Georgetown

Chadwick's

Chadwick's happy hour runs from 4 to 7pm, when domestic beer is $1.95, and rail drinks and house wine are $2.50. Chicken wings, something from the appetizer menu (white pizza, crab dip, potato skins, and such), and the chef's choice are only $3 per order during happy hour. Unless you have an appetite like Henry VIII, you can drink and graze for less than $10.

3205 K St. NW (between 32nd and 33rd sts.). ☎ *202/333-2565. **Metro:** Foggy Bottom, then walk north on 23rd St. to Pennsylvania Ave. and board any no. 30 bus headed for Georgetown. Get off at Wisconsin Ave. and M St., walk south on Wisconsin Ave. 2 blocks, right at K St., and continue 1 long block.*

Mr. Smith's

At Mr. Smith's, one of Georgetown's oldest saloons, happy hour lasts from 4 to 7pm. Beer and rail drinks are $1 off, items from the light-fare menu are half price, and a featured daily appetizer is only 50¢.

3104 M St. NW. ☎ *202/333-3104. **Metro:** Foggy Bottom, then walk north on 23rd St. to Pennsylvania Ave. and board any no. 30 bus bound for Georgetown. Get off at M and 31st sts. and cross the street.*

Part 5

Ready, Set, Go! Exploring Washington, D.C.

Unpack your bags, grab a bite to eat, and let's go. It's time to take in some American history, admire works by some of the world's greatest artists, see the government in action, and even do some shopping. The following chapters are designed to take the guesswork out of choosing what attractions to see and figuring out how best to see them.

If you're like most visitors, you'll set aside time for shopping. I've picked a lot of D.C. brains, added their tips to my own, and come up with a list of favorite shopping haunts in chapter 15.

If you're feeling overwhelmed by the choices, fast forward to chapter 16 for a handful of suggested itineraries. Since time is of the essence and you won't want to waste precious minutes crisscrossing the city in an illogical pattern, merely tap into one of these itineraries and go.

Chapter 12

Should I Just Take a Guided Tour?

In This Chapter

➤ Whirlwind tours

➤ Walking tours

➤ Architecture and historical tours

➤ Cruises

➤ Bike tours

When traveling I always find it helpful to check out the forest before inspecting the trees. For first-time visitors, those on a tight schedule, and individuals with limited mobility (or impediments such as children), a guided tour makes good sense. Not only can it save you legwork but it also provides an excellent overview of the city. Then, as time permits, you can visit the sights that pique your interest most.

D.C. tour guides are, in most instances, knowledgeable pros who delight in injecting a little humor into their patter. So you're bound to pick up a slew of interesting tidbits along the way. Several special-interest tours are also worth looking into.

Capitalizing on the Capital: Orientation Tours

Several companies offer general city tours. The expertise and delivery of these operators vary from guide to guide, but for the most part, guides are well trained and take pride in their calling.

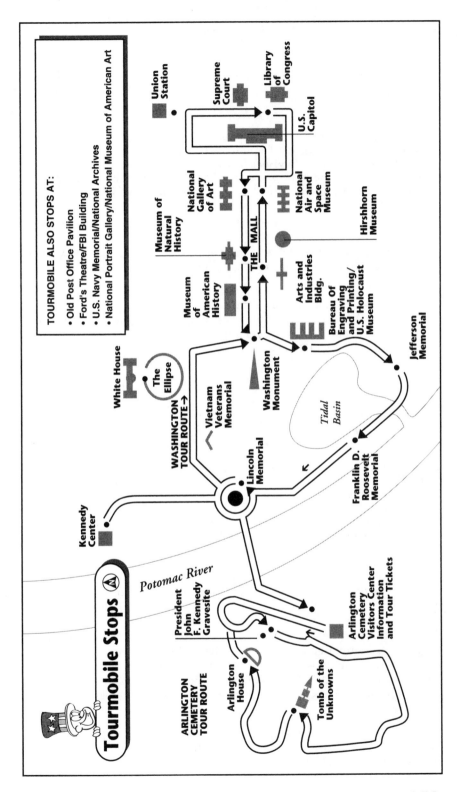

Tourmobile Stops

TOURMOBILE ALSO STOPS AT:
- Old Post Office Pavilion
- Ford's Theatre/FBI Building
- U.S. Navy Memorial/National Archives
- National Portrait Gallery/National Museum of American Art

Union Station

Supreme Court

Library of Congress

U.S. Capitol

National Gallery of Art

National Air and Space Museum

Museum of Natural History

THE MALL

Hirshhorn Museum

Museum of American History

Arts and Industries Bldg.

Bureau Of Engraving and Printing/U.S. Holocaust Museum

White House

The Ellipse

WASHINGTON TOUR ROUTE →

Vietnam Veterans Memorial

Washington Monument

Jefferson Memorial

Tidal Basin

Kennedy Center

Lincoln Memorial

Franklin D. Roosevelt Memorial

Potomac River

President John F. Kennedy Gravesite

Arlington Cemetery Visitors Center Information and Tour Tickets

ARLINGTON CEMETERY TOUR ROUTE

Arlington House

Tomb of the Unknowns

153

Hear Ye! Hear Ye!

If you're on an orientation tour and your guide suddenly spots the prez running through the streets, you'll want to be the first to see him before he fades into the distance. How can you make sure that you won't miss a thing? *Fight for a seat at the front of the bus (or tram) and stay close to the guide on walking tours so that when something unusual happens you'll be the first to know.*

Tourmobile (☎ 202/554-5100) stops at 21 places on or near the Mall and four spots at Arlington Cemetery. See the map on p. 153 for a list of complete stops.

You can get on and off the red, white, and blue sightseeing trams all day long. Options include the combined Washington/Arlington Cemetery tour or Arlington-only tour. The combined tour makes for a grueling day, especially with kids in tow. While it's cheaper, I advocate the divide-and-conquer plan.

Balancing the Budget

It's exhausting to visit all the important sights in 1 day. Fortunately, Tourmobile has devised an economical/not-too-stressful way to explore the city. You can buy an advance ticket after 3pm from June 15 through Labor Day, or after 1pm the rest of the year, that is valid for the rest of the afternoon plus the following day; these tickets cost $16 per adult, $8 for children 3 to 11. Well-trained narrators give commentaries about sights along the route and answer questions.

You can ride the trams for a whole day for one fare ($14 for age 12 and older, $7 for kids 3 to 11 on the combined tour; $4.75 and $2.25, respectively, on the Arlington Cemetery tour). Children 2 and under always ride free. Purchase a ticket when boarding or at the Arlington Cemetery Visitor Center. To get to Arlington Cemetery, take the Metro Blue line to the Arlington Cemetery stop. Or, for a small surcharge, you can order tickets in advance from Ticketmaster (☎ 800/551-SEAT). Some visitors remain aboard for an entire figure-8 loop, decide where they want to go, and then get off on the second go-around.

Tourmobile also offers round-trips to Mount Vernon, departing from the Arlington Cemetery Visitor Center and Washington Monument three times a day. The price is $20 for those 12 and older, $10 for kids 3 to 11, and includes admission to George Washington's riverfront home. Be sure to ask about other tours, some of which require advance reservations.

Another offering (June 15 to Labor Day) is the **Frederick Douglass National Historic Site Tour,** which includes a guided tour of Douglass's home, Cedar Hill, located in southeast Washington. Departures are from Arlington National Cemetery at noon, with a pickup at the Washington Monument shortly thereafter. Those 12 and older pay $7, and children 3 to 11 pay $3.50. A 2-day Combination Frederick Douglass Tour and Washington/Arlington National Cemetery Tour is also available at $28 for those 12 and older, $14 for children 3 to 11. For both the Mount Vernon and Frederick Douglass tours, you must reserve in person at either Arlington Cemetery or the Washington Monument at least an hour in advance.

Hear Ye! Hear Ye!

Visitors over the years have grappled with a very important question. Tourmobile or Old Town Trolley? There's no wrong or right answer. The major difference between the two is that the Tourmobile stops are mainly on the Mall. Old Town Trolley travels way beyond the Mall. It goes to Georgetown, Dupont Circle, Union Station, Washington Park Gourmet (near the National Zoo), and some hotels. Visitors should check their itineraries and see where their sightseeing is concentrated, and then decide. Consult the "Tourmobile Stops" map on p. 153 for more information on where the Tourmobile actually stops.

Old Town Trolley is similar to Tourmobile's fixed-price, get-on-and-off-as-often-as-you-like service. Old Town Trolley Tours alight at 18 D.C. locations including Georgetown and a stop near the National Zoo. Purchase your ticket when boarding the trolley, which stops at each site about every half hour. The full tour takes 2 hours and costs $18 for adults, $9 for kids 4 to 12, and is free for tots 3 and under. A **Washington After Hours Tour** passes the major memorials and federal buildings, dramatically lit for nighttime viewing. Call and ask for the pick-up point closest to your hotel and departure time (☎ **202/832-9800**).

Gray Line Sightseeing Tours conducts narrated bus tours, from 3 hours' to 2 days' duration (to the Maryland and Virginia hinterlands). Buses depart from the Gray Line terminal in Union Station. City tours run from $20 to $40. Gray Line has been in business forever and has an extensive fleet manned by well-informed guides. Multilingual, black heritage, and Washington After Dark tours (☎ **202/289-1995**) are also available.

Museum Bus provides minibus transportation between nearly 30 member museums in and around the city, from Union Station near the Capitol to the National Zoo several miles away. A $5 pass includes admission to those

Washington Slept Where?

When considering a tour operator other than those suggested here, call the **Guild of Professional Tour Guides** (☎ 202/ 298-1474). This tight association of more than 200 licensed guides will steer you in the right direction.

museums that charge and a discount in museum shops and restaurants. If you can live without the running commentary between stops, this is a good deal and an efficient way to travel between sights. For more information, call ☎ **202/588-7470.**

Walk This Way: Walking Tours

If your feet are up to the task and you'd like an in-depth look at different aspects of the city's history and culture, consider a walking tour. It's easy to view many of D.C.'s historic dwellings, architectural gems, and famous scandal sites when pounding the pavement on your own. It's a good idea when doing your homework to ask about the group size. Experience has taught me that smaller is better. The more adventurous are invited to chart their own course after preliminary research and/or consulting the book *Frommer's Memorable Walks in Washington, D.C.*

Architectural & Historical Walking Tours

British transplant **Anthony S. Pitch** pitches history during walking tours of the Adams–Morgan neighborhood and Georgetown on alternate Sundays. For the 2-hour tours, the amiable and well-informed author and guide charges $10 per head (☎ **301/294-9514**).

Hear Ye! Hear Ye!

Scandal Tours (☎ 202/ 783-7212), led by the local comedy troupe Gross National Product (GNP), leaves tourists rolling in the aisles. The narrated bus tour, departing Saturday (April to September) at 1pm from the Old Post Office Pavilion at 11th Street and Pennsylvania Avenue NW, takes in more than 100 scandalous sites. The cost is $30. The laughs are free.

Yolanda Robinson Darricarre leads tours of 1 to 4 days' duration, Wednesday through Saturday from May to October, "for the culturally and intellectually curious." A 1-day tour with **D.C. Walking Tours** (which scrupulously avoids tourist traps) is $65. Call ☎ **202/ 237-7534** or visit the Web site at **www. dcwalkingtours.com**.

Anita Allingham, an independent tour guide with more than 20 years' experience under her belt, will tailor a walking tour (with Metro transport when necessary) for your contingent that runs between $20 and $25 per person depending on the itinerary. One of the most requested is the Illuminated Night Tour that takes in the Lincoln Memorial, with its view of the eternal flame marking

John F. Kennedy's grave; the Jefferson Memorial; and the Kennedy Center rooftop's commanding view of downtown and the Potomac (☎ **301/ 493-8568**).

Rollin' on the River

Since Washington enjoys a riverfront setting, it'd be a shame to miss the capital's face from its most flattering side. While not all cruises are guided tours (some are water-based wheels; others are floating restaurants), they all afford a refreshing break from landlubbing sightseeing.

Capitol River Cruise's ***Nightingale II*** (☎ **800/405-5511**), a 150-year-old steel riverboat, departs Washington Harbour, at the south end of 31st Street NW, where it meets the river in Georgetown for narrated cruises, hourly from noon to 8pm (sometimes later on weekends), April through October. The 50-minute tour, which glides by monuments and memorials, is $10 for adults, $5 for kids 3 to 12. Picnic baskets are welcome and there's a snack bar onboard.

The Potomac Riverboat Company runs two narrated cruises on the Potomac. The ***Matthew Hayes*** cruises past several monuments and memorials for 90 minutes. Tickets are $14 for adults, $12 for seniors, $6 for kiddies 6 to 12. The ***Admiral Tilp*** ferries passengers to Mount Vernon and back again after they've toured George's estate. The cost is $7 for adults, $6 for seniors, $4 for children 2 to 12. Both depart from the foot of King Street, behind the Torpedo Factory in Old Town Alexandria. Reservations are strongly suggested (☎ **703/548-9000**). To get here, take the Metro to King Street, then a Dash bus to King and Fairfax. From there it's a short walk.

🦆 **DC Ducks's** (☎ **202/966-3825**) vintage World War II amphibious carriers quack me up. Roughly half of the 90-minute narrated tour is land-based, departing from the main entrance of Union Station, 50 Massachusetts Ave. NE (Metro: Union Station). After cruising the Mall, this hermaphrodite plunges into the Potomac at the Columbia Island Marina for a half hour before surfacing near Reagan National Airport for the return ride. Departures are daily at 11am, 1pm, and 3pm from April through October. Tickets, sold in Union Station, are $20 for adults, $10 for children 5 to 12, free for those under 5. Reservations are required at least a day in advance.

Breaking Away: Bicycle Tours

Bike the Sites (☎ **202/966-8862**) runs several guided bike tours on 21-speed Treks through D.C. On the 10-mile Capital Sites Ride, which begins and ends at the Freer Gallery of Art on the Mall, bikers pass scores of sights and gobble up history with their power bars. To get to the Freer Gallery, take the Metro to the Smithsonian stop. The $35 fee also covers helmets and water bottles. Kids under 14 must be accompanied by an adult.

Chapter 13

The Top Sights from A to Z

In This Chapter

➤ Attractions indexed by location and type

➤ Neighborhoods worth exploring

➤ Full write-ups of all the top attractions in town

➤ Your personal Greatest Hits list and a worksheet for making your choices

---

This chapter starts off with indexes listing all the top sights by location and type (museums, parks, bars—just wanted to see if you were paying attention—and so on). There's a method to this madness. For example, if you exit the Air and Space Museum, scratch your head, and wonder what else there is to see nearby, you can turn to the Mall listing and find out the National Gallery of Art is within spitting distance. (Well, almost.)

Although there's more on this list than you could possibly see during a normal visit, you can scribble your relative level of interest in the margins next to the reviews. Go ahead, write in the book. I give you permission! And I won't tell your first-grade teacher. Rank the sights on a scale of 1 to 5, no. 1's being primo, numero uno, the big kahuna; no. 5's being the sights you can live without, like your Aunt Muriel's meat loaf. Cheating is allowed, so if you prefer, assign the sights a no. 1 or a no. 5 and skip the numbers in between. Simple, no? I've provided a chart at the end of the chapter where you can list all your choices and decide what to cut and what you absolutely can't miss. In chapter 16 I give some pointers on linking these sights logically, so you don't end up cruising one of D.C.'s infamous circles or wandering around the National Mall for a fortnight. In chapter 17 you'll find help in narrowing your choices. So many sights, so little time!

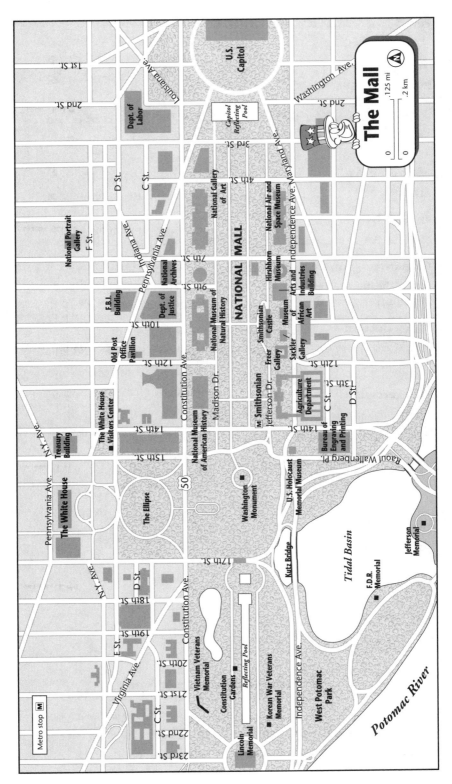

The Mall

N

0   .125 mi
0   .2 km

U.S. Capitol

Capitol Reflecting Pool

Dept. of Labor

NATIONAL MALL

National Gallery of Art

National Air and Space Museum

Hirshhorn Museum

Arts and Industries Building

Museum of African Art

Sackler Gallery

Smithsonian Castle

Freer Gallery

M Smithsonian

Jefferson Dr.

Agriculture Department

Bureau of Engraving and Printing

National Portrait Gallery

National Archives

F.B.I. Building

Dept. of Justice

Old Post Office Pavilion

National Museum of Natural History

National Museum of American History

Madison Dr.

Constitution Ave.

The White House Visitors Center

Treasury Building

The White House

Pennsylvania Ave.

N.Y. Ave.

The Ellipse

Washington Monument

U.S. Holocaust Memorial Museum

Tidal Basin

F.D.R. Memorial

Jefferson Memorial

Raoul Wallenberg Pl.

Kutz Bridge

Constitution Gardens

Reflecting Pool

Vietnam Veterans Memorial

Korean War Veterans Memorial

West Potomac Park

Lincoln Memorial

Potomac River

Constitution Ave.

Virginia Ave.

Independence Ave.

Maryland Ave.

Washington Ave.

Pennsylvania Ave.

Indiana Ave.

Louisiana Ave.

1st St.

2nd St.

3rd St.

4th St.

7th St.

9th St.

10th St.

12th St.

14th St.

15th St.

17th St.

18th St.

19th St.

20th St.

21st St.

22nd St.

23rd St.

D St.

C St.

F St.

E St.

D St.

50

M Metro stop

![kids] Note that I've indicated sights especially suited to travelers with kids in tow, so everybody will be a happy camper.

Quick Picks: Washington, D.C.'s Top Attractions at a Glance
The Top Sights by Location

Arlington, Va.
Arlington National Cemetery

Capitol Hill
National Postal Museum

Chinatown/Convention Center
Ford's Theatre & Lincoln Museum/Petersen House

Foggy Bottom
Rock Creek Park
Theodore Roosevelt Island

Georgetown
C&O Canal and Towpath
Dumbarton Oaks Gardens

Government Buildings
FBI
U.S. Capitol
U.S. Supreme Court

National Mall (hereinafter, the "Mall")
Enid A. Haupt Victorian Garden
Lincoln Memorial
National Air and Space Museum
National Archives

National Gallery of Art
National Museum of American History
National Museum of Natural History
Smithsonian "Castle"
Vietnam Veterans Memorial
Washington Monument

Tidal Basin
Bureau of Engraving and Printing
Franklin Delano Roosevelt Memorial
Holocaust Memorial Museum
Jefferson Memorial
Potomac Park (East and West)

War Monuments (or Memorials)
Arlington National Cemetery
Vietnam Veterans Memorial

White House Area
Lafayette Square
White House

Woodley Park
National Zoological Park

Index by Type of Attractions

Museums
Bureau of Engraving and Printing
Ford's Theatre & Lincoln Museum/Petersen House

Holocaust Memorial Museum
National Air and Space Museum
National Archives
National Gallery of Art

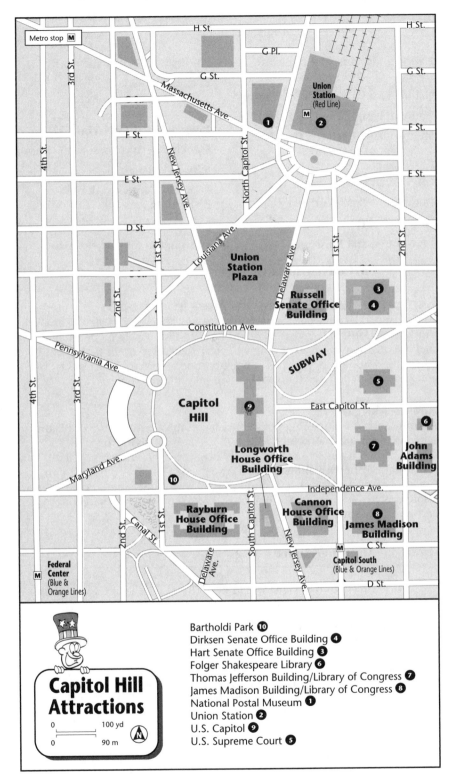

Metro stop **M**

H St.

G Pl.

G St.

Massachusetts Ave.

F St.

E St.

D St.

3rd St.

4th St.

New Jersey Ave.

North Capitol St.

Louisiana Ave.

Delaware Ave.

1st St.

2nd St.

Union Station (Red Line) **M**

①

②

Union Station Plaza

Russell Senate Office Building

Constitution Ave.

Pennsylvania Ave.

SUBWAY

③
④

⑤

Capitol Hill

⑨

East Capitol St.

⑥

⑦

John Adams Building

Longworth House Office Building

4th St.

3rd St.

Maryland Ave.

⑩

Independence Ave.

Rayburn House Office Building

2nd St.

Canal St.

1st St.

Delaware Ave.

South Capitol St.

New Jersey Ave.

Cannon House Office Building

James Madison Building

⑧

C St.

M Capitol South (Blue & Orange Lines)

M Federal Center (Blue & Orange Lines)

D St.

Capitol Hill Attractions

0   100 yd
0   90 m

N

Bartholdi Park **⑩**
Dirksen Senate Office Building **④**
Hart Senate Office Building **③**
Folger Shakespeare Library **⑥**
Thomas Jefferson Building/Library of Congress **⑦**
James Madison Building/Library of Congress **⑧**
National Postal Museum **①**
Union Station **②**
U.S. Capitol **⑨**
U.S. Supreme Court **⑤**

National Museum of American History

National Museum of Natural History

National Postal Museum

Smithsonian "Castle"

Parks

C&O Canal and Towpath

Dumbarton Oaks Gardens

Enid A. Haupt Victorian Garden

Lafayette Square

National Zoological Park

Potomac Park (East and West)

Rock Creek Park

Theodore Roosevelt Island

Presidential Material

Franklin Delano Roosevelt Memorial

Jefferson Memorial

Kennedy Center for the Performing Arts

Lincoln Memorial

Washington Monument

White House

Exploring Washington by Neighborhoods

Some visitors decide what they want to see and then plan their day around those attractions. Other visitors might want to pick a neighborhood and then spend a few hours exploring whatever sights pop up in their path. If you're the wandering type, pick a neighborhood from the descriptions below and go crazy—you never know what you may stumble upon.

Adams–Morgan

Adams–Morgan is a melting pot, with a large African-American and Latino population. The name, coined in the 1950s by local civic groups for the mostly white Adams school and largely black Morgan school, says it all. In a town that is otherwise homogenized (except for Chinatown and Dupont Circle), Adams–Morgan is refreshingly alive, with funky shops and bars, and numerous ethnic eateries. Locals come to soak up the bohemian atmosphere and give their suits a rest.

Hear Ye! Hear Ye!

On Saturday morning, locals and visitors flock to the open-air produce market in Adams–Morgan, which takes place in front of the Crestar Bank at the intersection of 18th Street and Columbia Road NW. To get here, take Metro to Woodley Park/National Zoo, walk south 1 block to Calvert Street, and go left, continue over the Duke Ellington Bridge and then a couple of blocks to the end of Calvert Street, then hang a right and continue 1 block to the intersection of 18th Street and Columbia Road, the hub of Adams–Morgan.

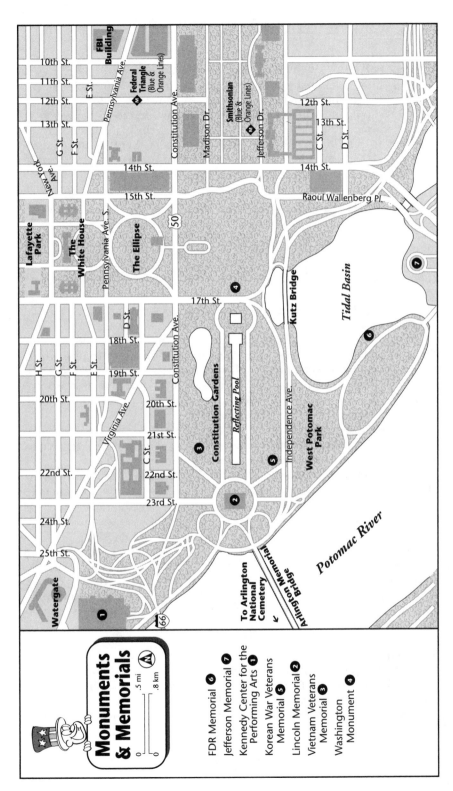

Monuments & Memorials

0 — .5 mi
0 — .8 km

FDR Memorial **6**
Jefferson Memorial **7**
Kennedy Center for the Performing Arts **1**
Korean War Veterans Memorial **5**
Lincoln Memorial **2**
Vietnam Veterans Memorial **3**
Washington Monument **4**

FBI Building
Federal Triangle (Blue & Orange Lines)
Smithsonian (Blue & Orange Lines)
10th St.
11th St.
12th St.
13th St.
E St.
Pennsylvania Ave.
Constitution Ave.
Madison Dr.
Jefferson Dr.
12th St.
13th St.
14th St.
C St.
D St.
14th St.
15th St.
Raoul Wallenberg Pl.
New York Ave.
G St.
F St.
Lafayette Park
The White House
Pennsylvania Ave. S.
The Ellipse
50
17th St.
Tidal Basin
Kutz Bridge
D St.
18th St.
19th St.
H St.
G St.
F St.
E St.
Constitution Ave.
Constitution Gardens
Reflecting Pool
Independence Ave.
West Potomac Park
20th St.
20th St.
21st St.
C St.
22nd St.
22nd St.
23rd St.
Virginia Ave.
24th St.
25th St.
Watergate
66
To Arlington National Cemetery
Arlington Memorial Bridge
Potomac River

Capitol Hill

The U.S. Capitol dominates this neighborhood, inhabited largely by those working on the Hill. The area has another face, however. Victorian row houses line residential streets, lending a small-town feel to the neighborhood. Locals and those with Hill business frequent the many restaurants and watering holes in the shadow of the Capitol dome. Other than the Capitol itself, the area does not hold as much draw for visitors as other D.C. neighborhoods. And it's not the place to be wandering aimlessly after dark.

Chinatown

Compared to San Francisco and New York, D.C.'s Chinatown is minuscule (it occupies the blocks between G, H, 5th, and 8th streets NW) and a bit rough around the edges. Most come here to attend sports events and concerts at the MCI Center, to eat, and to peruse the shops selling Chinese folk medicines, herbs, spices, and teas. Take Metro to Gallery Place/Chinatown, and you've arrived.

Dupont Circle

Chess games are ongoing in the small park—the hub of this bustling area—in the middle of one of the city's confounding traffic circles. With its many bookstores (some open all night), galleries, restaurants, and movie theaters, Dupont Circle is fun any time of the day or night. Come here to experience Washington at its most unbuttoned.

Foggy Bottom

The West End of D.C. abutting Georgetown is a short stroll from the White House. Site of the Kennedy Center, State Department, and George Washington University, the villagelike neighborhood is distinguished by charming row houses with street-front gardens. An oasis in a city of marble and concrete, Foggy Bottom is made for walking.

Georgetown

Perhaps D.C.'s best-known address, Georgetown was once a tobacco port and is the federal city's oldest neighborhood. Wisconsin Avenue and M Street are filled with boutiques, restaurants, bars, and an overabundance of record stores and T-shirt shops. You'll find Georgetown University and Dumbarton Oaks Gardens here as well as Georgian and Federal-style homes on cobblestone streets off the main drag.

The Mall

The only shopping in this Mall is in the museum stores. The 2-mile-long parklike space between the Lincoln Memorial and U.S. Capitol is the epicenter for tourists and a haven for joggers, bikers, and kite-flyers. Most of the Smithsonian museums front the Mall and many other attractions are a short distance away.

The Top Sights

Arlington National Cemetery
Arlington, Va.

The final resting place for more than 240,000 war dead and veterans (and their dependents), Arlington commands a view of the capital city from the Virginia side of Memorial Bridge. A memorial honoring the nearly 2 million women who have served in the military since the American Revolution greets visitors just inside the cemetery entrance. Pick up a map at the Visitor Center, which is a Tourmobile stop and also a good place for a pit stop since there are no bathrooms between here and **Arlington House** (the former Custis–Lee Mansion that was the home of Robert E. Lee and Martha Washington's great-granddaughter—it's okay, they were married). Free self-guided tours of Arlington House, a hybrid of 18th-century Greek Revival and plantation styles, are ongoing from 9:30am to 4:30pm, except January 1 and December 25, when the mansion is closed.

Perhaps the most moving scene, aside from the panorama of sweeping lawns punctuated by rows of simple markers, is the changing of the guard at the **Tomb of the Unknowns** (between Memorial and Roosevelt drives). The guards change every hour on the hour (round the clock) from October through March and every half hour April through September.

Pierre L'Enfant's grave is near Arlington House, with a primo view of the city he planned, and below are the grave sites of John F. Kennedy, Jacqueline Kennedy Onassis, and Robert F. Kennedy (see page 170 for map of specific sites). A good mile north (near the Ord and Weitzel Gate) you'll find the famous Marine Corps Memorial of the marines raising the flag on Iwo Jima, and the Netherlands Carillon, sight of weekend concerts April through September.

Arlington, Va., west side of Memorial Bridge (Honest Abe's memorial anchors the east side of the bridge). ☎ *703/607-8052.* **Metro:** *Arlington National Cemetery. Also accessible by Tourmobile.* **Open:** *Apr–Sept daily 8am–7pm; Oct–Mar daily 8am–5pm.* **Admission:** *Free.*

⭐Kids **Bureau of Engraving and Printing**
Tidal Basin.

The buck stops here! It also starts here. If you wanna see where 22.5 million notes are printed daily (that's about $77 billion per year), you'll have to rise and shine early, and make it your first stop. This is such a top-dollar attraction that April through September visitors line up before 8am at the kiosk on Raoul Wallenberg Place (15th Street SW) for same-day, timed tickets for the guided tour. The bureau also prints Treasury bonds and White House invitations (mine keep getting lost in the mail). Sorry, no samples on the way out.

14th and C sts. SW (enter on 14th St.) ☎ *202/622-2000.* **Metro:** *Smithsonian, then walk west on Independence Ave. 1 long block to left at 14th St. (entrance) or 2 blocks to 15th St. (kiosk).* **Open:** *Mon–Fri 9am–2pm. Extended summer hours. Closed federal holidays, Jan 1, Dec 25.* **Admission:** *Free.*

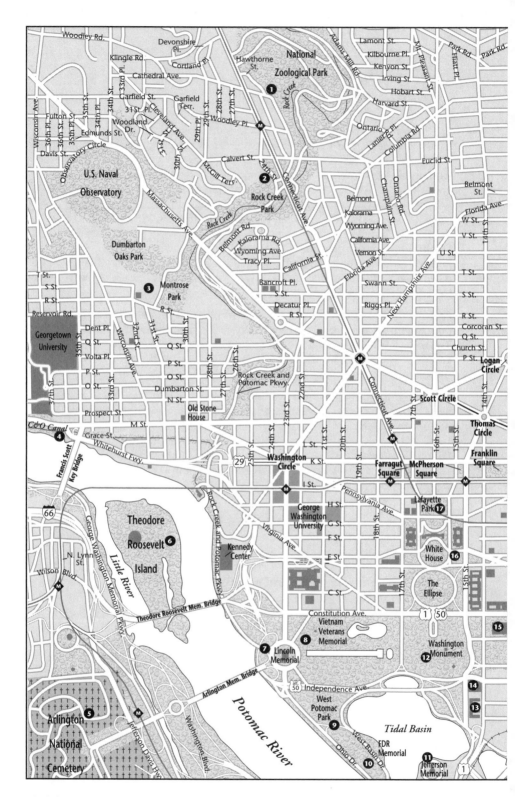

National Zoological Park

Rock Creek Park

U.S. Naval Observatory

Dumbarton Oaks Park

Montrose Park

Georgetown University

Theodore Roosevelt Island

Little River

Arlington National Cemetery

Potomac River

Tidal Basin

The Ellipse

White House

Lafayette Park

Washington Monument

Jefferson Memorial

FDR Memorial

West Potomac Park

Lincoln Memorial

Vietnam Veterans Memorial

Kennedy Center

George Washington University

Washington Circle

Farragut Square

McPherson Square

Franklin Square

Scott Circle

Thomas Circle

Logan Circle

Old Stone House

C&O Canal

The Top Sights in Washington, D. C.

0		.25 mi
0		.4 km

Arlington National Cemetery **5**
Bureau of Engraving
  and Printing **13**
C & O Canal **4**
Dumbarton Oaks Gardens **3**
FBI **19**
Ford's Theatre &
  Lincoln Museum **18**
Enid A. Haupt
  Victorian Garden **23**
FDR Memorial **10**
Jefferson Memorial **11**
Lafayette Square **17**
Lincoln Memorial **7**
National Air and
  Space Museum **24**
National Archives **21**
National Gallery of Art
  (East Building) **26**
National Gallery of Art
  (West Building) **25**
National Museum of
  American History **15**
National Museum of
  Natural History **20**
National Zoological Park **1**
Potomac Park **9**
Rock Creek Park **2**
Theodore Roosevelt Island **6**
Smithsonian "Castle"
  (Smithsonian
  Institution Building) **22**
U.S. Holocaust Memorial
  Museum **14**
Washington Monument **12**
White House **16**
Vietnam Veterans Memorial **8**

⭐Kids C&O Canal and Towpath
Georgetown.

Joggers, walkers, and bikers vie for space on the tree-lined paths along the old Chesapeake and Ohio Canal (and Potomac River), built in the 1800s to link Washington and Cumberland, Maryland, 185 miles away.

At **Thompson's Boat Center,** across from the infamous Watergate, you can rent a boat and paddle around the Potomac (☎ **202/333-4861**). Rentals average $20 to $25 per boat per day. Or, for a change of pace, board the *Georgetown,* a 19th-century canal boat berthed in the heart of Georgetown, between 30th and Thomas Jefferson streets NW (☎ **202/653-5844**). The canal cruise runs from mid-April through October, Wednesday through Sunday, and costs $4 for adults, $3.50 for kids 3 to 13 and senior citizens 62 and over. On Sunday afternoon in the summer, concerts play behind the Foundry (canal between 30th and Thomas Jefferson streets; ☎ **202/653-5190**).

30th and K sts. NW. ☎ 202/653-5844. **Metro:** *Foggy Bottom, then board any bus bound for Georgetown, or hoof it north on 23rd St. to Washington Circle, left at Pennsylvania to M St. Continue on M St. to 30th St., left to canal. If you're not up to the 15-minute walk, take a taxi.* **Open:** *All the time, but I don't recommend a visit after dark.* **Admission:** *Free. Charge for boat rental, canal boat ride.*

⭐Kids Dumbarton Oaks Gardens
Georgetown.

It's a little out of the way if your time is limited, but it's well worth a visit, especially when shopping or dining in Georgetown. While the former Robert Woods Bliss mansion is a gem for its collection of Byzantine and pre-Colombian art, the 16-acre garden, with its formal terrace design, wisteria-covered arbors, flower beds, and magnolia and cherry trees, is, in a word, breathtaking. Spring is especially glorious when daffodils and tulips bloom in a riot of colors. The terrain is hilly. You'd do well to leave the 3-inch heels and flip-flops behind.

1703 32nd St. NW (entrance on R St. between 31st and 32nd sts.). ☎ 202/339-6400. **Metro:** *Foggy Bottom is more than a mile away. Walk from anywhere in Georgetown or take a taxi; parking is a bear.* **Open:** *Daily 2–5pm. (Note: The mansion is open Tues–Sun 2–5pm.) Closed national holidays and sometimes during inclement weather.* **Admission:** *Free.*

Enid A. Haupt Victorian Garden
Mall.

Covering the underground Sackler Gallery and Museum of African Art is this charming 4-acre park with seasonal flowers spilling from baskets hanging from lampposts. The central flower garden replicates the colorful rose window of the Smithsonian Castle. Enter the island garden through a moon gate and rest on benches framed by weeping cherries. The tea roses and magnolias are a sight for sore eyes in summer. A brass sundial, built by two Museum of American History staffers, marks Washington's 40-degree latitude. Please report any inconsistencies at once! And please don't walk on the grass.

10th St. and Independence Ave. SW (between the Freer Gallery and Arts and Industries Building; also accessible from the Sackler). ☎ *202/357-2700.* **Metro:** *Smithsonian.* **Open:** *Memorial Day–Labor Day, daily 7am–8pm; rest of the year, daily 7am–5:45pm.* **Admission.** *Free.*

Kids FBI
Federal Triangle.

The image of J. Edgar Hoover running around in high heels and dresses aside, the FBI is an impressive organization, and a tour of its headquarters is one of the hottest tickets in town, especially with youngsters. An introduction to the Ten Most Wanted and short film start the guided tour, which wends its way by laboratories where a car's make and model are determined from a paint chip and technicians analyze hair, fibers, and blood for crime-solving clues. The bang-up finish in the firing range may leave your ears ringing. While kids often mention the FBI as their favorite D.C. sight, be advised that the gunfire may frighten those under 6. The hour-long tour begins every 15 minutes, Monday through Friday from 8:45am to 4:15pm. Unless you enjoy standing in lines, especially April through August, arrive by 8:30am. Even then, you may have a wait without VIP tickets.

Pennsylvania Ave. and 10th St. NW (tour entrance at E. St. between 9th and 10th sts.). ☎ *202/324-3447.* **Metro:** *Metro Center, then walk south on 12th St. 2 blocks to left on E St. 2 blocks; Gallery Place, National Archives, Federal Triangle stations are about equidistant.* **Open:** *Mon–Fri 8:45am–4:15pm. Closed weekends and federal holidays.* **Admission:** *Free.*

Kids **Ford's Theatre & Lincoln Museum/Petersen House**
Chinatown.

As you may have heard, on April 14, 1865, an ornery John Wilkes Booth shot the 16th president as he watched *Our American Cousin.* This did not help business, and Ford's closed for more than 100 years. In 1968 it reopened (bet the popcorn was stale) and has been packin' 'em in ever since. The presidential box is furnished as it was that fateful April night. You can visit the booth when rehearsals and matinees are not in progress. Call ☎ **202/ 347-4833** to find out the theater's schedule. Exhibited in the basement of the Lincoln Museum are Lincoln's death mask and Booth's derringer along with other related memorabilia.

The mortally wounded Lincoln was taken to the **Petersen House,** across the street at 516 10th St. NW, where he died in the small bedroom at 7:22am on April 15. The time is frozen on the bedside clock in the little house, whose decor hasn't changed since that time either. The Petersen House is open free to the public every day but December 25 from 9am to 5pm.

517 10th St. NW (between E and F sts.). ☎ *202/426-6925.* **Metro:** *Gallery Place/Chinatown, then walk 1 block south on 7th St., right at F St., left at 10th St.* **Open:** *Daily 9am–5pm. Closed Dec. 25.* **Admission:** *Free.*

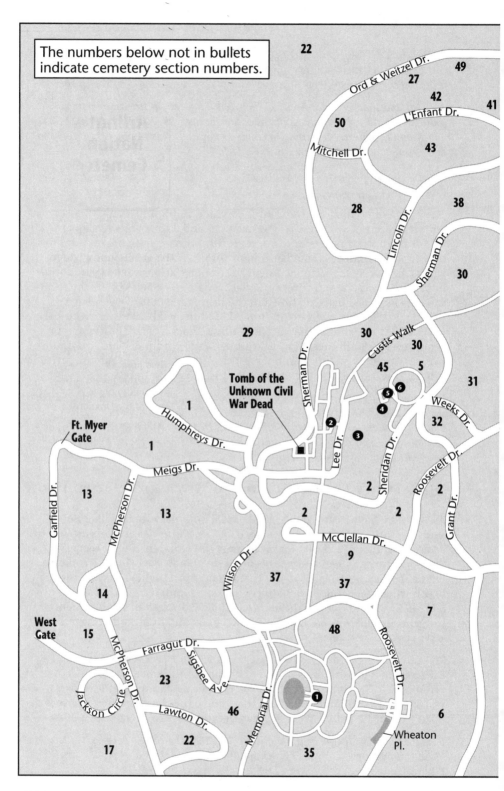

The numbers below not in bullets indicate cemetery section numbers.

22

Ord & Weitzel Dr.

49

27

42

41

50

L'Enfant Dr.

Mitchell Dr.

43

Lincoln Dr.

38

28

Sherman Dr.

30

29

Sherman Dr.

30

Custis Walk

30

45

5

Tomb of the Unknown Civil War Dead

Lee Dr.

❷

❺ ❻

❹

31

❸

Weeks Dr.

32

Humphreys Dr.

1

Ft. Myer Gate

1

Meigs Dr.

Sheridan Dr.

Roosevelt Dr.

2

Garfield Dr.

McPherson Dr.

13

13

2

2

2

Grant Dr.

Wilson Dr.

McClellan Dr.

9

14

37

37

7

West Gate

15

48

Roosevelt Dr.

McPherson Dr.

Farragut Dr.

Sigsbee Ave.

23

Jackson Circle

Lawton Dr.

46

Memorial Dr.

❶

6

Wheaton Pl.

17

22

35

170

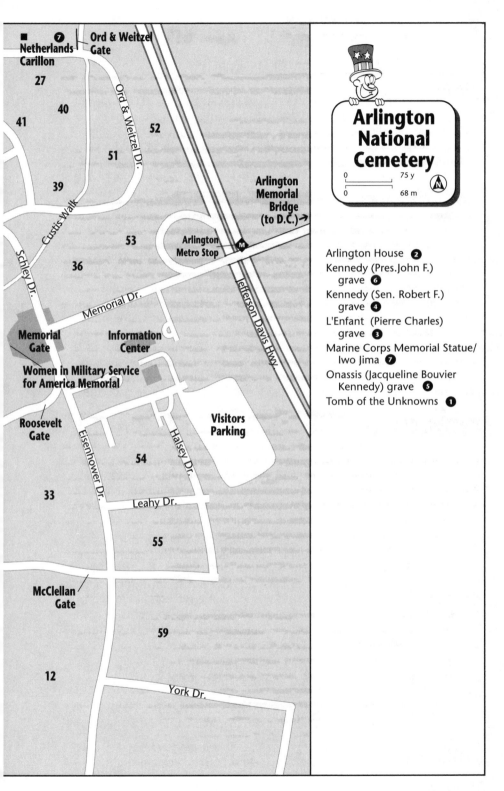

Arlington National Cemetery

0 ——— 75 y
0 ——— 68 m

Arlington House ❷
Kennedy (Pres. John F.) grave ❻
Kennedy (Sen. Robert F.) grave ❹
L'Enfant (Pierre Charles) grave ❸
Marine Corps Memorial Statue/ Iwo Jima ❼
Onassis (Jacqueline Bouvier Kennedy) grave ❺
Tomb of the Unknowns ❶

Netherlands Carillon ❼
Ord & Weitzel Gate
27
40
41
Ord & Weitzel Dr.
52
51
39
Custis Walk
Arlington Memorial Bridge (to D.C.)→
53
Arlington Metro Stop M
36
Schley Dr.
Memorial Dr.
Jefferson Davis Hwy.
Memorial Gate
Information Center
Women in Military Service for America Memorial
Roosevelt Gate
Eisenhower Dr.
Halsey Dr.
Visitors Parking
54
33
Leahy Dr.
55
McClellan Gate
59
12
York Dr.

Franklin Delano Roosevelt Memorial
Tidal Basin.
The latest presidential monument to clutter, I mean enhance, D.C., opened to great fanfare in May 1997. And it's been receiving rave reviews ever since for its grandeur and design. The site, marked by granite, fountains, waterfalls, and meditative areas, is near the Jefferson Memorial (two for the price of one!) and celebrates the contributions of our 32nd president. Exhibits deal with the Great Depression, World War II, and other aspects of Roosevelt's 12-year reign. Larger-than-life-size statues of Eleanor and Fala are easily distinguishable. You'll find FDR's wheelchair and other memorabilia in the Information Center. Rest rooms anchor both ends of the fortresslike monument, the length of three football fields.

South end of 15th St. SW in West Potomac Park. ☎ *202/426-6821.* **Metro:** *Smithsonian, then walk west along Independence Ave. until you're ready to plotz (about 15 minutes). Also a Tourmobile stop. Or take a taxi.* **Open:** *Daily 8am–midnight. Closed Dec. 25.* **Admission:** *Free. Fala reproductions extra.*

Holocaust Memorial Museum
Tidal Basin.
I haven't met a soul who was unmoved by a visit to this museum. And although is may be moving, it's not easy to spend 5 or 6 hours here. I am maxed out—emotionally drained—after 3. Because this is strong stuff, the museum recommends that children under 11 stay behind, except to visit two exhibits described below. Parents of older children would do well to prepare their offspring ahead.

The national memorial to the 6 million Jews and millions of others exterminated during the Holocaust documents this obscene chapter of history in multimedia exhibitions with interactive videos and films. Visitors pick up an identity card of a Holocaust victim on the way in, adding to the immediacy of the experience.

The self-guided tour begins on the 4th floor, which documents the rise of Nazism. On the third floor, where the Nazis' "Final Solution" is depicted, visitors board a freight car used to transport Jews to Treblinka and listen to recordings of survivors. Take tissues. The 2nd floor is dedicated to the liberation of the camps and the many non-Jews, who, at great risk, hid Jews during the war. Time-specific tickets are required to view the above. They're available at the museum beginning at 10am daily (get there early) or by calling Protix (☎ 800/400-9373).

Visitors are allowed into the special exhibit areas on the first floor and concourse without tickets. Among these special exhibits is Daniel's Story, a watered-down version of the Holocaust appropriate for children under 11. The Children's Wall (the colorful tiles were painted by American schoolchildren) commemorates the 1.5 million children who perished in the Holocaust.

100 Raoul Wallenberg Place (formerly 15th St. SW, near Independence Ave. and the southwest corner of the Mall). ☎ *202/488-0400.* **Metro:** *Smithsonian, then walk*

west 2 blocks on Independence Ave. and left at Raoul Wallenberg Place.
Open: *Daily 10am–5:30pm. Closed Yom Kippur (usually in Sept) and Dec 25.*
Admission: *Free, but small surcharge for tickets through Protix (see above for number).*

Kids Jefferson Memorial
Tidal Basin.

The accomplishments of this Renaissance man—author of the Declaration of Independence, third U.S. president, and founder of the University of the Virginia, to name a few—are etched in a marble monument aptly resembling the Pantheon in Rome. Jefferson was so fond of the columned rotunda design, he used it at the University of Virginia and his beloved Monticello home. Poised at the edge of the Tidal Basin, it enjoys a view of the Capitol, Washington Monument, and Lincoln Memorial. Nobody asked, but for my money it's the most beautiful monument in Washington, especially when framed in spring by the cherry blossoms or illuminated at night. Let me know what you think.

Tidal Basin, south end of 15th St. SW, in West Potomac Park. ☎ ***202/426-6821.***
Metro: *Smithsonian, then head west on Independence Ave. to the Tidal Basin (watch the traffic!) and south along the Tidal Basin path. It's about a 15-minute walk from Metro, so you may want to take a taxi or Tourmobile to get here.*

D.C. Dirt

If you're boppin' down Pennsylvania Avenue and the flag is flying at the White House, it means the president is home. Wave. Maybe he'll invite you in for milk and cookies. You can call ☎ **202/456-2343** for recorded information on the president's daily schedule. (In light of Zippergate, don't you think the unscheduled events would make for a more interesting recording?)

Lafayette Square
White House Area.

Once part of the White House gardens, and long a haven for the homeless, protestors, pigeons, squirrels, and brown-bagging policy wonks, the pretty public park across from the White House is now a good place to enjoy a snack and stretch out on the grass before trudging on. Although named for the Marquis de Lafayette who visited the site in 1824, the equestrian statue of General Andrew Jackson dominates the park and Lafayette is relegated to the southeast corner (go figure).

H St. NW to the north, Pennsylvania Ave. to the south, between 15th and 17th sts. (east and west). **Metro:** *McPherson Square, then walk south on Vermont Ave. to the "back side" of the square.*

173

Kids **Lincoln Memorial**
Mall.

Although plans for a memorial to the 16th president were talked about in 1867, 2 years after Lincoln's death, another 45 years passed before Henry Bacon's design was accepted in 1912, and 10 years more before the monument's dedication in 1922. It took Daniel French 28 blocks of marble and 4 years to complete the seated statue of a contemplative Lincoln gazing across the Reflecting Pool and Mall to the Capitol. I'd say it was worth the rocks and time. How about you?

Excerpts of the Gettysburg Address and Second Inaugural Address are carved into the limestone walls, and the 36 Doric columns represent the number of states in the Union at Lincoln's death in 1865. A visitor center beneath the memorial holds Lincoln memorabilia as well as photographs of the protests and civil rights events that have taken place on the monument grounds. Check out the views from the front and back after dark!

West end of Mall at 23rd St. NW (between Constitution and Independence aves.). ☎ *202/426-6895.* **Metro:** *Foggy Bottom, then walk south 7 blocks on 23rd St.* **Open:** *24 hours. Park staff on duty 8am–midnight.* **Admission:** *Free. (Is this a great city, or what?)*

Kids **National Air and Space Museum**
Mall.

If it has wings or it's flown, it's here. The Wright brothers' *1903 Flyer,* Charles Lindbergh's *Spirit of St. Louis,* John Glenn's *Friendship 7,* and the *Enola Gay* are a tiny sampling of aviation's milestones housed at Air and Space. Go early or late to miss the crowds and pick up a floor plan at the information desk on entering. Exhibits, many with interactive displays, cover a broad spectrum, from the earliest flying machines to rockets and flight in the computer age. In the Langley Theater, flight-related movies play on a 5-story IMAX screen. *To Fly* is still a stunner after more than 20 years. If you do nothing else, buy tickets as soon as you enter and see it. That's an order. Two programs alternate in the Albert Einstein Planetarium, one of which is geared to kids 4 to 8. You could spend hours perusing the books and souvenirs in the Museum Gift Shop, where the freeze-dried ice-cream sandwiches are always a hit with youngsters.

Time Savers

It's a bird! It's a plane! It's even larger than two football fields! No, it's not Superman. It's the National Air and Space Museum—which, by the way, is the most visited museum in the world. Better get there early.

South side of the Mall at Independence Ave. SW and 7th St. (enter at Independence Ave. for the full effect). ☎ *202/357-2700.* **Metro:** *L'Enfant Plaza (Smithsonian museums exit), then walk north 2 blocks on 7th St. SW to the pale marble edifice the length of two football fields.* **Open:** *Daily 10am–5:30pm. Closed Dec 25.*

Admission: Free. Charge for tickets ($5 for adults, $3.75 for ages 2–21 and seniors 55 and over) to Langley Theater and Einstein Planetarium.

National Archives
Mall.

Three very important pieces of paper—the Declaration of Independence, Constitution of the United States (and Bill of Rights), and a 1297 (that's no typo; 1-2-9-7) version of the Magna Carta—are on display. Get here near closing time when the documents are lowered into an underground vault said to be impervious to an atom bomb. The archives stored in the imposing building, with its 72 Corinthian columns and bronze doors, are often called "the nation's memory," and for good reason. Billions of other pieces of paper documenting more than 200 years of our nation's official life reside here: federal documents, passport applications, census figures, photographs, and more. Much more. (Phew! How do they do it? I have trouble organizing my desktop papers.)

Many trace their genealogy here. In fact, this is where author Alex Haley began his research for his bestseller *Roots*. Kids under 8 may find the archives boring.

Constitution Ave. and 8th St. NW. ☎ *202/ 501-5000.* **Metro:** *Archives.* **Open:** *Daily 10am–5:30pm, usually with extended hours Apr–Labor Day.* **Admission:** *Free.*

National Gallery of Art
Mall.

I was going to wait to tell you about this fabulous museum until the next chapter, but I couldn't wait. (For other art museums, see chapter 14.) One of the world's top cultural attractions, the National Gallery of Art is actually two separate buildings connected by an underground moving walkway.

The **West Building** is a treasure trove of 12th- to 20th-century paintings and sculptures. Among the masters whose works hang in the West Wing are Bosch, El Greco, Gainsborough, Giotto, Holbein, Rembrandt, and Vermeer. The portrait of Ginevra de'Benci, the only Leonardo da Vinci painting hanging outside a European gallery, is here. Sculpture by Daumier, Degas, and Rodin fill a ground-floor gallery. Only a portion of the sizable collection is on view at any one time, augmented by special exhibitions. With the help of computer screens, visitors can literally zoom in on their favorite works to view the artist's brush strokes in the Micro Gallery. The gift shop sells reasonably priced prints worthy of framing, gorgeous books, and stationery. John Russell Pope's architecture is glorious.

Time Savers

If you want to know when the seals lunch at the National Zoo, or on what floor of the Natural History Museum the Hope Diamond dazzles, phone the Smithsonian at ☎ **202/357-2700.** (It's worth dialing just to talk to a real person instead of someone's voice mail, or a recording thanking you for your patience.)

The **East Building,** a trapezoid designed by I. M. Pei, features a soaring ground-level central court dominated by a humongous Calder mobile. The museum overflows with a wealth of 20th-century masterworks, and a visit always produces a mood-elevating high. When your soul seeks nourishment, head here for Mondrian's grids, Lichtenstein's campy *Look Mickey,* Matisse's enchanting *Large Composition with Masks,* Picasso's *The Tragedy* (from his blue period), and special shows, which eat up much of the gallery space. If you are partial to a particular artist, it would be wise to call ahead. Most of the gallery's holdings are under wraps at any given time, as Pei's design emphasizes public over gallery space. Passes are usually required for special exhibitions. Ask at the information desk to find out what's goin' on.

North side of the Mall (between 3rd and 7th sts. NW; entrances at 6th St. and Constitution Ave. or Madison Dr.) ☎ *202/737-4215.* ***Metro:*** *Archives, then walk south 1 block on 7th St. and left 1 block.* ***Open:*** *Mon–Sat 10am–5pm, Sun 11am–6pm. Closed Jan 1 and Dec 25.* ***Admission:*** *Free.*

🌟Kids National Museum of American History
Mall.

You want Americana? You've come to the right place. Three floors of this huge repository are crammed with examples of the cultural, technological, and scientific advances that helped shape our country's character. First Lady memorabilia, the Star-Spangled Banner, Dorothy's ruby slippers, a 280-ton steam locomotive, and a hands-on history room geared to youngsters are among the top draws. Do take a break and stop in the Palm Court, an authentic Victorian ice-cream parlor, for a malt or sundae before tackling the next museum. Arrive early or late, especially on weekends when it's a zoo by early afternoon.

14th St. and Constitution Ave. NW (entrances on Constitution Ave. and Madison Dr.). ☎ *202/357-2700.* ***Metro:*** *Smithsonian (Mall exit), then cut north across the Mall to the museum on your left; or Federal Triangle, and walk south on 12th St. NW 1 block, then right at Constitution Ave.* ***Open:*** *Daily 10am–5:30pm. Closed Dec 25.* ***Admission:*** *Free.*

🌟Kids National Museum of Natural History
Mall.

After countless visits over more than 35 years, I still get a kick from this museum. There's talk of removing the 8-ton African bush elephant who greets visitors in the marble-pillared rotunda. They'll have to deal with me first.

Books have been written about the wonders of the natural world displayed here. We'll have to content ourselves with some highlights. Like the Hooker Hall of Geology, Gems and Minerals, with the 45.5-karat Hope Diamond and even more dazzling mineral collection. And the O. Orkin Insect Zoo, home to many creepy-crawlers and interactive displays. And the skeletal remains of our prehistoric relatives in Dinosaur Hall. And the 92-foot replica of a blue whale and giant squid in Sea Life Hall. With children in tow, this museum is a must. Enjoy!

Constitution Ave. and 10th St. NW (2nd entrance on Madison Dr.). ☎ *202/ 357-2700.* **Metro:** *Federal Triangle, then walk south on 12th St. 2 blocks to left at Constitution Ave.; or Smithsonian, and cut across Mall to museum on your right.* **Open:** *Daily 10am–5:30pm.*

D.C. Dirt

The 45.5-karat Hope Diamond on display at the National Museum of Natural History wasn't always a museum piece. Once the eye of a Hindu Idol in India, the diamond was stolen in the 17th century, and the gods put a curse on all future wearers. Future owners included Marie Antoinette and Evalyn Walsh McLean. You know what happened to Marie Antoinette. But Evalyn Walsh McLean? Her husband went insane, her marriage dissolved, and then her eldest son was killed in an accident. McLean continued to wear the diamond—her family suffered from financial ruin during the Depression, and her only daughter later died of a drug overdose. McLean died in 1947 and her friends and family had a hard time getting rid of the diamond. The jeweler Harry Winston finally bought it in 1949 to pay McLean's estate taxes. When Winston donated the stone to the Smithsonian 9 years later, it's said that the postman who delivered it had his leg crushed in a truck accident, his wife and dog died soon thereafter, and his house burned to the ground. Maybe diamonds aren't a girl's best friend?

 National Postal Museum
Capitol Hill.
Everything you ever wanted to know about the history of stamps and the postal service—and more—is attractively served up in this museum, a joint project of the Postal Service and Smithsonian Institution. Now if they could only deliver the mail more efficiently.

Tour a Southern Railway mail car, ogle the floating laser images and holograms in the Customers and Consumers Gallery, send a special souvenir postcard, or learn about the big business of direct mail ("junk" in most lexicons) that plugs your mailbox. The museum is chockablock full of interactive areas and video games that delight children of all ages.

2 Massachusetts Ave. NE (next to Union Station in the City Post Office Building). ☎ *202/357-2700.* **Metro:** *Union Station.* **Open:** *Daily 10am–5:30pm.* **Admission:** *Free.*

National Zoological Park
Woodley Park.

The National Zoo (3 Metro stops away from Metro Center) is home to several thousand animals representing more than 500 species. The 163-acre verdant parcel of winding paths and forested hills fills quickly with busloads of schoolchildren and families, so a morning or late afternoon visit is advisable, especially spring through fall. The animals, for the most part, inhabit spacious enclosures reminiscent of their natural habitats. Three miles of trails crisscross the hilly terrain, so comfortable, nonskid shoes are strongly suggested. At the **Education Building** near the main Connecticut Avenue entrance, you can pick up a map and schedule of special programs.

Several highlights I have yet to outgrow include the elephants, who demonstrate a trunkload of tricks twice most mornings, the sea lions' performance (in exchange for fish) around 11:30am, and the giant panda, Hsing-Hsing, who dines around 11am and 3pm. The rest of the time, he's dull as dishwater, preferring to nap in the bamboo. If you enter the **Great Outdoor Flight Cage,** which supports many of our feathered friends, watch your head. If you get nailed by droppings, remember, it's good luck! **Amazonia** is a stunningly re-created rain forest. Watch the macaques and orangutans in the **Think Tank** (not to be confused with downtown think tanks inhabited by less-animated pinstripers). A trip to the zoo never disappoints, but I can't say the same about the food. With kids, I recommend toting sandwiches or snacks. You can rent a stroller for a few bucks.

3001 Connecticut Ave. NW. ☎ *202/673-4800.* **Metro:** *Woodley Park/National Zoo, then northbound L-2 or L-4 bus, or walk three-tenths of a mile (warning: it's uphill).* **Open:** *Buildings, May to mid-Sept daily 10am–6pm; rest of the year, daily 10am–4:30pm. Grounds, May to mid-Sept daily 6am–8pm; rest of the year, daily 6am–6pm.* **Admission:** *Free. Fee for parking.*

Potomac Park (East and West)
Tidal Basin.

Though the two sections of 700-acre Potomac Park are designated East and West, on a map East is more South, and West is more North. Oh well, this is Washington, and reason doesn't always prevail. **West Potomac Park** is basically the area around the Tidal Basin and Jefferson Memorial. **East Potomac Park** is, um, south of the Tidal Basin. (Don't tell me you're confused—look at the map.)

More than 3,000 cherry trees, especially when blooming, are the park's main claim to fame. Because of D.C.'s fickle weather, the blossoms appear anywhere from late March to mid-April, but April 5 is the average. You have a better chance of winning the lottery than pinpointing the bloomin' date. What can I say? Life ain't a bowl of cherries. Besides, this is a lovely place to stroll any time of year.

West Potomac Park is an easy walk from the Mall and surrounds the Lincoln, Roosevelt, Korean, and Vietnam Veterans memorials; Reflecting

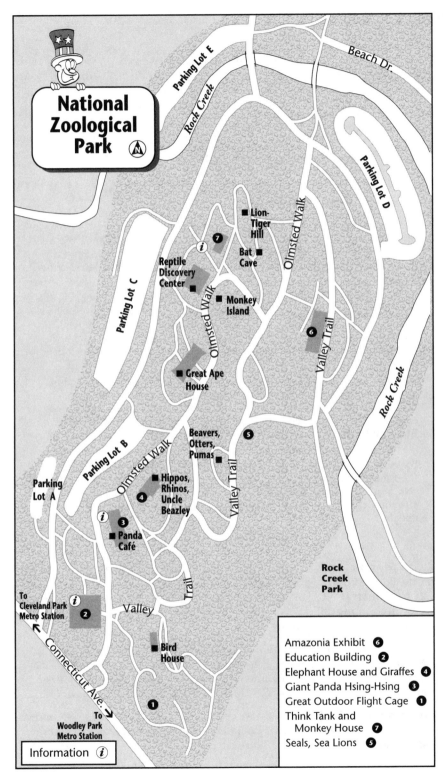

National Zoological Park

Beach Dr.

Parking Lot E

Rock Creek

Parking Lot D

Olmsted Walk

■ Lion-Tiger Hill

❼

ⓘ

Reptile Discovery Center ■

Bat Cave ■

■ Monkey Island

Olmsted Walk

❻

Valley Trail

Parking Lot C

■ Great Ape House

■ Beavers, Otters, Pumas

❺

Parking Lot B

Olmsted Walk

❹ ■ Hippos, Rhinos, Uncle Beazley

Valley Trail

Parking Lot A

ⓘ ❸

■ Panda Café

Rock Creek

Rock Creek Park

To Cleveland Park Metro Station

ⓘ

❷

Valley Trail

Connecticut Ave.

■ Bird House

❶

To Woodley Park Metro Station

Information ⓘ

Amazonia Exhibit ❻
Education Building ❷
Elephant House and Giraffes ❹
Giant Panda Hsing-Hsing ❸
Great Outdoor Flight Cage ❶
Think Tank and
    Monkey House ❼
Seals, Sea Lions ❺

179

Pool; and Constitution Gardens, with a pond visited by a stray duck or two. You can rent a paddleboat and cruise the Tidal Basin from 10am to an hour before sunset. Two-seaters go for $7 an hour; four-seaters cost $14.

Good Thing George Washington Didn't Cut Down That Cherry Tree

Mention Washington, D.C., and most people think of cherry trees. A harbinger of spring when they embrace the Tidal Basin in their pale, lacy arms, the trees were a gift from Japan in 1912. The original trees were planted by First Lady Helen Herron Taft and the Viscountess Chinda of Japan. (Never heard of her? Neither had I.)

Of the original 3,000 white- and soft-pink-blossomed Yoshino trees, fewer than 200 survive. More have been added over the years, along with Akebonos, with single pale pink flowers, and Kwansans, with deeper pink pompomlike blossoms. Every spring more than 3,700 trees flower, gracing the Tidal Basin, East Potomac Park, and the Washington Monument grounds with their delicate beauty.

The Yoshinos bloom first, usually in early April, followed by the Kwansans a week or two later. It all depends on the kindness—or severity—of Mother Nature. The trees have blossomed as early as mid-March and as late as mid-April. So, if you're planning a visit during the 2-week **National Cherry Blossom Festival** (beginning in late March), you have a 50–50 chance of seeing the trees at their peak.

For more information, call the **Park Service** (☎ **202/619-7222**) or check the cherry trees' very own Web site: **www.nps.gov/nacc/cherry/index.htm**. (No, you can't e-mail the trees directly.) Also, watch the *Washington Post* and local newscasts in the weeks preceding the festival for budding and flowering updates.

East Potomac Park is much larger and has golf courses, tennis courts, picnic areas, a swimming pool, and hiking and biking paths. I know of no easy way to get here, except by car or taxi. The peninsula is a beautiful place for a scenic drive along Ohio Drive, which fronts the Washington Channel to the east and Potomac River to the west.

West Potomac Park: *Constitution Ave. to the north, 14th St. to the east, Jefferson Memorial to the south, Potomac River to the west.* ☎ ***202/619-7222.*** ***Metro:*** *Smithsonian, then head west on Independence Ave., young man, head west. (It's about a 10-minute walk.)* ***Open:*** *Dawn to dusk.* ***Admission:*** *Free.*

East Potomac Park: *Ohio Dr. SW, south of the Tidal Basin and Independence Ave.* ☎ ***202/426-6765.*** ***Metro:*** *Uh-uh (take a taxi).* ***Open:*** *Dawn to dusk.* ***Admission:*** *Free. Charge for golf, tennis, etc.*

Rock Creek Park
Foggy Bottom into Chevy Chase, Md.

The granddaddy of D.C. parks stretches for nearly 12 miles from the Potomac River north into Maryland and is flush with natural wonders. Besides hiking, biking, and fitness trails, the park has an 18-hole golf course, horseback riding, 25 tennis courts, a nature center and planetarium, playgrounds, picnic areas, and the remnants of several forts built to protect Washington during the Civil War.

In summer, **Carter Barron Amphitheater** audiences applaud their favorite musical groups and Shakespeare in the Park. The men's Legg Mason Tennis Classic is played at the park's H. G. FitzGerald Tennis Center (16th and Kennedy streets NW) the third week in July, invariably the hottest week of the summer (☎ **202/291-9888**). The Carter Barron Amphitheater is located at 16th Street and Colorado Avenue NW (☎ **202/260-6836**). Metro: Silver Spring, then transfer to the S2 or S4 bus headed south on 16th Street for Federal Triangle. Ask the driver for the stop nearest the amphitheater.

Because the sprawling park eats up more than 2,000 acres, filling D.C. like ham in a sandwich, it's not easily accessible by Metro. Your best bet is to focus on one area of the park and then, if you're familiar with the roads, drive (free parking is available throughout the park)—or take a taxi.

5000 Glover Rd. NW (Visitor Information Center). ☎ *202/282-1063.* **Metro:** *Friendship Heights, then transfer to E1 or E3 bus to Military Rd. and Oregon Ave./Glover Rd.* **Open:** *To vehicular traffic around the clock; on foot, dawn to dusk.* **Admission:** *Free.*

D.C. Dirt

You can thank the wealthy English scientist James Smithson (1765–1829) for all the free Smithsonian museums in Washington. Why would the illegitimate son of the Duke of Northumberland bequeath his fortune to a country he never visited? He was probably concerned that the new nation across the ocean was lacking in established cultural institutions. In 1836, Smithson's gift, a shipment of 105 bags of gold sovereigns (worth about half a million dollars!) arrived at the U.S. Mint in Philadelphia. In 1846, President James Polk signed an act into law, which established the Smithsonian Institution and provided "for the faithful execution of said trust, according to the will of the liberal and enlightened donor." The law authorized a board to receive "all objects of art and of foreign and curious research, and all objects of natural history, plants, and geological and mineralogical specimens . . . for research and museum purposes."

With the help of subsequent donations and congressional appropriations, the Smithsonian now includes a complex of 14 museums in Washington, D.C., the National Zoological Park, and two museums in New York. Think about that as you ogle the Hope Diamond or marvel at a 3.5-billion-year-old fossil.

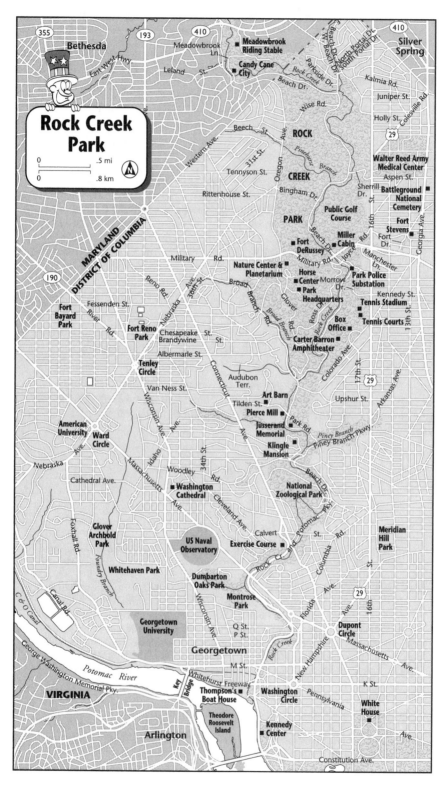

Rock Creek Park

0   .5 mi
0   .8 km

355
193
410
410

Bethesda

Silver Spring

Meadowbrook Ln.
Meadowbrook Riding Stable
Candy Cane City
East West Hwy.
Leland St.
Beach Dr.
W. Beach Dr.
North Portal Dr.
South Portal Dr.
Parkside Dr.
Beach Dr.
Rock Creek
Wise Rd.
Kalmia Rd.
Juniper St.
Holly St.
29
Colesville Rd.

Western Ave.
31st St.
Oregon Ave.
Beech St.
ROCK
CREEK
PARK
Pinehurst Branch
Tennyson St.
Rittenhouse St.
Bingham Dr.

Walter Reed Army Medical Center
Aspen St.
Sherrill Dr.
Battleground National Cemetery
Georgia Ave.

Public Golf Course

Fort Stevens
Fort Dr.
16th Rd.

Military Rd.
Fort DeRussey
Miller Cabin
Joyce Rd.
Manchester Ln.

Nature Center & Planetarium
Horse Center
Park Headquarters
Mortow Dr.
Ross Dr.
Park Police Substation
Kennedy St.
Tennis Stadium
13th St.

Broad Branch Rd.
Glover Rd.
Buck Creek
Box Office
Tennis Courts

Carter Barron Amphitheater

Colorado Ave.
17th St.
29
Arkansas Ave.
Upshur St.

American University
Ward Circle
Wisconsin Ave.
Massachusetts Ave.
Reno Rd.
Nebraska Ave.
36th St.
Broad Branch Rd.
Connecticut Ave.

Fort Bayard Park
River Rd.
Fessenden St.
Fort Reno Park
Chesapeake St.
Brandywine St.
Albermarle St.
Tenley Circle
Van Ness St.
Audubon Terr.
Tilden St.
Art Barn
Pierce Mill
Jusserand Memorial
Klingle Mansion
Park Rd.
Piney Branch
Piney Branch Pkwy.

MARYLAND
DISTRICT OF COLUMBIA
190
Military Rd.

Nebraska Ave.
Cathedral Ave.
Idaho Ave.
34th St.
Woodley Rd.
Washington Cathedral
Cleveland Ave.
National Zoological Park
Beach Dr.
Rock Creek and Potomac Pkwy.
Meridian Hill Park

Glover Archbold Park
Foxhall Rd.
Whitehaven Park
Foundry Branch
US Naval Observatory
Exercise Course
Calvert St.
Columbia Rd.
Florida Ave.
16th St.
29
Dupont Circle
Massachusetts Ave.

Dumbarton Oaks Park
Montrose Park
Georgetown University
Wisconsin Ave.
Q St.
P St.
Georgetown
Rock Creek
New Hampshire Ave.

C & O Canal
Canal Rd.
George Washington Memorial Pkwy.
Potomac River
VIRGINIA
Arlington
Key Bridge
Whitehurst Freeway
M St.
Thompson's Boat House
Washington Circle
Pennsylvania Ave.
K St.
White House
Theodore Roosevelt Island
Kennedy Center
Constitution Ave.

Kids **Smithsonian "Castle"**
Mall.

Formally known as the Smithsonian Institution Building, the Castle is the flagship of this esteemed institution and a good place to begin a D.C. visit. You can pick up reams of information on attractions, including a daily list of special events, and watch the 20-minute video giving an overview of Smithsonian museums. Kids delight in accessing information from the video-display monitors. Go ahead, ask the staff your most obscure question. The remains of James Smithson, the Brit whose bequest got this ball rolling, are interred in a crypt off the Jefferson Drive entrance.

1000 Jefferson Dr. SW. ☎ *202/357-2700. **Metro:** Smithsonian (duh!). **Open:** Daily 9am–5:30pm. Closed Dec 25. **Admission:** Free.*

Theodore Roosevelt Island
Smack in the middle of the Potomac River, between D.C. and Virginia.

The 88-acre preserve dedicated to the old Rough Rider himself and his numerous conservation efforts was once inhabited by Native Americans. The diverse ecosystem is now home to rabbits, chipmunks, fox, and owls, and numerous other species of flora and fauna. More than 2 miles of foot trails weave through a pristine setting marred by the roar of airplanes descending into Reagan National Airport. A bronze statue of Roosevelt overlooks a moat-encircled terrace. Picnicking is allowed on the grounds near the island, but no food is allowed once you enter. June through September, bring insect repellent. You'll thank me.

Off the Virginia side of G. W. Memorial Parkway between Key and Roosevelt bridges. ☎ *703/289-2530. **Directions:** Roosevelt Bridge to G. W. Memorial Parkway north. (You cannot get to the island if you're traveling southbound on the parkway. Trust me. I learned the hard way and spent an unscheduled week in Virginia.) You can also walk here from D.C.'s West End. Walk across the Theodore Roosevelt Memorial Bridge (it's a continuation of Constitution Avenue) to the parking lot for Theodore Roosevelt Island. Don't worry, it's a short bridge. From here, there's another short bridge that'll take you right into the park. Occasional visitors: Don't even try to drive here. Take a taxi. Or paddle over from Thompson's Boat Center (☎ 202/333-4861). To get to Thompson's, take Metro to Foggy Bottom, walk south on New Hampshire Ave. 3 blocks, right at Virginia Ave., go 3 blocks to Rock Creek Parkway, and cross at the light only (the traffic zips along here) to Thompson's on the river. It's opposite the north end of the Watergate complex. Open daily from 9:30am to dusk.*

Kids **U.S. Capitol**
Capitol Hill.

I think the Capitol should be a required stop for all visitors. In a word, it is awesome: for its architecture, history, as a symbol of our government, and for the many art treasures housed within its hallowed halls. During the Civil War it was used as a hospital and barracks for Union troops. Bread baked in

Time Savers

Last-minute passes for morning VIP tours of the Capitol are sometimes available if you show up at your senator's office (no appointment necessary). If you left your Rolodex at home or the office location is not on the tip of your tongue, call ☎ **202/224-3121.**

ovens beneath the West Wing fed soldiers stationed at nearby forts. The 180-foot-high dome (resembling a giant chocolate-covered cherry) dominates the Washington landscape. The cherry stem atop the dome is the statue *Freedom*. If the sight doesn't accelerate your pacemaker, your battery needs recharging.

Beneath the dome, with its allegorical fresco by Constantino Brumidi, lies the **Rotunda,** where nine presidents (and two heroic federal officers, who defended the Capitol from the attack of a paranoid gunman) have lain in state. In **Statuary Hall,** once the House of Representatives, statues of prominent Americans—political and otherwise—fill the room. I hope I've whetted your appetite sufficiently. Start your visit with the half-hour guided tour (Monday through Saturday from 9:30am to 4:30pm, sometimes with extended hours), then strike out on your own.

East end of the Mall (entrance on E. Capitol St. and 1st St. NE). ☎ *202/ 225-6827.* **Metro:** *Capitol South, then walk north 3 blocks on 3rd St., left at E. Capitol St. (don't trip over the steps).* **Open:** *Daily 9am–4:30pm (often with extended hours Mar–Sept as determined annually by Congress). Closed Jan 1, Thanksgiving, Dec 25.* **Admission:** *Free (ain't Washington grand?).*

Hear Ye! Hear Ye!

Here's some free advice on how to get tickets to tour the Capitol. From March through October, all visitors must pick up free entry tickets next to the center grand staircase on the east side of the Capitol (facing the Supreme Court building). There are two lines: one for those taking guided tours; the other for those touring on their own. Ask a police officer if you're not sure which line is which. Tickets are not required from November through February. If you arrive on a weekday at 9:15am or around 3pm, the wait shouldn't be too bad. Saturdays are a zoo, as you might expect. Guides are stationed in the Rotunda to help those taking self-guided tours.

U.S. Supreme Court
Capitol Hill.
The nation's highest court doesn't make the top 10 list of most visitors, but as an emblem of the judicial branch of our government, it's worth a look see. Cases are heard Monday through Wednesday from the first Monday in

October through April (but not all weeks), and visitors may sit in on the proceedings. If you want to sit in, call ☎ **202/479-3211** or check the *Washington Post*'s Supreme Court calendar for the docket. Arrive an hour early (by 9am); earlier for highly publicized cases. Cases are heard from 10am to noon and occasionally from 1 to 2pm.

The judges release orders and opinions from mid-May to early July. Free lectures (every hour on the half hour between 9:30am and 3:30pm) and a film on the workings of the Court are offered year-round. Take in the view of the Capitol from the entrance steps.

1st St. and Maryland Ave. NE (opposite the Capitol). ☎ ***202/479-3000.*** **Metro:** *Capitol South, then walk north 3 blocks on 1st St. NE.* **Open:** *Mon–Fri 9am–4:30pm. Closed holidays.* **Admission:** *Free.*

Vietnam Veterans Memorial
Mall.
The Wall, as it is known, is a low-slung V-shaped monument near the Lincoln Memorial in Constitution Gardens. Etched on 140 black granite panels are the names of those who lost their lives during the Vietnam War. (Remember when it was called "a conflict"? Some conflict.) Friends and relatives come from all over the world to leave mementos near the names of loved ones. The war dead are listed chronologically from the first skirmish in 1959 to the last in 1975. The scene is a moving one, even for those with no personal connection to the war. The Wall continues to be one of the most visited sites in Washington. The astute will notice that you can't see the Wall until you approach it; and, that it is angled in such a way that it points directly to the Lincoln Memorial on one side and the Washington Monument on the other—the leaders of the two most important wars fought on American soil. Friendly, knowledgeable park rangers are on hand to answer questions.

Northeast of the Lincoln Memorial near 21st St. and Constitution Ave. NW. ☎ ***202/634-1568.*** **Metro:** *Foggy Bottom, then walk south on 23rd St. 7 blocks, left at Constitution Ave. 2 blocks.* **Open:** *24 hours. Park rangers on duty 8am–midnight.* **Admission:** *Free.*

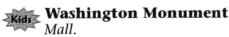 ## Washington Monument
Mall.

Surely, even if you recently returned from Pluto, you'll recognize the towering marble obelisk. I've seen the lines for the elevator up to the top snaking around the base in midwinter, so arrive early or late for the shortest wait. For $1.50 you can order a ticket in advance through Ticketmaster (☎ **800/505-5040**). The same timed-admission tickets are also available free at the monument starting at

Tourist Traps

During the summer at the Washington Monument, it's not unusual to find all the tickets gone by early afternoon. The ticket booth opens at 7:30am, so if you don't get a ticket, you only have yourself to blame.

7:30am. Military bands play on the grounds on summer evenings, and the monument is a dramatic backdrop for the spectacular 4th of July fireworks. Gridlike scaffolding worthy of Spider Man veils the monument, undergoing repairs, until sometime in 2000. And although the scaffolding affects the exterior appearance of the monument, the view from the observation level is still awesome.

15th St. and Constitution Ave. NW. ☎ *202/426-6839.* **Metro:** *Smithsonian, then walk north 2 blocks on 12th St., left at Madison Dr. (on the Mall) 2 blocks.* **Open:** *Apr–Labor Day daily 8am–midnight, rest of the year, daily 9am–5pm.* **Admission:** *Free. Closed July 4 and Dec 25.*

High Crimes and Misdemeanors?

Aside from Washington and Kennedy, the list of known presidents who did not respect their marriage vows continues to spread like Potomac fever. Psychologists have linked politicians' voracious desire for power with their other expanded appetites. Here are a few to consider.

Warren G. Harding enjoyed Nan Britton's company in the Oval Office (sound familiar?). Britton claimed that when Harding was a senator he fathered her illegitimate daughter. Harding also carried on with Carrie Fulton Phillips, the wife of a good friend. **FDR** was busy with Missy Lehand and Lucy Mercer, who was with the president when he died in Warm Springs, Georgia. **Eisenhower** had Kay Summersby. Although the affair was never confirmed by anyone except Summersby, those in the know say it happened. Despite his alleged infidelity and the busywork associated with leading the Allied forces in Europe, Eisenhower wrote Mamie 319 letters during his 3 years abroad. **Lyndon B. Johnson** had a rep as the consummate womanizer. Surely it wasn't for his good looks. My deep throats tell me that **George Bush** carried on a long-term relationship with a suburban Virginia matron. **President Clinton** I don't have to tell you about. Can't wait to read his 20-volume memoir. Now, what do you think Congress and the American people would do to a female president who cheated on her spouse? Stay tuned.

 ## White House
White House Area.

You can't tour the Oval Office where President Clinton and "that woman" allegedly conducted after-hours business, but you can view the public areas. Unless you have VIP tickets, you'll have to stop into the White House Visitor Center (8am is not too early; 7am will guarantee a ticket), 1450 Pennsylvania Ave. NW (☎ **202/208-1631**) from March to September for same-day tickets to the Maison Blanche. The half-hour video, *Inside These Walls,* may give you a closer look of the interior of the presidential mansion than the actual tour. Late fall and winter, visitors queue up at the East Visitors Gate on East

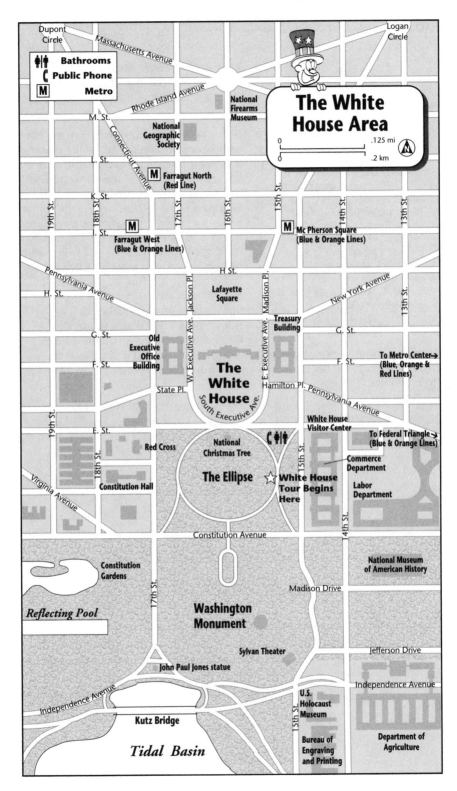

The White House Area

0 — .125 mi
0 — .2 km

Dupont Circle

Massachusetts Avenue

Bathrooms
Public Phone
M **Metro**

Rhode Island Avenue

Logan Circle

National Firearms Museum

M. St.

National Geographic Society

Connecticut Avenue

L. St.

M Farragut North (Red Line)

K. St.

19th St.
18th St.
17th St.
16th St.
15th St.
14th St.
13th St.

I. St.

M Farragut West (Blue & Orange Lines)

M Mc Pherson Square (Blue & Orange Lines)

Pennsylvania Avenue

H. St.

H St.

Lafayette Square

New York Avenue

Jackson Pl.
Madison Pl.

13th St.

G. St.

Treasury Building

G. St.

Old Executive Office Building

W. Executive Ave.
E. Executive Ave.

F. St.

The White House

F. St.

To Metro Center→ (Blue, Orange & Red Lines)

State Pl.

Hamilton Pl. Pennsylvania Avenue

South Executive Ave.

E. St.

19th St.
18th St.

Red Cross

National Christmas Tree

White House Visitor Center

To Federal Triangle→ (Blue & Orange Lines)

Commerce Department

Constitution Hall

The Ellipse

15th St.

☆ **White House Tour Begins Here**

Labor Department

Virginia Avenue

Constitution Avenue

Constitution Gardens

National Museum of American History

Reflecting Pool

17th St.

Washington Monument

Madison Drive

Jefferson Drive

Sylvan Theater

John Paul Jones statue

Independence Avenue

Independence Avenue

Kutz Bridge

15th St.

U.S. Holocaust Museum

Tidal Basin

Bureau of Engraving and Printing

Department of Agriculture

187

Time Savers

Don't rush. If your timed ticket to the White House is for 10:20am, you won't have to get on line until at least 10:30am. Why? Time is not of the essence at the White House, and for some reason the tours always run late. So, instead of waiting on line, have that second cup of coffee. Or bring a newspaper while you wait.

Executive Avenue, adjacent to the prez's place. Be advised that the White House is closed Sunday and Monday to prying eyes.

If you're a U.S. citizen, you own a piece of the rock, er, house. And what a house it is, with priceless art and furnishings that reflect the tastes and contributions of its residents, current and past. The tour covers the ground and main public floors and bores the pants off most kids under 8. Be advised that the big house is only open to the public for 2 hours and visitors are herded through like cattle. For this reason, I find anything but a VIP tour unsatisfying. If you can swing it, opt for the spring or fall garden and house tours (see "Washington, D.C., Calendar of Events" in chapter 1 for dates and more information). The grounds are beautiful and infused with history. The Children's Garden bears the imprints of former presidents' children and grandchildren.

1600 Pennsylvania Ave. NW (as if you needed to be told). ☎ ***800/717-1450.*** **Metro:** *McPherson Square, then south on 15th St. to Pennsylvania Ave. and hang a right to the biggest house on the block; left off 15th St. at Pennsylvania Ave. for the Visitor Center.* **Open:** *Tues–Sat 10am–noon. Closed some days for official functions (call first!).* **Admission:** *Free.*

Worksheet: Your Must-See Attractions

Enter the attractions you most would like to visit to see how they'll fit into your schedule. Then use the date book below to plan your itinerary.

Attraction and location	Amount of time you expect to spend there	Best day and time to go

DAY 1

Morning:

Lunch:

Afternoon:

Dinner:

Evening:

DAY 2

Morning:

Lunch:

Afternoon:

Dinner:

Evening:

DAY 3

Morning:

Lunch:

Afternoon:

Dinner:

Evening:

DAY 4

Morning:

Lunch:

Afternoon:

Dinner:

Evening:

DAY 5

Morning:

Lunch:

Afternoon:

Dinner:

Evening:

Chapter 14

More Fun Stuff to Do

> **In This Chapter**
>
> ➤ Special sights for architectural enthusiasts, history buffs, art lovers, kids, bookworms, and more
>
> ➤ Scandalous sights
>
> ➤ Places to visit outside of the city

Visitors take note: There's a heck of a lot more than bureaucratic red tape, marble statues, and space modules in D.C. Read on, my friends, there's a lot to see while you're here.

If You're Interested in Buildings of All Shapes and Sizes

The **National Building Museum** (formerly the Pension Building) is an architectural wonder dedicated to architecture and building history. The Renaissance-style palazzo design and majestic Great Hall with 75-foot-high columns have to be seen to be believed. A permanent exhibition, *Washington: Symbol and City,* focuses on the construction of the capital city. The television special, *Christmas in Washington,* is filmed here annually, and it has been the site of numerous inaugural balls. The building fills the north side of Judiciary Square at 401 F St., NW (☎ **202/272-2448**). It's open Monday through Saturday from 10am to 4pm, Sunday from 1 to 4pm. Admission is free. Take Metro to Judiciary Square, ride the escalator (up, please), and you've arrived.

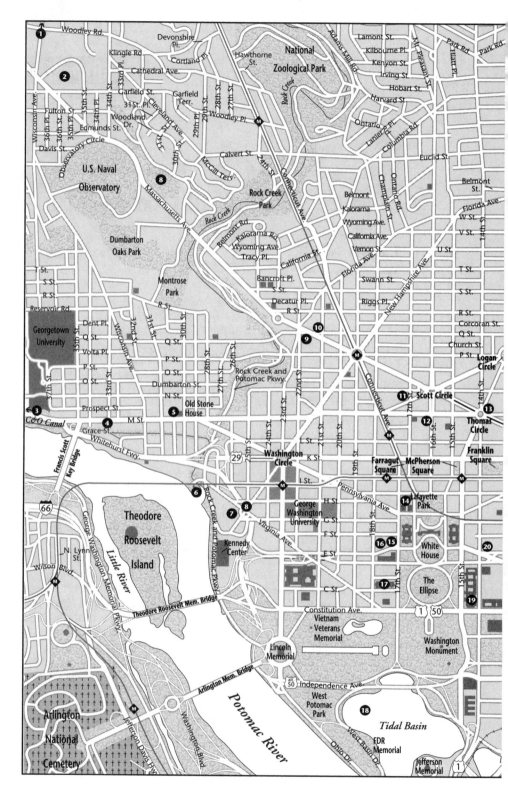

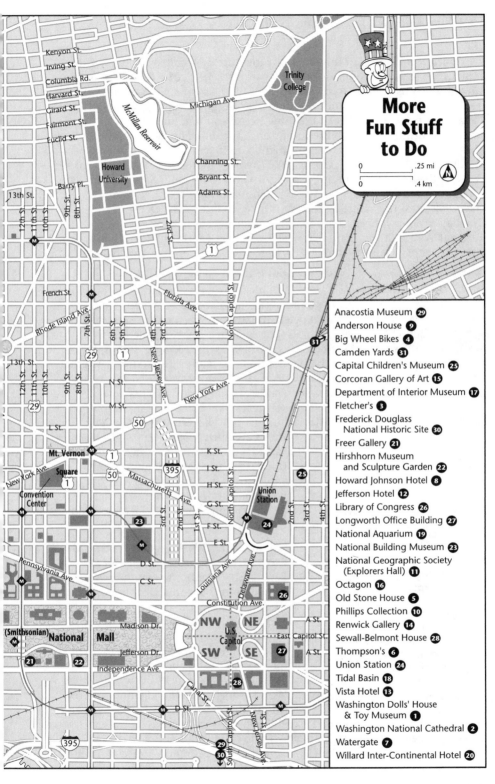

More Fun Stuff to Do

0   .25 mi
0   .4 km

Anacostia Museum **29**
Anderson House **9**
Big Wheel Bikes **4**
Camden Yards **31**
Capital Children's Museum **25**
Corcoran Gallery of Art **15**
Department of Interior Museum **17**
Fletcher's **3**
Frederick Douglass
    National Historic Site **30**
Freer Gallery **21**
Hirshhorn Museum
    and Sculpture Garden **22**
Howard Johnson Hotel **8**
Jefferson Hotel **12**
Library of Congress **26**
Longworth Office Building **27**
National Aquarium **19**
National Building Museum **23**
National Geographic Society
    (Explorers Hall) **11**
Octagon **16**
Old Stone House **5**
Phillips Collection **10**
Renwick Gallery **14**
Sewall-Belmont House **28**
Thompson's **6**
Union Station **24**
Tidal Basin **18**
Vista Hotel **13**
Washington Dolls' House
    & Toy Museum **1**
Washington National Cathedral **2**
Watergate **7**
Willard Inter-Continental Hotel **20**

197

The **Octagon** belongs to the American Institute of Architects, who used the building as its headquarters for many years until 1973. The Federal-style town home was built by John Tayloe, a wealthy Virginia plantation owner, in 1800. The architect, William Thornton, also designed the Capitol. Today the Octagon is open to visitors as a historic house and museum of architecture. Period furnishings decorate the rooms once inhabited by Tayloe and his 15 children. Note that the house is misnamed, as it actually has six sides. Guess it's too late to call it the Hexagon. Take the half-hour guided tour to learn some of the home's fascinating history, involving several U.S. presidents. The Octagon is at 1799 New York Ave. NW, an itsy-bitsy piece of New York Avenue west of the White House (☎ **202/638-3105**). The Octagon is open Tuesday to Sunday from 10am to 4pm. Admission is $3. Take Metro to Farragut West, I Street exit. Walk west 1 block on I to 18th Street, then south (toward Pennsylvania Avenue) 5 blocks to the corner of New York Avenue.

Kids **Union Station** has become a top D.C. attraction since its restoration in the late 1980s. Who'd'a thunk it? Daniel Burnham's beaux-arts neoclassical design provides a stunning and auspicious welcome to arriving Amtrak passengers. Modeled after the Diocletian Baths and Arch of Constantine in Rome, the station is replete with 50-foot columns, graceful galleries, mahogany banisters, coffered ceilings brushed with 22-karat gold leaf, stenciled skylights, and fields of marble flooring. Aside from the station's original purpose and as a site for special events, federal workers, tourists, area teens, and families flock here for the 100 retail and food shops on three levels, nine-screen cinema complex, and lower-level food court with more than 20 stalls. Union Station is at 50 Massachusetts Ave. NE (☎ **202/371-9441**). The shops are open Monday through Saturday from 10am to 9pm, Sunday from 10am to 6pm. Restaurants have varying hours. Admission is free, but you'll be hard-pressed not to spend money during your visit. Take Metro to Union Station and you've arrived!

Hear Ye! Hear Ye!

Chances are you probably won't see the president wandering around the streets of Washington. If you're really desperate to catch a glimpse of him, note that there's a helipad in the White House back yard, so if you stand near the Ellipse (behind the White House), you might be able to catch him coming or going.

The imposing **Washington National Cathedral** (Cathedral Church of St. Peter and St. Paul) is the sixth-largest cathedral in the world. How imposing? Well, for starters the nave is 518 feet long and the vaulted ceiling is 102 feet high. Though Episcopal, it serves as a national house of prayer. And it is awesome. The foundation of the English Gothic-style cathedral was laid in 1907, but the pesky World Wars (I and II) and empty coffers interrupted construction several times before the dedication in 1990. Resembling a cross in design (you weren't expecting the Star of David, were you?), the cathedral dominates the D.C. skyline, surpassed only by the U.S. Capitol and Washington Monument. It anchors the intersection of Wisconsin and Massachusetts avenues NW—nice piece of real estate, huh? With a prime location, about a mile north of Georgetown, it shares nearly 60 lush acres with gardens, four private schools, a greenhouse, and Herb Cottage, where locals pick up dried herbs and teas they can't find on the grocer's shelves. If you do nothing else, check the view from the Pilgrim Observation Gallery. The Children's Chapel is furnished with a pint-sized pipe organ and chairs. The medieval-inspired Bishop's Garden is south of the cathedral (ask a groundskeeper if you forgot your compass). For information on Tuesday and Wednesday afternoon tea, see chapter 11.

You can't miss the National Cathedral (visible from several locations in and around D.C.) at Massachusetts and Wisconsin avenues (☎ **202/537-6200**). Visit the cathedral Monday through Saturday from 10am to 4:30pm, Sunday from 12:30 or 4:30pm, or attend services (held several times every day). Free 45-minute guided tours begin about every 15 minutes (except on major holidays) Monday through Saturday from 10am to 3:15pm and Sunday from 12:30 to 2:45pm (☎ **202/537-6207**). Admission is free. Take Metro to Dupont Circle, then an N bus up Massachusetts Avenue NW; or take Metro to Tenleytown and then hop on any 30-series bus south on Wisconsin Avenue.

If You're Looking for a Historic Home Away from Home

Kids **Old Stone House,** in the heart of Georgetown, is the only pre-Revolutionary house still standing in the District. Dating back to 1765, the small fieldstone house is furnished as it was in the late 18th century during Georgetown's heyday as a thriving tobacco port. Park rangers are on hand to answer questions. The best part of this historic site is the sloping lawn and lovely English-style garden out back, a popular picnicking spot for locals. The house is located at 3051 M St. NW (☎ **202/426-6851**) and is open from 9am to 5pm daily from Memorial Day to Labor Day; from 9am to 5pm Wednesday to Sunday from Labor Day to Memorial Day. Admission is free. Take Metro to Foggy Bottom. Walk north on 23rd Street to Washington Circle and west on Pennsylvania Avenue (ask anyone you see if you're headed toward Georgetown). Continue on M Street (the two merge) to the house between 30th and 31st streets. (Figure on a 20-minute walk if you don't get lost.) Or, at Pennsylvania Avenue, board any bus traveling over M Street to Georgetown.

Head for the handsome red brick **Sewall–Belmont House,** said to be the oldest house on Capitol Hill, to bone up on suffragist and feminist history. The Federal/Queen Anne–style home, part of which dates to 1680, was the residence of Alice Paul, author of the original Equal Rights Amendment to the Constitution and founder of the National Women's Party in 1913. Portraits and busts of suffragists and those who were active in the equal rights movement decorate the rooms. The house is located a few blocks from the U.S. Capitol at 144 Constitution Ave. NE (☎ **202/546-3989**), and is open Tuesday to Friday from 10am to 3pm, Saturday from noon to 4pm, Sunday from noon to 4pm, March through October only. Docent-led tours are ongoing. Admission is by donation (your call!). Take Metro to Union Station and cross Massachusetts Avenue to 1st Street NE (ask a taxi driver or baggage handler) and walk south 3 blocks (toward the Capitol), then left at Constitution Avenue 1 block.

Step into the past at the **Woodrow Wilson House** at 2340 S St. NW (☎ **202/387-4062**). Take Metro to Dupont Circle, walk north up Massachusetts Avenue, take a right on 24th Street, go half a block to S Street NW, and turn right. Wilson, the lead promoter of the League of Nations, lived in this Georgian Revival home after he left office as the 28th president of the United States in 1921, until his death in 1924. The house remains very much the same as it was when he lived in it. Unlike today when presidents have to give over all gifts they receive in office (for fear of a subpoena), when Wilson was prez he kept all the gifts, which are now nicely displayed in a drawing room. This is a great way to see how the other half lived in the '20s. The house is open Tuesday to Sunday from 10am to 4pm; admission is $5 for adults, $4 for seniors, and $2.50 for students. The hourly docent-led tours share a true glimpse into the life of a statesman and president.

The **Anderson House** is an Italianate mansion at 2118 Massachusetts Ave. NW (☎ **202/785-2040**). Take Metro to Dupont Circle and walk north up Massachusetts Avenue. The former home of a career diplomat and his heiress wife, the house brims with furnishings and art (spanning five centuries) collected by the couple. You're welcome to drool over, but not on, the 18th-century chairs from Versailles, Spanish wood carvings, Flemish silk tapestries, and so on, Tuesday through Saturday from 1 to 4pm. Admission is free.

If You Want to Get to the Art of the Matter

Besides the National Gallery of Art, mentioned in chapter 13, Washington is known for its many other preeminent art museums and galleries, many of which are part of the Smithsonian conglomerate. A number of private galleries color Georgetown, Dupont Circle, and 7th Street NW between D and H streets.

A hop, skip, and jump from the White House, the **Corcoran Gallery of Art** is Washington's first private art museum. A large collection of American art spanning the 18th through 20th centuries rotates in changing exhibits on two floors. The gallery is on a small scale as museums go, and unintimidating. Among the Corcoran's riches are paintings by the Hudson River School artists and portraits by Cassatt, Sargent, Whistler, and Homer. Although the emphasis is decidedly American, works by Flemish and Dutch masters and French Impressionists are on display, as well as Renaissance tapestries and photography. The Corcoran offers free tours daily at noon and also at 7:30pm on Thursday when the museum is open until 9pm. A cafe is open for lunch Monday through Saturday, for tea and dinner on Thursday, and for Sunday brunch (☎ **202/639-1786**). The marble staircase and double atrium on the first floor are worth the price of admission.

The Corcoran is around the corner from the White House at 500 17th St. NW between D and E streets (☎ **202/639-1700**). Hours are from 10am to 5pm on Friday through Wednesday; Thursday the doors stay open until 9pm. Suggested donations are $3 adults, $1 students, $5 per family. Take Metro to Farragut West and walk south on 17th Street NW 5 blocks.

The **Freer Gallery,** with its Renaissance-style facade and tranquil courtyard, is, in my totally subjective thinking, one of the most beautiful buildings in all D.C. And what's inside isn't exactly chopped liver. The world's largest collection of works by James McNeill Whistler is at home in the Freer, a gift of Whistler's patron, industrialist Charles Lang Freer. Try to catch the docent-led tour of Whistler's *Harmony in Blue and Gold: The Peacock Room,* for the story behind this extraordinary dining room. The museum is also internationally known for its collection of Asian art spanning 6,000 years. At any given time only 10% of the Freer's permanent collection is on view. You'll find the Freer at Jefferson Drive and 12th Street SW, on the south side of the Mall (☎ **202/357-2104**). Hours are 10am to 5:30pm daily. Admission is free. Take Metro to the Smithsonian, walk 1 block north on 12th Street (toward the Mall), and right at Jefferson Drive.

The **Hirshhorn Museum and Sculpture Garden** opened in 1974 with Joseph Hirshhorn's little gift of six thousand 20th-century paintings, drawings, and sculptures. The museum's collection continues to grow with gifts from other donors. Among the artists represented in the doughnutlike galleries are Rodin, Degas, O'Keeffe, and Pollack. Pick up a calendar for information on free films, lectures, and concerts. The Sculpture Garden is a delightful place to decompress amid works by Calder, Moore, and other masters of the mallet and chisel. A self-service outdoor cafe is open from Memorial Day to Labor Day. The Hirshhorn is at Independence Avenue and 7th Street SW, on the south side of the Mall (☎ **202/357-2700**). The museum is open from 10am to 5:30pm daily. You may visit the Sculpture Garden from dawn to dusk. The price of admission is just your own finely chiseled features. Take Metro to L'Enfant Plaza (Smithsonian exit) and walk north on 7th Street 3 blocks to left at Independence Avenue.

The **Phillips Collection** features a stunning collection of French Impressionism, Post-Impressionism, and modern masterpieces in the former home of collector and benefactor Duncan Phillips. The Phillips is also the site of free Sunday concerts, tours, and gallery talks. No art lover should bypass this stop. Works by Renoir, Matisse, Klee, and Picasso are among the jewels. The museum is at the lower end of Embassy Row at 1600 21st St. NW (at Q Street; ☎ **202/387-0961**). Hours are from 10am to 5pm Tuesday, Wednesday, and Friday through Sunday; Thursday until 8:30pm. Summer hours are usually extended. Admission is $6.50 Saturday and Sunday; free for children 18 and under. At other times a contribution is suggested. Take Metro to Dupont Circle (Q Street exit) and walk west on Q Street to 21st Street.

Contemporary crafts and decorative arts are showcased in the **Renwick Gallery,** a stunning 19th-century French Second Empire–style building

201

Hear Ye! Hear Ye!

Exhibits come and exhibits go, but you can always count on the **Smithsonian Information Line** (☎ 202/357-2020) to hear a recorded message about special events and exhibits taking place at the Smithsonian while you're in town.

across from the White House. Check out the Ghost Clock, carved from a solid piece of mahogany, and Larry Fuente's colorful *Game Fish,* with glittering scales of game pieces and toys. Washington's first private art museum anchors the northeast corner of 17th Street and Pennsylvania Avenue NW (☎ 202/357-2700). Hours are from 10am to 5:30pm daily. Admission is free. Take Metro to Farragut West, walk east 1 block on I Street, then right at 17th Street. Continue 2 blocks to Pennsylvania Avenue.

If You're Kiddin' Around

The **Capital Children's Museum** at 800 3rd St. NE (at H Street; ☎ 202/675-4120), which is located a few blocks from Union Station, is a hit with kids under 12—but, unfortunately, often overlooked. Learning is fun at the CCM with its many hands-on exhibits and interactive displays focused on world cultures, communication, and technology. In the T.V. studio, pint-sized Sam Donaldsons can enjoy their 15 minutes of fame and test state-of-the-art special-effects equipment. The museum hosts special weekend activities, workshops, and performances. The opportunities for learning at this struggling private museum far outweigh the peeling paint and location. The museum is open from 10am to 5pm from Labor Day to Easter, from 10am to 6pm the rest of the year. Admission is $6 for adults and children 3 and older, free for kids 2 and under. The nearest Metro is Union Station. Even though the museum is nearby, I strongly suggest taking a taxi. This isn't the greatest neighborhood.

Washington Dolls' House & Toy Museum gives Santa's workshop a run for its money. Tucked away in a northwest corner of D.C. near the Chevy Chase, Maryland, border (no passport required to cross), this wonderland of dollhouses and antique toys attracts kids up to 80 and beyond. Collectors will find periodicals on dolls and dollhouses, and miniature accessories (new and consigned) in the second-floor shops. The Dolls' House is at 5236 44th St. NW (☎ 202/244-0024). Hours are Tuesday to Saturday from 10am to 5pm, Sunday from noon to 5pm. Admission is $4 for grown-ups, $2 for rugrats under 12. Take Metro to Friendship Heights and walk west on Western Avenue (toward Lord & Taylor). Turn left at L&T, then right at 44th Street. It may sound like a trek, but it's no more than a 7-minute walk.

The **National Aquarium** is one of the first D.C. sights that area parents introduce their wee ones too. Sharks, eels, and koi (Japanese carp) get along swimmingly in 50 tanks at the nation's oldest aquarium. Luckily for them, the piranhas have their own tank. Don't expect a multilevel state-of-the-art aquarium with all the bells and whistles. No matter. Kids enjoy getting their hands wet in the touch tank. It's not every day of the week they can pet a horseshoe crab. Yuck. The aquarium is located at 14th Street and Constitution Avenue NW (inside the Department of Commerce Building). Fish and federal commerce? Makes sense to me. A piranha or two occasionally feed on the federal payroll. The telephone number is ☎ 202/482-2825 and hours are daily from 9am to 5pm. Admission is $2 adults, 75¢ for those 2 to 10, free if you're 1 or under. Take Metro to Federal Triangle. Walk south on 12th Street 1 block to Constitution Ave. Go right to 14th Street. Right again to the U.S. Department of Commerce.

National Geographic Society's **Explorers Hall** is an oft-overlooked attraction that merits a visit, especially with children over 6. Human evolution, global and space expeditions, and ancient civilizations are the focus in the society's headquarters. Interactive displays and videos encourage visitors to "touch, play, and learn." Orbital flight 23,000 miles above Earth is simulated in the Earth Station One amphitheater. The book and gift shop sells beautiful collections of nature photography, globes, maps, and back issues of *National Geographic* magazine. The museum is near the bustling Connecticut Avenue–K Street crossroads at 17th and M streets NW. The telephone number is ☎ **202/783-5000;** hours are Monday to Saturday from 9am to 5pm, Sunday from 10am to 5pm. Admission is free. Take Metro to Farragut North (Connecticut Avenue and L Street exit). Walk east on L Street 1 block to left at 17th Street and continue 2 blocks to the entrance.

If You Want to See Other Cultures

Anacostia Museum, at 1901 Fort Place SE (off Martin Luther King Jr. Ave; ☎ 202/287-3382), is a national resource devoted to promoting public understanding and knowledge of the African-American experience, with a special focus on the Washington, D.C., area. Historic documents, art, and sheet music are part of the large permanent collection overseen by the Smithsonian, which is augmented by special exhibitions, talks, workshops, and educational programs. With advance reservations, visitors can take a short guided walk along the George Washington Carver nature trail on the museum grounds. Otherwise, forgo walking in this neighborhood. The museum is a bit out of the way, so allow sufficient travel time. The hours are from 10am to 5pm daily. Take Metro to Anacostia, then board a W1 or W2 bus to the museum's door.

Adult visitors need a photo ID (driver's license will do it) to enter the **Department of Interior Museum.** This is not a government decorating firm. Instead, many aspects of Interior business—the National Park Service, Geological Survey, and Bureau of Indian Affairs, to name a few—are displayed here. The exhibits relating to Native American life are most interesting, with pottery, artifacts, crafts, and beadwork. A Native American docent is usually on hand to answer questions and tell stories. The Indian Craft Shop across the hall in Room 1023 is a good spot for gift and souvenir shopping. You'll find the museum near DAR Constitution Hall at 1849 C St. NW

(☎ 202/208-4743). Hours are Monday to Friday from 8am to 4pm. Another D.C. freebie. Take Metro to Farragut West. Walk south 5 blocks on 18th Street, right at C Street, and continue 1 short block.

Frederick Douglass National Historic Site, at 1411 W St. SE (☎ 800/ 365-2267), commemorates the contributions of the abolitionist and orator who called Cedar Hill home. The 20-room Victorian house on the Anacostia River is filled with many of the original furnishings and Douglass memorabilia. In the visitor center a film gives an overview of Douglass's life. The hill out front offers a sweeping view of the Anacostia River, Washington Navy Yard, U.S. Capitol, and Washington Monument. Special programs are ongoing during Black History Month (February). Hours are from 9am to 4pm mid-October to mid-April, from 9am to 5pm the remaining 6 months. Admission is $3 if you're between 7 and 61, $1.50 for age 62 and over, free for kids 6 and under. Take Metro to Anacostia, then hop on a B2/Mt. Rainier bus (8 blocks). Tourmobile also has a special tour that stops here.

If You Want to Read Your Rights

Book lovers will find additional sources for their addiction in chapter 15.

You can't borrow books from the **Library of Congress** (☎ 202/ 707-8000), the nation's—and world's—largest library, but if you're over high-school age, you can use them for research. And you can admire the Great Hall. I wish I had a dime for every hour I spent in the Jefferson Building's Main Reading Room as a college student. Books fill more than 500 miles of shelves, so it's a big improvement over what the public library has to offer. I recommend nonresearchers join the hour-long guided tour. Then take a gander at the Gutenberg Bible and Giant (we're talkin' big, friends) Bible of Mainz on the main floor along with exhibits of posters, music, and photographs. Pierre L'Enfant's blueprint for Washington is in the second-floor Southwest Gallery. Famous icons of pop culture, such as Bert and Ernie, Barbie, and Star Wars masks, reside on the 4th floor of the Madison Building, a block away. The Library of Congress is on Capitol Hill at 1st Street SE between Independence Avenue and E. Capitol Street. It's open Monday through Saturday from 10am to 5pm. Admission is free. Take Metro to Capitol South, then walk north on 1st Street 2 blocks.

If You're Wondering What Happened Here

Where to start? Scandals almost outnumber bureaucrats in Washington. It's hard to pick up a newspaper without learning the sordid details of some congressman's (or president's) illegal or salacious escapades. To round out your visit—and education—I can't pass up the opportunity to share a few scandal sites with you. They're grouped by location.

If You're in Foggy Bottom

At the **Watergate,** 2600 Virginia Ave. NW, in the wee small hours of June 17, 1972, a security guard found a taped-over lock to the bugged offices of the Democratic Party's national headquarters. Inside, five cowering rubber-gloved "burglars" (bunglers is closer to the truth) clutched $100 bills and binoculars. Between that fateful evening and Richard M. Nixon's resignation on August 4, 1974, 25 members of the president's staff were slapped with jail terms by Judge "Maximum John" Sirica.

And, of course, the Watergate is where Monica Lewinsky lived with her mother while a White House intern and special friend to President Clinton. I can add nothing to the overabundance of nauseating media coverage. To catch a glimpse of the Watergate (maybe you'll see the Doles milling about), take Metro to Foggy Bottom. Walk south 3 blocks on New Hampshire Avenue and cross Virginia Avenue.

Across the street at the **Howard Johnson Hotel,** 2601 Virginia Ave., G. Gordon Liddy did his dirty work on behalf of the Watergate caper. The former counsel to the Committee to Re-elect the President ("CREEP"; how's that for an apt acronym?) collected $235,000 for his Watergate efforts.

High Crimes and Misdemeanors?

Now, most people don't think of the father of our country as a sex symbol, but George had a wandering eye. And greasy palms. Sorry to burst your bubble. When he was a mere general, h͝e awarded himself an 8-year expense account of $449,261. He also shared his military plans with one of his mistresses, Mary Gibbons, who snitched to William Tryon, the royal governor of New York. Oops.

If You're Wandering Around the Tidal Basin

Police stopped Rep. Wilbur Mills (the former and dearly departed Arkansas congressman and chairman of the powerful House Ways and Means Committee) at 2am on October 7, 1974, for speeding in a car without head-lights. With Mills was his date for the evening, Fanne (no "i") Foxe, a strip-per who performed under the moniker "the Argentine firecracker." Miss Foxe panicked and dove into the Tidal Basin under the watchful gaze of Mr. Jefferson. Mills later resigned from Ways and Means and did not seek reelec-tion in 1976. (What is it with these Arkansas boys?)

If You're at the Jefferson Hotel

Here at 16th and M streets NW, Dick Morris, former political consultant to President Clinton, kept company with Sherry Rowlands, a $200-an-hour prostitute. The twosome were caught on camera snuggling on the balcony of Suite 205 at this elegant downtown hotel. Sherry claimed that Morris shared insider secrets with her and let her listen in on conversations with Bill and Hill.

If You're at the Willard Hotel

At this venerable address at 1455 Pennsylvania Ave. NW, **Ulysses S. Grant** met with influence peddlers over brandy and cigars in the old Willard lobby (hence the term *lobbyist*). Robber barons wheeled and dealed here, buying politicians' votes in exchange for whisky and cash during the Civil War.

If You're at the Vista Hotel (1400 M St. NW—on Scott Circle)

Vowing that "the bitch set me up," hizzoner **Marion Barry** (the former D.C. mayor, druggie, and womanizer) was caught on videotape in an FBI sting, in Room 727, January 18, 1990, taking hits from a crack pipe. Hey, it's a pressured job. A guy has to relax once in a while. At his side was former model Rasheeda Moore (a.k.a. "the bitch"). At the trial, where he faced 14 separate drug charges, sordid details of Barry's frequent forays into drugs and sex came to light. He was convicted only on one count of cocaine possession. During his 6-month incarceration in Petersburg, Virginia, he rid himself of stress in the prison's visiting room (in plain view of about 40 inmates and their families) at the hands of a prostitute. Now comes the surreal conclusion: Despite his "poor judgment," and despite the pathetic showing of his administration (14 members censured for fiscal wrongdoing), the people of the District of Columbia reelected Marion Barry. I am not making this up. He was sworn in for a fourth term on January 2, 1995. Definitely fodder for "Ripley's Believe It or Not." The good news is he is not back for a fifth term. In January 1999, Anthony A. Williams was sworn in as D.C.'s new mayor. Attila the Hun would have been an improvement.

If You're on the Hill

Here's a frame of reference, as you peruse the following section. If you face the west facade of the Capitol (actually the back, which overlooks the Mall), the House of Representatives is to the right of the dome; the Senate is to the left.

At the **Longworth Office Building** on Independence and New Jersey avenues SE, Elizabeth Ray earned $14,000 a year (not bad in 1974) in Room 1506 as a secretary to Rep. Wayne Hays of Ohio. Trouble was, she didn't type or answer phones and, after 2 years, had grown tired of his shenanigans. Motivated by fear that she would lose her job after Hays married another of his secretaries, Ray went to the *Washington Post* with her story. Hays was real upset. His career ended abruptly and he subsequently overdosed on prescription medication (unsuccessfully). Just another shining example of our tax dollars at work.

Stephen Gobie, one-time boyfriend and housekeeper of **Rep. Barney Frank,** Democratic congressman from Massachusetts, ran a male escort service (how's that for a euphemism?) out of Frank's Capitol Hill residence. And Frank didn't have a clue. Right. And I'm the Mayflower Madam.

If You Want to Burn Off Some Steam

Chances are that hoofing it between museums will provide you with sufficient exercise during your visit. But if you still have energy to burn, take a power walk around the Tidal Basin or Mall, swim laps in the hotel pool, tone up your thumb on the remote, or try one of the following.

If You Have Two Wheels

Bike the Sites, Inc. (☎ 202/966-8662) has four biking tours of the city. The hour-long Early Bird Fun Ride on 21-speed Trek Hybrids is moderately paced and costs $25. Guides lead the way while imparting historical information. If you want to strike out on your own, rent a bike and head for the C&O Canal towpath, which begins in Georgetown. Bike rentals run about $20 a

Hear Ye! Hear Ye!

Hiking paths abound in and around Washington. Break in those new boots along the C&O Canal, the 20 miles of trails in Rock Creek Park, or the short-but-rugged $2\frac{1}{2}$-mile trail on Theodore Roosevelt Island. (See the parks listed in chapter 13.)

day for a 10-speed. Call **Big Wheel Bikes** (☎ 202/337-0245) in Georgetown. You can cycle all the way from Georgetown to Seneca, Maryland, 23 miles away, and be back in time for the 11 o'clock news (maybe). Or pick up the trail along the George Washington Memorial Parkway on the Virginia side of Memorial Bridge. But please, I beg you, don't ride on Washington, D.C., streets unescorted unless you have a strong death wish. It's a short pedal over to the C&O Canal. Traffic is horrific around here, so be careful and remember to look both ways before crossing Canal Road.

If You Want to Row, Row, Row Your Boat

From late March through October you can burn calories on the Potomac River while enjoying Washington at its most photogenic. Rent a canoe or rowboat at **Thompson's,** Rock Creek Parkway and Virginia Avenue NW, across from the Watergate and a short walk from the Foggy Bottom Metro station (☎ 202/333-4861), or **Fletcher's,** 4940 Canal Rd. NW (☎ 202/244-0461)—take a taxi. Hourly rates vary but average $20 to $25 per boat per day. Tone your legs in a paddleboat on the Tidal Basin, near the Jefferson Memorial; $7 per hour for a two-seater, $14 for a four-seater (☎ 202/484-0206).

Hear Ye! Hear Ye!

Do you want to root, root, root for the home team? Well, better head out to Camden Yards in Baltimore to see the American League's Baltimore Orioles (☎ 410/685-9800). Camden Yards is a cool ballpark, fashioned from a warehouse to resemble old-time fields of dreams. MARC trains whip fans from Union Station in D.C. directly to the stadium. O's tickets are snatched up way in advance (☎ 800/551-SEAT). There's also a D.C. ticket office at 914 17th St. NW (☎ 202/296-2473).

If You'd Like to See the House That George Built

Rightly so, many feel that no trip to Washington, D.C., is complete without a visit to Georgie Porgie's riverfront estate. **Mount Vernon** (☎ 703/780-2000) lies (but never *lies*) 16 miles south of D.C. To reach Mount Vernon by car, cross the Potomac—any bridge will do—into Virginia and pick up the George Washington Memorial Parkway south to the plantation. If you're without wheels, you can still get there from here. April through October only, **Tourmobile buses** (☎ 202/554-5100) depart daily from Arlington National Cemetery and the Washington Monument. The round-trip fare of $20 ($10 for kids 3 to 11; free for children under 3) includes admission to the estate. Other options are **Gray Line bus tours** (☎ 202/289-1995) and **Spirit of Washington Cruises** (☎ 202/554-8000; every month but November and December).

Many of the original furnishings remain in rooms painted in George's favorite colors. Exemplary of 18th-century architecture and the lifestyle of that era's rich and famous, the home sits on 500 acres (originally 8,000) of prime waterfront property. The father of our country rode horseback on the lawn and oversaw every facet of the plantation's operation. Some of the trees he planted thrive in front of the mansion. Washington retired here in 1797 and died 2 years later. He's buried in the family tomb, along with Martha and other kinfolk.

Tours of the home are self-guided, but docents are strategically located to answer questions. Thirty-minute walking tours of the slave burial ground and gardens are offered April through October at 10am, noon, 2pm, and 4pm. Outside the main gate are a snack bar and the Mount Vernon Inn restaurant (☎ 703/780-0011), with three fireplaces and wait staff in 18th-century garb. Picnicking is allowed in Riverside Park, 1 mile north of the estate. If you're driving, you may want to stop midway between Washington and Mount Vernon in Old Town, Alexandria, with scores of restaurants, shops, and historic sites.

If You Want to Visit an Old Town

One could easily spend a day in this charming seaport town of Old Town, Virginia, settled in the mid-18th century by Scottish tobacco merchants.

Tourist Traps

When planning a trip to Alexandria, you should keep in mind that a lot of the attractions are closed on Monday.

Despite massive urban renewal, much of the colonial ambience is intact. For information, call or stop at the **Alexandria Convention and Visitors Association,** in the Ramsay House, at 221 King St. (☎ 703/838-4200).

To get to Old Town by car, take the Arlington Memorial or 14th Street Bridge into Virginia and the George Washington Memorial Parkway south. In Old Town, the parkway becomes

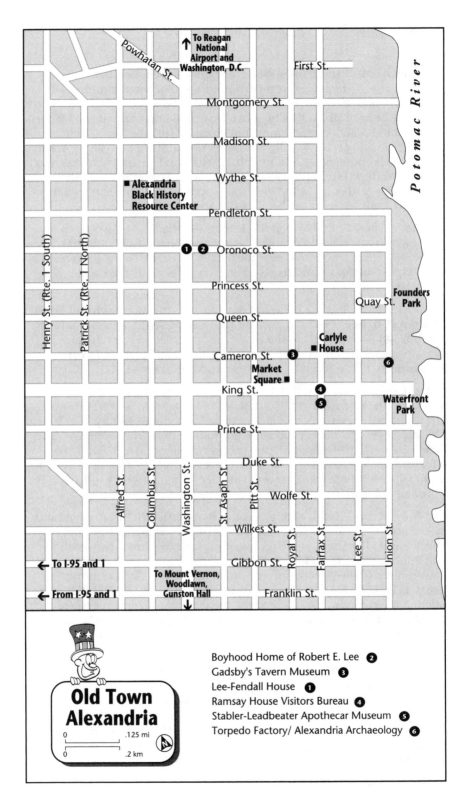

Powhatan St.

To Reagan National Airport and Washington, D.C.

First St.

Montgomery St.

Madison St.

Wythe St.

■ Alexandria Black History Resource Center

Pendleton St.

① **②** Oronoco St.

Princess St.

Queen St.

Quay St.

Founders Park

Carlyle House

Cameron St. **③** ■

Market Square ■

King St. **④**

⑤

⑥

Waterfront Park

Prince St.

Duke St.

Wolfe St.

Wilkes St.

← To I-95 and 1

Gibbon St.

To Mount Vernon, Woodlawn, Gunston Hall

← From I-95 and 1

Franklin St.

Henry St. (Rte. 1 South)

Patrick St. (Rte. 1 North)

Alfred St.

Columbus St.

Washington St.

St. Asaph St.

Pitt St.

Royal St.

Fairfax St.

Lee St.

Union St.

Potomac River

Old Town Alexandria

0   .125 mi

0   .2 km

Boyhood Home of Robert E. Lee **②**
Gadsby's Tavern Museum **③**
Lee-Fendall House **①**
Ramsay House Visitors Bureau **④**
Stabler-Leadbeater Apothecar Museum **⑤**
Torpedo Factory/ Alexandria Archaeology **⑥**

209

Washington Street and crosses King Street, the neighborhood's main east–west artery. The tourist area lies within a grid between Washington Street and the waterfront (7 blocks to the east), and for about 6 blocks north and south of King Street. Pick up a free 1-day parking permit at the Visitors Association (see above), good for complimentary parking at any 2-hour meter. Street and garage parking are also available. It's less hassle, especially on weekends and holidays, when traffic is thick and parking is scarce, to take **Metro's Yellow Line** to the King Street station. Then catch a DASH bus (AT2 or AT5) eastbound to the Visitors Association. Otherwise, it's about a mile walk from Metro to the heart of Old Town.

Pick up brochures and a map at the Visitors Association and strike out on your own, or take a guided walking tour. **Alexandria Tours** (☎ 703/ 461-0955) offers 1-hour overview tours daily. The **Old Town Experience** (☎ 703/836-0694) tour visits several historic sites along the cobblestone streets, by advance reservation only.

Among the many historic buildings open to visitors is the **Boyhood Home of Robert E. Lee** at 607 Oronoco St. (between St. Asaph and Washington; ☎ 703/548-8454). Tours of the Federal-style mansion are given daily. Washington, Jefferson, and Madison broke bread at **Gadsby's Tavern Museum,** at 134 N. Royal St. (at Cameron; ☎ 703/838-4242).

In the **Torpedo Factory,** 105 N. Union St. (between King and Cameron streets on the waterfront; ☎ 703/838-4565), 160 artists and craftspeople create and sell their wares in a former torpedo shell–case factory. A visit to the Torpedo Factory is an experience not to be missed when touring Old Town. Exhibits on Alexandria's past are also displayed here, courtesy of **Alexandria Archaeology** (☎ 703/838-4399). Shopping is primo in Old Town where boutiques and gift and antiques shops cluster on and around King and Cameron streets.

Old Town is chockablock with places to eat, from storefront carry-outs and cafes to cozy pubs and fine restaurants. Pick up a sandwich at the **Deli on the Strand,** The Strand no. 5 (entrance on S. Union Street, between Duke and Prince streets; ☎ 703/683-5340), and picnic under an awning or on the grassy shores of the Potomac. Catch up on news from the U.K. at the **Tea Cosy,** 1119 S. Royal St. (between King and Prince streets; ☎ 703/836-8181), offering finger sandwiches and scones, shepherd's pie, Cornish pasties, and British ales. **Chadwick's,** at 203 S. Strand St. (☎ 703/836-4422), has good hamburgers and other well-priced, palatable pub fare in an attractive, family-friendly eatery.

Before or after the 30-minute tour of the Tavern Museum, visitors can dine in the authentically re-created **Gadsby's Tavern,** 134 N. Royal St. (at Cameron; ☎ 703/838-4242). The wait staff, in colonial duds, serve Sally Lunn bread and G.W.'s favorite—roast duckling with fruit stuffing. Stained glass and murals depict scenes from *The Hobbit* at **Bilbo Baggins,** 208 Queen St. (at Lee; ☎ 703/683-0300). Imaginative vegetarian dishes, pasta, and seafood star in this cozy, two-story restaurant featuring 30-plus wines by the glass.

Where to Shop 'til You Drop

Okay, so you came to Washington to visit some monuments and memorials, get a firsthand look at Archie Bunker's chair, and see government in action, but shopping shouldn't be relegated to the bottom of your list. Washington may not be known as a shopping mecca like, say, New York, but there are plenty of places where you can whip out your plastic or find some good deals. If you're looking for major department stores, you'll have to head out to the suburbs, but for some unique finds in the city, read on, and I'll show you the best way to go Mall-to-mall shopping.

Prime Shopping Hours

It'd be nice for us shoppers if all the stores got together and decided on the same hours. But that's as realistic as government bigwigs giving up their VIP parking spaces at Reagan National Airport.

Business hours vary widely by type of shop and location. Most shops open at 9 or 9:30am and close at 5:30 or 6pm. Some stay open later one or more evenings. But you have to remember that Washington is not a late-night town. After dark, most D.C. workers exit the city like passengers on the *Titanic*. They're either burning the midnight oil or unwinding behind picket fences miles away. Many businesses in heavily trafficked areas, such as

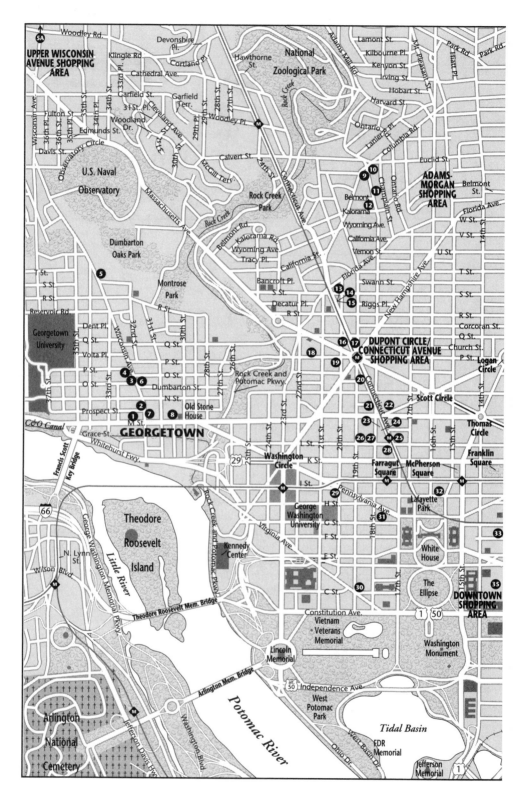

UPPER WISCONSIN
AVENUE SHOPPING
AREA

Woodley Rd.

Devonshire
Pl.

Klingle Rd.

Cortland Pl.

Cathedral Ave.

Garfield St.

Garfield
Terr.

31st St.

Cleveland Ave.

Woodland
Dr.

Edmunds St.

Davis St.

Fulton St.

Observatory Circle

U.S. Naval

Observatory

Dumbarton
Oaks Park

Massachusetts Ave.

Reservoir Rd.

Georgetown
University

Dent Pl.

Q St.

Volta Pl.

P St.

O St.

Prospect St.

Dumbarton St.

N St.

M St.

C&O Canal

Grace St.

Whitehurst Fwy.

GEORGETOWN

Old Stone
House

Montrose
Park

T St.

S St.

R St.

Rock Creek
Park

Rock Creek

Rock Creek and
Potomac Pkwy.

Calvert St.

McGill Terr.

Woodley Pl.

Belmont Rd.

Wyoming Ave.
Tracy Pl.

Kalorama Rd.

California St.

Bancroft Pl.

S St.

Decatur Pl.

R St.

Connecticut Ave.

National
Zoological Park

Hawthorne
St.

Rock Creek

Lamont St.

Kilbourne Pl.

Kenyon St.

Irving St.

Hobart St.

Harvard St.

Adams Mill Rd.

Mt. Pleasant St.

Park Rd.

Park Rd.

Hiatt Pl.

Ontario Pl.

Lanier Pl.

Columbia Rd.

Euclid St.

ADAMS-
MORGAN
SHOPPING
AREA

Belmont
St.

Belmont

Kalorama

Wyoming Ave.

California Ave.

Vernon St.

Ontario Rd.

Champlain St.

Florida Ave.

W St.

V St.

U St.

New Hampshire Ave.

Florida Ave.

Swann St.

Riggs Pl.

T St.

S St.

R St.

Corcoran St.

Q St.

Church St.

P St.

Logan
Circle

DUPONT CIRCLE/
CONNECTICUT AVENUE
SHOPPING AREA

Scott Circle

Thomas
Circle

Franklin
Square

McPherson
Square

Farragut
Square

Washington
Circle

Washington
Circle

Pennsylvania Ave.

Lafayette
Park

White
House

The
Ellipse

DOWNTOWN
SHOPPING
AREA

Washington
Monument

Francis Scott
Key Bridge

66

N. Lynn
St.

Wilson Blvd.

Arlington

National

Cemetery

Theodore

Roosevelt

Island

Little River

George Washington Memorial Pkwy.

Theodore Roosevelt Mem. Bridge

Rock Creek and Potomac Pkwy.

Kennedy
Center

George
Washington
University

Virginia Ave.

H St.

G St.

F St.

E St.

C St.

Constitution Ave.

Vietnam
Veterans
Memorial

Lincoln
Memorial

Arlington Mem. Bridge

Jefferson Davis Hwy.

Washington Blvd.

Potomac River

Independence Ave.

West
Potomac
Park

Tidal Basin

FDR
Memorial

Jefferson
Memorial

West Basin Dr.

Ohio Dr.

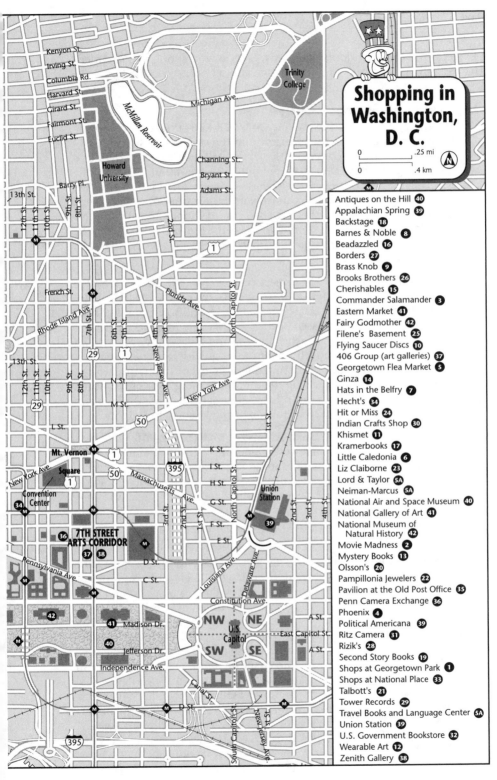

Shopping in Washington, D. C.

0   .25 mi
0   .4 km

Antiques on the Hill **40**
Appalachian Spring **39**
Backstage **18**
Barnes & Noble **8**
Beadazzled **16**
Borders **27**
Brass Knob **9**
Brooks Brothers **26**
Cherishables **15**
Commander Salamander **3**
Eastern Market **41**
Fairy Godmother **42**
Filene's Basement **25**
Flying Saucer Discs **10**
406 Group (art galleries) **37**
Georgetown Flea Market **5**
Ginza **14**
Hats in the Belfry **7**
Hecht's **34**
Hit or Miss **24**
Indian Crafts Shop **30**
Khismet **11**
Kramerbooks **17**
Little Caledonia **6**
Liz Claiborne **23**
Lord & Taylor **5A**
Neiman-Marcus **5A**
National Air and Space Museum **40**
National Gallery of Art **41**
National Museum of Natural History **42**
Movie Madness **2**
Mystery Books **13**
Olsson's **20**
Pampillonia Jewelers **22**
Pavilion at the Old Post Office **35**
Penn Camera Exchange **36**
Phoenix **4**
Political Americana **39**
Ritz Camera **31**
Rizik's **28**
Second Story Books **19**
Shops at Georgetown Park **1**
Shops at National Place **33**
Talbott's **21**
Tower Records **29**
Travel Books and Language Center **5A**
Union Station **39**
U.S. Government Bookstore **32**
Wearable Art **12**
Zenith Gallery **38**

213

Georgetown, keep their doors open later, especially in spring and summer. The best advice I can offer is to call before you set out.

Department Stores Galore

➤ **Hecht's.** 12th and G sts. NW (☎ 202/628-6661). Take Metro to Metro Center and ride the escalator into the store. At this spacious emporium, which is conveniently located at Metro Center, you'll find a mix of conservative (D.C.'s favored nonstyle) and trendy. The strongest departments are cosmetics, housewares, lingerie, and men's casual wear and furnishings. If your last pair of pantyhose has a run or you need a tie or lipstick in a hurry, this is a good place to shop. Actually, it's the only downtown place to shop if you seek the breadth offered by a department store. Hecht's has suburban branches in Maryland and Virginia too.

➤ **Filene's Basement.** 1133 Connecticut Ave. NW (☎ 202/872-8430). Take Metro to Farragut North (L Street exit), walk west a few doors to Connecticut Avenue, and right. Although I'm still wearing a $49 blazer I purchased at a Boston-based Filene's 7 years ago, more recent visits have proved less successful. The clothing and accessories—for men and women, no kidswear—run the gamut from quality to shlock. Sometimes you have to rummage through mountains of tightly packed merchandise to find the big bargain (sort of like kissing a lot of toads to find a prince). Filene's is also in the Mazza Gallerie at 5300 Wisconsin Ave. NW (☎ 202/966-0208). Take Metro to Friendship Heights.

➤ **Lord & Taylor.** 5225 Western Ave. NW (☎ 202/362-9600). Metro to Friendship Heights and walk west 1 block on Western Avenue to the big white building at the corner of Jenifer Street. An offshoot of the New York chain, Lord & Taylor's women's wear and accessories and children's clothing are the strongest departments. I loved to shop here when my kidlets were young and willing to wear what I picked out. Lord & Taylor's sales are legendary (there's usually a sale going on in at least one department); lots of quality merchandise with swell markdowns.

➤ **Neiman–Marcus.** Mazza Gallerie, 5300 Wisconsin Ave. NW (☎ 202/966-9700). Take Metro to Friendship Heights, then walk south on Wisconsin Avenue, a block or so. I don't get it. Every time I'm in Neiman's you could shoot a cannon off. How do they stay in business? Although there's plenty of well-displayed upscale (and expensive) merchandise, I'm thankful that it doesn't cost a farthing to look. The salespeople are so pleasant and helpful, they'll pick you up when you faint after looking at the price tags. It's fun shopping for wedding gifts here, as the china and crystal are noteworthy. Serious shoppers circle like buzzards at the half-yearly sales.

A Taxing Issue

The sales tax in Washington is 5.75%. It probably took a task force of 300 to come up with the number. Why don't they round it off and make everyone's life simpler?

You'll find no recliners, little print housedresses, or $2 kitchen gadgets. (Neiman's and Filene's in the same mall? From the sublime to the ridiculous.)

Good Bill Hunting—Prime Shopping Areas

During your visit, perhaps as a break from museum brain drain, you may want to peruse the following shopping areas. Each wears its own distinctive aura.

Adams–Morgan

Perhaps the liveliest and most ethnically diverse of D.C. neighborhoods radiates from the crossroads of 18th Street and Columbia Road NW. While you'll find more restaurants and clubs than retail stores, there are plenty of second-hand and one-of-a-kind shops. Maybe while you're walking off dinner or people-watching, you'll pick up a trinket or two. **Flying Saucer Discs,** 3218 18th St. NW (☎ **202/265-DISC;** Metro: Dupont Circle), sells used jazz, pop, rock, and classical CDs from its basement store. Decorators and do-it-yourselfers love to mine the **Brass Knob,** 2311 18th St. NW (☎ **202/ 332-3370;** Metro: Dupont Circle), for architectural finds salvaged from demolished houses and office buildings. Colorful garments, made of African-inspired textiles, by designer Millee Spears of Ghana, fill **Khismet Wearable Art,** 1800 Belmont Rd. NW (☎ **202/234-7778;** Metro: Dupont Circle or Woodley Park/National Zoo). Parking is impossible in Adams–Morgan and it's an uphill schlepp from the Dupont Circle Metro station. Unless you're in great shape, do yourself a favor and take a taxi, especially after dark.

Hear Ye! Hear Ye!

You'll find some of the best and most diverse shopping—for quality crafts, books, and souvenirs—in the museum and gallery shops. Since you'll already be visiting the museums, you'll have a head start on emptying your wallet of all that excess paper. Here are some of my favorites:

➤ **John F. Kennedy Center for the Performing Arts,** 2700 F St. NW (☎ **202/416-8350**), for posters, performing arts memorabilia, videos, and CDs.

➤ **National Air and Space Museum,** Independence Ave. and 7th St. SW (☎ **202/357-1387**), for flight-related books, posters, and souvenirs.

➤ **National Gallery of Art,** Constitution Ave. between 4th and 6th sts. NW (☎ **202/737-4215**), for art posters, books, and stationery.

➤ **National Geographic Society,** 17th and M sts. NW (☎ **202/ 857-7588**), for maps, globes, and back issues of *National Geographic* magazine.

➤ **National Museum of Natural History,** 10th St. and Constitution Ave. NW (☎ **202/357-1537**), for crafts, books, clothing, and jewelry.

Connecticut Avenue/Dupont Circle

Stores on the lower end of Connecticut Avenue, around K Street NW, reflect the armies of tasteful suits scurrying up the ladder around D.C.'s equivalent of Wall Street. So it's no surprise to find such bastions of conservatism as **Brooks Brothers,** 1840 L St. NW (☎ **202/659-4650**); **Talbot's,** 1227 Connecticut Ave. NW (☎ **202/887-6973**); **Burberry's,** 1155 Connecticut Ave. NW (☎ **202/463-3000**); or **Liz Claiborne,** 1144 Connecticut Ave. NW (☎ **202/785-8625**). For casual wear, mosey into my favorite *couturier,* the **Gap,** 1120 Connecticut Ave. (☎ **202/429-0691**). Women invited to a formal affair at the White House, with nothing to wear, head for **Rizik's,** 1100 Connecticut Ave. NW (☎ **202/223-4050**), for designer duds and expert service. For affordable office-appropriate and casual wear, try **Hit or Miss,** 1140 Connecticut Ave. (☎ **202/223-8231**).

The mood alters noticeably as you approach Dupont Circle, with fewer ties and briefcases, more jeans and multipierced anatomy. Scour the galleries, bookstores, secondhand shops, and gay boutiques in this laid-back neighborhood that's D.C.'s equivalent of Greenwich Village. Try **Kramerbooks & Afterwords** for books and a cappuccino, at 1517 Connecticut Ave. NW (☎ **202/387-1400**); **Cherishables,** 1608 20th St. NW (☎ **202/785-4087**), for American folk art, furniture, and quilts; or **Backstage,** 2101 P St. NW (☎ **202/775-1488**), for scripts, sheet music, and theatrical makeup (some of which is great for masking imperfections on nontheatrical faces). At **Beadazzled,** 1522 Connecticut Ave. NW (☎ **202/265-BEAD**), the staff will help you assemble a necklace from the large selection of beads. You can outfit yourself in a kimono and fan at **Ginza,** 1721 Connecticut Ave. NW (☎ **202/331-7991**).

Downtown/Federal Triangle

On a stretch of Pennsylvania Avenue between 11th and 14th streets NW, dominated by federal and district office buildings, is the elegant Willard Inter-Continental Hotel at the corner of 14th Street. Nearby are the National Press Club, National Theater, and J. W. Marriott, as well as the **Shops at National Place** (enter on F Street NW between 13th and 14th streets; ☎ **202/783-9090**). The four-level mall in the National Press Building has **Electonique** (electronic gadgets), **Capitol Image** (souvenirs), **Curious Kids** (toys), and **B. Dalton** (books), as well as numerous places to purchase clothing, shoes, and accessories. The Food Hall on the top level hawks a variety of fast foods and desserts. Metro Center is only a block away.

A visit to the **Pavilion at the Old Post Office,** Pennsylvania Ave. and 11th St. NW (☎ **202/289-4224**), is most worthwhile for the architecture and elevator ride to the clock tower for a stunning view of the city. Touristy shops sell souvenirs and glorified junk for the most part. Maybe that's why kids enjoy coming here. More-than-adequate chow (try the spicy chicken wings and bleu cheese dip) is available at a variety of food stands, which offer mouthwatering specialties ranging from sandwiches and hamburgers to Indian and Oriental fare.

🌟 Georgetown

I must admit that I liked Georgetown better during my student days when there were fewer record stores and less-scruffy-looking youths; no mall; and more boutiques, parking spaces, and properly attired blue-haired ladies. Georgetown still has a certain cache, however, and shoppers of all ages enjoy spending money here.

Shops line both sides of M Street NW, from 28th to 36th streets, and Wisconsin Avenue, from the C&O Canal (below M Street) north to R Street, as well as many of the side streets. On the down side, the nearest Metro station, Foggy Bottom, is a mile away, and street parking is scarce. There are a few lots, but they fill up quickly, especially on weekends. A strict disciple of the K.I.S.S. (Keep it simple, stupid) philosophy, I humbly suggest taking a taxi from wherever you're staying.

Besides an overabundance of record stores and branches of national chains (**Gap, Banana Republic, Benetton,** and **Original Levi's Store**), there are some treasured old-timers in Georgetown that bear mentioning. **Movie Madness,** 1222 Wisconsin Ave. (☎ 202/337-7064), sells movie posters. At **Commander Salamander,** 1420 Wisconsin Ave. (☎ 202/337-2265), you can purchase the latest in black leather or have your hair streaked with DayGlo orange. The original **Hats in the Belfry,** 1237 Wisconsin Ave. (☎ 202/342-2006), sells a large selection of stylish and outlandish chapeaux out of its closet-sized but highly successful shop. Since 1955, **The Phoenix,** 1514 Wisconsin Ave. NW (☎ 202/338-4404), has been selling Mexican folk art and bric-a-brac, handcrafted silver jewelry, and those gauzy peasant blouses favored by Joan Baez disciples. My all-time favorite Georgetown shop is still **Little Caledonia,** 1419 Wisconsin Ave. (☎ 202/333-4700), in business for more than 60 years. I could spend days browsing through the Lilliputian rooms crammed with china, home and kitchen furnishings, and toys. If Little Caledonia closes, I'm giving up my citizenship.

Balancing the Budget

If you insist on driving into Georgetown after all my warnings, you should park in the garage beneath Georgetown Park (enter on Wisconsin Avenue, just below M Street). The garage gives a break on parking with proof of a $10 purchase from one of the shops in the mall.

And then there's the **Shops at Georgetown Park,** 3222 M St. NW (☎ 202/342-8180), a handsome mall done in brick, brass, and potted plants. Well-heeled travelers, diplomats, and matrons (urban and suburban) frequent the galleries and pricey boutiques for art and fine leather goods, imported children's clothing, overpriced toys, and new threads. The rest of us head for **Mrs. Field's** for a double-chocolate-chip cookie and bury

217

ourselves in the stacks at **Waldenbooks.** This is a fine place for browsing unless you have deep pockets. Very deep.

Kids Union Station

For some of us, shopping is secondary in this magnificent choo-choo station, restored in the 1980s at great expense, and worth every greenback dollar, I'd say. Please look around before bolting for the 75 shops. Many are offshoots of national chains, like **Brookstone** (gadgets), **B. Dalton** (books), and **The Nature Company** (environmentally themed books and tchotchkes). Elsewhere you'll find everything from women's wear to political memorabilia and handcrafted jewelry. You'd be way off track to bypass the **Great Train Store** on the main floor. Some very good restaurants are located throughout the station (I'm partial to B. Smith's), and the quintessential food court is on the lower level, with better-than-average food. The shops are open Monday through Saturday from 10am to 9pm, Sunday from 10am to 6pm. Restaurants have varying hours. Union Station is near the U.S. Capitol at 50 Massachusetts Ave. NE (☎ **202/371-9441**). The Union Station Metro station is downstairs.

Upper Wisconsin Avenue NW

An exclusive shopping corridor crosses the line between Washington and Chevy Chase, Maryland. Known as Friendship Heights, the largely residential area boasts a score of upscale and designer shops on Wisconsin Avenue (**Tiffany's, Gianni Versace, Cartier, Saks–Jandel,** to name a few). On the Maryland side, to the north, is **Saks Fifth Avenue.** Within D.C.'s border are **Lord & Taylor** (see "Department Stores Galore" above) and two malls: the **Mazza Gallerie,** 5300 Wisconsin Ave. NW (☎ **202/966-6114**), with **Neiman–Marcus, Filene's,** and numerous specialty shops; and **Chevy Chase Pavilion,** 5345 Wisconsin Ave. NW (☎ **202/686-5335**), with a wide range of offerings, from the classic, tailored clothing at **Country Road Australia** to the consummate container store, **Hold Everything.** One of the area's most popular and well-populated restaurants, the Cheesecake Factory, is here.

Where to Find That Little Something: Specialty Stores

Antiques

You'll find beautiful old furniture, art, jewelry, and the like at antique shops throughout the area, but few bargains. Within D.C., the greatest concentration is on Capitol Hill and in Georgetown. Further afield, head for Antique Row in Kensington, Maryland, or Old Town Alexandria, Virginia. At Antique Row more than 40 antiques and collectibles shops line up like tin soldiers along Howard Avenue, off Upper Connecticut Avenue, in suburban Kensington, Maryland. It's worth the half-hour drive from the District for good deals on everything from accessories to furniture. If you're driving, go north on Connecticut Avenue (County Road no. 185) into Maryland, about

5½ miles past the D.C. line. Turn right at Howard Avenue (there's a Safeway on the corner). Or take a northbound L8 (Aspen Hill) bus from the Friendship Heights Metro station at Wisconsin and Western avenues NW.

If you're going to stay a closer to the District, begin your search at **Antiques-on-the-Hill,** 701 North Carolina Ave. SE (☎ **202/543-1819;** Metro: Eastern Market), with a little of this and a little of that, or the **Brass Knob,** 2311 18th St. NW (☎ **202/332-3370;** Metro: Dupont Circle), for architectural finds salvaged from demolished houses and office buildings.

Art Galleries

While galleries are scattered throughout the city, the majority can be found in Dupont Circle, Georgetown, and on 7th Street NW (known in official circles as the 7th Street Arts Corridor) between D and H streets (Metro: Gallery Place/Chinatown).

Among my favorites are the **Addison/Ripley Gallery, Ltd.,** 9 Hillyer Ct. NW (☎ **202/328-2332;** Metro: Dupont Circle), for works by contemporary artists (some local). Along the **7th Street Arts Corridor** you'll find a wealth of contemporary paintings, prints, and drawings, by national and international artists at the **406 Group,** 406 7th St. NW. The spacious old building is shared by **David Adamson Gallery** (☎ **202/628-0257**), **Baumgartner Gallery** (☎ **202/232-6320**), and **Touchstone Gallery** (☎ **202/347-2787**), a 15-member co-op. Across the street is the **Zenith Gallery,** 413 7th St. NW (☎ **202/783-2963**). Much of the contemporary art here is by locals. The Zenith is probably best known for its annual neon and humor shows.

Bookstores

Washington is a bookish town with a number of chain bookstores, such as B. Dalton, Barnes & Noble, Borders, Crown (dwindling after major financial woes caused by Haft family's rifts), and Walden. Don't overlook the museum stores for a wide selection of special-interest books.

If you're looking to while away the hours by browsing at a Barnes & Noble or Borders superstore, you're in luck. More than 150,000 titles fill the three-level **Barnes & Noble** in Georgetown, 3040 M St. NW (between 30th and 31st streets; ☎ **202/965-9880**). Housed in an old warehouse, B&N has a coffee bar, extensive newsstand, and plenty of comfy seating. The closest Metro is Foggy Bottom. Walk north on 23rd street to Pennsylvania Avenue, cross the street and catch any no. 30 bus to 30th and M streets, or walk the 7 blocks from 23rd Street.

At last count, **Borders,** 1800 L St. NW (at 18th Street; ☎ **202/466-4999**), stocked 200,000 titles, as well as videos, tapes, and CDs, in its megastore in the heart of Downtown. While the kiddies attend the Saturday morning story hour for preschoolers, parents enjoy a few quiet moments perusing the shelves or sipping a latte from the cafe/coffee bar. Take Metro to Farragut North, walk south half a block on Connecticut Avenue, right at L Street, and 1 block to Borders.

Hear Ye! Hear Ye!

The National Air and Space Museum may be the most visited museum in the world, but it's not the top draw in the D.C. area. What could be more popular? Over 13,000 buses (that's not including individuals who drive) a year bring visitors to **Potomac Mills** located in Prince William, Virginia. And for good reason. Shoppers flock to the outlet stores here, which offer incredible bargains. Stores of interest include: **Ikea, Barney's New York,** a **Nordstrom** outlet, a **Spiegel** outlet, a **Saks Fifth Avenue** outlet, **TJ Maxx**—the list goes on and on.

Potomac Mills is located 12 miles south of D.C.'s Capital Beltway, at exit 156 off of I-95. For $12 round-trip, you can take a shuttle bus that picks up shoppers at several Metro stations in downtown D.C.; call ATW Transportation at ☎ **703/551-1050** for a schedule and list of pickup points. If there's no answer, call the Potomac Mills information number at ☎ **800/VA-MILLS.**

Of the independent booksellers, I like the personal service at the four D.C. **Olsson'ses:** 1307 19th St. NW (off Dupont Circle; ☎ **202/785-1133;** Metro: Dupont Circle); 1200 F St. NW (at Metro Center; ☎ **202/347-3686;** Metro: Metro Center); 1239 Wisconsin Ave. NW (between M and N streets; ☎ **202/338-9544;** Metro: Foggy Bottom); 418 7th St. NW (in the Lansburgh Building, between D and E streets NW; ☎ **202/638-7610**). Some hardcovers and paperbacks are discounted, and the sales staff's recommendations are usually right on.

Fairy Godmother, 319 7th St. SE (on Capitol Hill; ☎ **202/547-5474;** Metro: Eastern Market), carries a wide selection of children's books and has story times for preschoolers. You can also buy toys from the Godmother.

Second Story Books, 2000 P St. NW (☎ **202/659-8884;** Metro: Dupont Circle), is the place for old and out-of-print books, used CDs, and advertising posters. Browsing is not only tolerated, it's encouraged.

If you didn't get your fill of Monica and Bill in 1998 and '99, you can purchase the unedited transcripts of their grand jury testimonies (unless sold out) at the **U.S. Government Bookstore,** 1510 H St. NW (between 15th and 16th streets; ☎ **202/653-5075;** Metro: McPherson Square). You can also pick up other, less-offensive government documents and publications generated by the Government Printing Office. (Makes for great bedtime reading. Zzzzz . . .). The store is open Monday through Friday from 8am to 4pm.

Travel Books and Language Center, 4437 Wisconsin Ave. NW (☎ **202/237-1322;** Metro: Tenleytown), is one of the *country's* foremost purveyors of travel-related books (guides, memoirs, diaries, fiction, and photography), maps, language dictionaries, and tapes. I spend so much time here, I'm thinking of renting space in the back.

Go to **Mystery Books,** 1715 Connecticut Ave. NW (☎ **202/483-1600;** Metro: Dupont Circle), to find out whodunit to whom, with what, even if you lack the first clue.

Cameras

Weekend shutterbugs and professionals head for **Penn Camera Exchange,** 915 E St. NW (☎ **202/347-5777;** Metro Center or Gallery Place), for discounts on brand names and quality processing. Penn also buys, trades, rents, and repairs used equipment.

Ritz Camera, 1740 Pennsylvania Ave. NW. (☎ **202/466-3470;** Metro: Farragut West; several other locations), is a one-stop photo shop with 1-hour photofinishing and an on-site enlarger for your favorite D.C. photos.

CDs & Tapes

Tower Records, 2000 Pennsylvania Ave. NW (☎ **202/331-2400;** Metro: Foggy Bottom), has the area's largest selection of music, as well as videos and laser discs. **Olsson's Books & Records,** with locations in Georgetown (☎ **202/338-9544**) on 19th Street below Dupont Circle (☎ **202/785-1133;** Metro: Dupont Circle), near Metro Center (☎ **202/347-3686**), and 7th Street NW (on the 7th Street Arts Corridor; ☎ **202/638-7610**), is strong in all categories (especially classical and folk), and the salespeople are always helpful.

Crafts

Appalachian Spring, Union Station, 50 Massachusetts Ave. NE. (☎ **202/682-0505;** Metro: Union Station), has quality crafts—rag rugs, pottery, kaleidoscopes, quilts (new), weavings, and more—all made in the US of A. Another branch is in Georgetown at 1415 Wisconsin Ave. NW. But the one at Union Station is easier to get to.

The **Indian Crafts Shop** in the Department of the Interior, 1849 C St. NW, Room 1023 (☎ **202/208-4056;** Metro: Farragut West), is a first-rate source for Native American crafts and handcrafted jewelry, priced from a few dollars to well over $1,000.

Farmers & Flea Markets

From Tuesday through Saturday at **Eastern Market,** 7th and C streets SE (south of North Carolina Avenue; ☎ **202/543-7293;** Metro: Eastern Market), stalls spill from the red brick market built in 1873. The atmosphere is part bazaar, part bizarre. Buy flowers and produce on Saturday, antiques, knickknacks, and junk on Sunday. Shops along 7th Street sell clothing and antiques, as well as food.

Every Sunday from March through December, bargain-hunters flood the parking lot on Wisconsin Avenue NW, between S and T streets, at Georgetown's north end, site of the **Georgetown Flea Market.** Close to 100 vendors sell furniture, clothing, antiques, and what my grandmother used to call "dust collectors." Poking around here is great fun. Getting here is not. If you take Metro to Foggy Bottom or Dupont Circle, it's at least a 30-minute walk. Unless you're a seasoned walker, take a taxi. Forget the bus, as Sunday service can be spotty.

Jewelry

Notice to all spouses, suitors, and significant others: Wondering what to get that special someone? Simple: a little bauble from **Pampillonia Jewelers,** at 1213 Connecticut Ave. NW (☎ **202/628-6305;** Metro: Farragut North); or Mazza Gallerie, 5300 Wisconsin Ave. NW (☎ **202/363-6305;** Metro: Friendship Heights). This family-owned business is the sine qua non of Washington jewelers, with traditional and custom-designed pieces for women and men.

Political Memorabilia

Political Americana, 50 Massachusetts Ave. NE (in Union Station; ☎ **202/547-1685;** Metro: Union Station), is prime hunting ground for souvenirs such as old campaign buttons, books, bumper stickers, and other politically inspired novelties. Other branches can be found at Georgetown Park, 3222 M St. NW (☎ **202/543-7300**), and 685 15th St. NW (between the McPherson Square Metro station and White House; ☎ **202/547-1817**).

Chapter 16

Divide & Conquer: Six Battle Plans for Seeing the Sights

In This Chapter

➤ Six suggestions for how to spend your day exploring Washington, D.C.

There's no need to zigzag from one end of town to the other, wasting time and wearing yourself out. Ricocheting through the city like a stray bullet gets old fast. I urge first-timers to take a guided tour for an overview, then draw up a battle plan for conquering the sights within a particular area; or follow one of the itineraries I've drummed up. Less is definitely more, so reduce your expectations, especially when limited to a 2- or 3-day visit. Allow break time for meals or snacks, shopping, and vegging out.

Each itinerary is designed to end by mid- to late afternoon, or when you cannot take another step—whichever comes first. Return to your hotel and people-watch in the lobby, or put your feet up—maybe catch some zzz's—in your room. Decompress and get in gear for a night on the town. After a day of pavement-pounding and brain drain, you've earned a rest. Rejuvenated, you'll be primed to enjoy dinner, a live performance, or an after-dark tour. Or maybe you'll just want to lick an ice-cream cone and stroll through Georgetown. For more information on each attraction, please refer to chapters 13 and 14. Refueling spots are covered in chapters 10 and 11.

Itinerary #1: Monuments, Memorials & More

If you want to take in all the top sights in 1 day, this is the battle plan for you. This itinerary will take you through the Bureau of Engraving and Printing or U.S. Holocaust Memorial Museum, National Museum of American History, Washington Monument, Lincoln and Vietnam Veterans memorials. I've even thrown in a stroll around the scenic Tidal Basin with

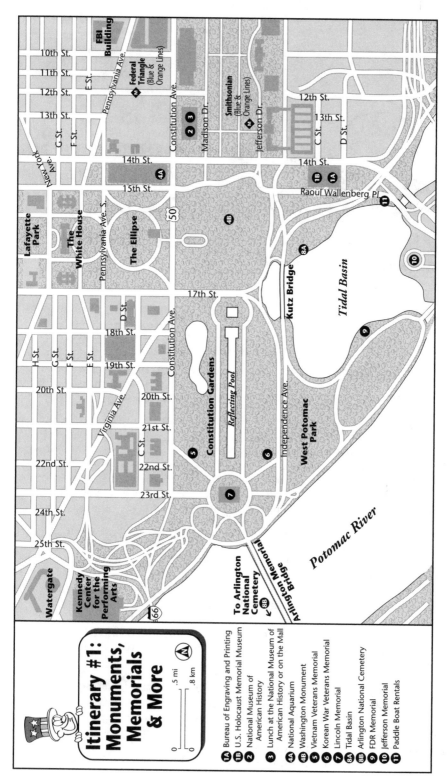

Itinerary #1: Monuments, Memorials & More

0   .5 mi
0   .8 km

1A Bureau of Engraving and Printing
1B U.S. Holocaust Memorial Museum
2 National Museum of American History
3 Lunch at the National Museum of American History or on the Mall
4A National Aquarium
4B Washington Monument
5 Vietnam Veterans Memorial
6 Korean War Veterans Memorial
7 Lincoln Memorial
8A Tidal Basin
8B Arlington National Cemetery
9 FDR Memorial
10 Jefferson Memorial
11 Paddle Boat Rentals

Map labels

FBI Building
Federal Triangle (Blue & Orange Lines)
Smithsonian (Blue & Orange Lines)
Pennsylvania Ave.
Constitution Ave.
Madison Dr.
Jefferson Dr.
10th St.
11th St.
12th St.
13th St.
14th St.
15th St.
E St.
G St.
F St.
New York Ave.
Lafayette Park
The White House
The Ellipse
Pennsylvania Ave. S.
Raoul Wallenberg Pl.
Tidal Basin
Kutz Bridge
17th St.
18th St.
19th St.
20th St.
21st St.
22nd St.
23rd St.
24th St.
25th St.
H St.
G St.
F St.
E St.
D St.
C St.
Virginia Ave.
Constitution Ave.
Constitution Gardens
Reflecting Pool
West Potomac Park
Independence Ave.
Watergate
Kennedy Center for the Performing Arts
To Arlington National Cemetery
Arlington Memorial Bridge
Potomac River
C St.
D St.
50
66

stops at the Jefferson and FDR memorials at no additional cost. Feel free to make substitutions without penalty. For example, you may wish to visit the Museum of Natural History or another Mall museum in place of American History. Or perhaps you'd rather scrap the Bureau of Engraving and Printing and Holocaust Memorial Museum in favor of an FBI tour. If so, if you get out of the FBI alive, hop on Metro at the Federal Triangle station and hop off at the Smithsonian station, which'll put you in proximity to the monuments and memorials described below. Refer to your handy map for help. Or ask a friendly-looking native. Or call me at home and I'll talk you through it. *One final bit of advice:* Get a good night's sleep and eat a hearty breakfast before you attempt this. And don't wear new shoes.

1A. Start with an early-morning tour of the **Bureau of Engraving and Printing,** 14th and C streets SW (☎ 202/874-3188), where $77 *billion* in currency is printed annually. Arrive by 8am at the kiosk around the corner, on Raoul Wallenberg Place (15th Street SW), for timed tickets (if you didn't order VIP tickets).

1B. Newly printed stacks of greenbacks don't turn you on? That's okay; substitute the **U.S. Holocaust Memorial Museum** around the corner at 100 Raoul Wallenberg Place (15th Street SW; ☎ 202/488-0400), for a sobering and meaningful experience. While same-day, timed tickets are issued at the museum beginning at 10am daily, it's best to secure them ahead through Protix (☎ 202/400-9373). Take a break in the **Holocaust Museum cafeteria-style cafe,** serving beverages, sandwiches, desserts, and fruit. (Allow 2 hours for either the Bureau of Engraving and Printing or the Holocaust Museum.) When you're done, walk north on 14th Street to Constitution Avenue. The building on the corner, to your right, is . . .

2. The **National Museum of American History** is a storehouse of machinery, artifacts, and cultural icons that helped shape our nation—from the original Star-Spangled Banner to exhibits on the changing roles of women. (Allow 1 hour.)

3. Lunchtime! Have a sandwich and ice-cream sundae or soda in the 1900s-style **Palm Court** cafe on the first floor of the Museum of American History, or hit the lower-level cafeteria-style **Main Street Cafes,** with h and h (hamburgers and hot dogs), pizza, deli sandwiches, hot entrees, desserts, but no wedding cake. Or exit the rear of the museum onto the Mall and pick up an el cheapo lunch from a street vendor. (Allow 30 minutes.)

4A. Detour. If you have kids in tow, cross Constitution Avenue at 14th Street and walk north to the **Commerce Department,** at 14th Street and Constitution Avenue NW (☎ 202/482-2825), where you'll find the **National Aquarium**—the nation's oldest—with touch tanks and shark or piranha feedings at 2pm. (Allow 1 hour.)

4B. Otherwise, stay on Constitution Avenue, heading west for a glimpse of the **Ellipse** and **White House** "backside" on your way to one of the most instantly recognizable monuments in the world: the **Washington Monument,** currently undergoing renovation. Wait in line to ride the elevator to the observation level or come back another time. Then head west (on the grass if it isn't wet) through **Constitution Gardens,** a lovely parklike parcel with a pond, the **Reflecting Pool,** and a drop-dead vista east to the Capitol. (Allow 1 hour.)

5. Head to the low-slung, two-part (does anyone else think it resembles a rifle or machine gun?) **Vietnam Veterans Memorial,** near 21st Street and Constitution Avenue NW. The polished black granite tablets are inscribed with the names of 60,000 war dead and MIAs. (Allow 15 minutes.)

6. Dead ahead, on the other side of the Reflecting Pool, is the **Korean War Veterans Memorial,** a striking, larger-than-life tableau of soldiers (here sculpted of stainless steel) on the march. (Allow 15 minutes.)

7. No visit to Washington would be complete without a respectful visit to the **Lincoln Memorial.** Don't let the scaffolding put you off. Although repairs are ongoing until sometime in 2000, visitors are welcome. Besides the spectacular view of the Mall from the steps, take in the vista from the rear of the monument, across the Potomac to Arlington National Cemetery. (Allow 30 minutes.)

8A. Head due south from the Lincoln Memorial 1 block, then east along Independence Avenue to the **Tidal Basin.** A stroll around the Tidal Basin takes about 45 minutes. It's beautiful and well worth it—also a great photo op. If it's springtime, it must be cherry blossom season. Rest your weary bod on a bench or the grass.

8B. Schwartzenegger types and serious hoofers should detour to **Arlington National Cemetery** over Memorial Bridge (behind the Lincoln Memorial). This is for the high-energy, I-want-to-do-everything-in-1-day type. Everyone else: You'd do better to visit Arlington another day, on your own or via Tourmobile. (Allow 2 hours if you choose to ignore my recommendation.)

9. If you take the Tidal Basin route, wander through the massive, sprawling **FDR Memorial** (on the southwest bank).

10. Take in the gleaming white marble **Jefferson Memorial** (south end).

11. If you want to work off some of those excess vacation calories, rent a **paddleboat** at the southeast corner of the Basin (15th Street SW and East Basin Drive), where you can also grab a soda, ice cream, or snack from a vendor. From the Tidal Basin, it's a 10- to 15-minute walk (east on Independence Avenue) back to the Mall and the Smithsonian Metro stop. (Allow 1½ hours.)

12. Sweet dreams. (40 winks—3 hours.)

Itinerary #2: Capitol Hill

Plan on spending the better part of a day touring Capitol Hill. Monday through Friday works best, since on weekends there's little action in the congressional offices, the restaurants in federal office buildings are closed, and you'll be competing for space with sightseeing locals, out in droves. Have breakfast at your hotel or in a nearby coffee shop, then take Metro to the Federal Center SW station.

1. On your way to the U.S. Capitol, stop at pretty **Bartholdi Park,** with its 30-foot-high fountain by Frederic Bartholdi, the French sculptor who designed the Statue of Liberty. The U.S. Botanic Garden, across the street, is closed for renovation until sometime in 2000. (Allow 15 minutes.)

2. It's off to the East Front of the **U.S. Capitol,** your first "official" stop. Line up for a guided tour at the foot of the steps, or climb them and enter the Rotunda, where you can pick up a brochure and tour on your own. Stop to share your views with your state's senator. If he or she is on the floor (of the Senate chamber, not passed out) or on the road, leave a message with an aide. (Allow 1 to 3 hours.)

3. Since you paid for it, you might as well ride the **subway** (not part of Metro; it's located in the basement) connecting the Capitol to the **Dirksen** and **Hart Senate office buildings.** The system, run by electromagnets, cost taxpayers $18 million. As you leave the Capitol, be sure to walk around to the **West Front** for an unobstructed view of the Mall to the Lincoln Memorial; definitely a Kodak moment. (Allow 30 minutes.)

4. Take a **lunch break** in the **Dirksen Senate Office Building South Buffet Room;** cafeteria or **Montpelier Dining Room** in the James Madison Building of the Library of Congress; or in a Hill cafe or pub. Keep an eye out for your senator. (Allow 1 hour.)

5. Walk off lunch on your way to the **Thomas Jefferson Building** of the **Library of Congress.** Catch the short orientation film before counting the volumes (more than 17 million catalogued books) and viewing the magnificent Main Reading Room of the world's largest library. The copyright office, with displays of pop culture icons, is located in the **Madison Building.** (Allow 1 hour.)

6. If the play's your thing, feast your eyes on the Elizabethan-style theater and Great Hall in the nearby **Folger Shakespeare Library** and pay your respects to Puck (in the garden) on the way out of the Library of Congress. (Allow 15 to 30 minutes.)

7A. Detour to one of the District's oldest homes, the **Sewall–Belmont House,** a repository of feminist and suffragist memorabilia on a residential street. (Allow 30 minutes.)

227

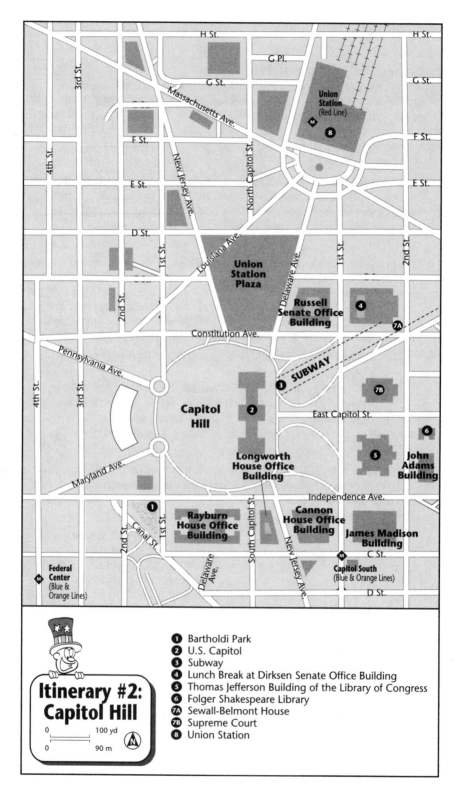

Itinerary #2:
Capitol Hill

0 ____ 100 yd
0 ____ 90 m

1 Bartholdi Park
2 U.S. Capitol
3 Subway
4 Lunch Break at Dirksen Senate Office Building
5 Thomas Jefferson Building of the Library of Congress
6 Folger Shakespeare Library
7A Sewall-Belmont House
7B Supreme Court
8 Union Station

228

7B. Otherwise, head directly for the **Supreme Court.** *Oyez! Oyez!* (Hear ye! Hear ye!). Attend the free lecture and/or see the short film on the Court's workings and take in the view from the steps.

8. Finish with shopping, a coffee or dessert break, and, perhaps, a late afternoon movie (cheaper before 6pm!) in **Union Station.** When the spirit moves you, catch Metro back to your hotel.

Hear Ye! Hear Ye!

If you want to hear a case being argued at the Supreme Court—roughly Monday through Wednesday mornings from October through April—reconfigure your battle plan and make this your first stop of the day. You can then easily go on to the Capitol.

Itinerary #3: Dupont Circle

Even if you deep-six the suggestions below and scrap the map, you're bound to enjoy Dupont Circle. The vibrant and colorful neighborhood is made (like Nancy Sinatra's boots) for walking. If you follow the program, do the Dupont Circle neighborhood Wednesday through Saturday, since some sights are closed at other times. Begin by 10am and expect to finish between 3 and 4pm. Breakfast in your hotel or take Metro to Dupont Circle and begin the day with a latte and bagel at **Afterwords,** the cafe in Kramerbooks. In nice weather, tote your java to . . .

1. **Dupont Circle Park.** Named for a Navy Civil War hero, Rear Admiral Samuel Francis duPont (see the small equestrian statue?), the park is an oasis for office workers, youths, chess-playing seniors, and musicians. (Allow 15 to 30 minutes.)

2. Get a taste of **Embassy Row** while walking to the **Phillips Collection,** a historic mansion full of dazzling modern art. (Allow 1½ hours.)

3. Break for a snack or early lunch in the Phillips cafe or wander over to **Pizzeria Paradiso** or **WrapWorks** for a quick bite. For a sit-down lunch, try **BeDuCi.** (Allow 1 hour.) Then resume your tour of Dupont Circle at . . .

4. **Anderson House.** Head to this Italianate mansion for a look at how diplomats live. The collection of art and furniture will take your breath away.

5. Take a leisurely *uphill* stroll along **Embassy Row** (Massachusetts Avenue) to admire the embassies and chanceries on your way to the **Woodrow Wilson House** for a tour of the post–White House residence of the 28th U.S. president. (Allow 1½ hours.)

6. Shop along **Connecticut Avenue.** Refuel with a snack and browse the stores, boutiques, and galleries on your way to the Dupont Circle Metro. (Allow 1 to 2 hours.)

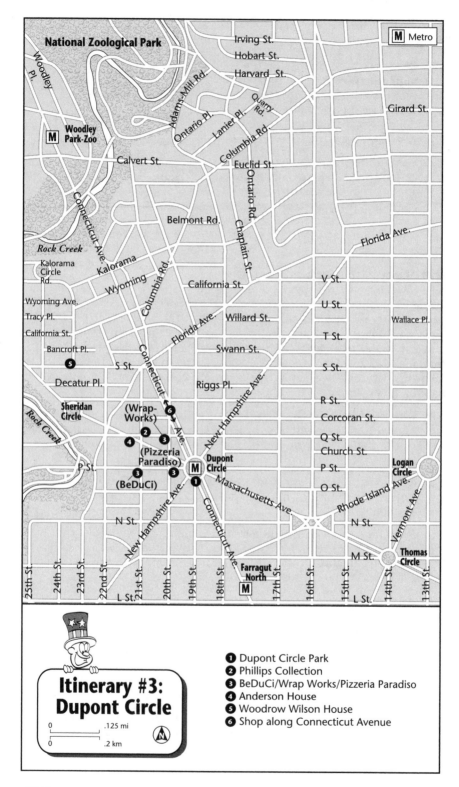

National Zoological Park

Irving St.
Hobart St.
Harvard St.
Girard St.

Woodley Pl.

M Metro

M Woodley Park-Zoo

Adams-Mill Rd.
Ontario Pl.
Lanier Pl.
Quarry Rd.
Columbia Rd.

Calvert St.

Euclid St.

Connecticut Ave.

Belmont Rd.

Ontario Rd.
Chaplain St.
Florida Ave.

Rock Creek

Kalorama Circle Rd.

Kalorama

Wyoming

California St.

V St.
U St.

Wyoming Ave.
Tracy Pl.
California St.

Columbia Rd.

Florida Ave.
Willard St.

Wallace Pl.

T St.

Bancroft Pl.

Swann St.

⑤

S St.

S St.

Decatur Pl.

Riggs Pl.

R St.
Corcoran St.

Sheridan Circle

(Wrap-Works)

⑥

New Hampshire Ave.

Rock Creek

②

③

Q St.
Church St.

④

(Pizzeria Paradiso)

P St.

Logan Circle

P St.

③

③

M Dupont Circle

O St.

Rhode Island Ave.

Vermont Ave.

(BeDuCi)

①

Massachusetts Ave.

N St.

New Hampshire Ave.

Connecticut Ave.

N St.

M St.

Thomas Circle

25th St.
24th St.
23rd St.
22nd St.
21st St.
20th St.
19th St.
18th St.
17th St.
16th St.
15th St.
14th St.
13th St.

Farragut North

M

L St.

L St.

Itinerary #3: Dupont Circle

0 _____ .125 mi
0 _____ .2 km

① Dupont Circle Park
② Phillips Collection
③ BeDuCi/Wrap Works/Pizzeria Paradiso
④ Anderson House
⑤ Woodrow Wilson House
⑥ Shop along Connecticut Avenue

230

Itinerary #4: Georgetown

A day in Georgetown is always a pleasure, but be forewarned: The streets are mobbed on weekends. For this reason, I prefer Georgetown on a weekday, but, judging by the crowds, many chant the mantra "the more the merrier." As noted earlier, Georgetown is about a 20-minute walk from the Foggy Bottom Metro. To conserve energy, catch any no. 30 bus from Pennsylvania Avenue. You have a choice here. If you prefer serenity, start out early with breakfast at Patisserie–Cafe Didier and conclude your foray into Georgetown early to midafternoon. On the other hand, you could sleep in, begin your visit around noon, and end with dinner and a taste of the nightlife scene. If you choose the latter, you may want to take a taxi back to your hotel.

1. Start with a stroll along the promenade at **Washington Harbour.** Drink in the waterfront scene (and if the time is right, an alfresco Bloody Mary at Sequoia, allowing 30 minutes to 1 hour).

2. **Old Stone House,** the only pre-Revolutionary edifice in Washington, with a lovely English-style garden in the back. (Allow 30 minutes.)

3. Cross M Street opposite the **Old Stone House,** at Thomas Jefferson Street, and head for the river. Walk along the canal, flush with wildlife and the roar of planes approaching Reagan National Airport. The *Georgetown,* a working canal boat, cruises the **C&O Canal** April through October. (Allow 15 minutes to 2 hours; the cruise is $1\frac{1}{2}$ hours.)

4. Browse the shops along **M Street** (allowing 30 minutes to 1 hour) and cross Wisconsin to

5. **Shops at Georgetown Park,** a glitzy mall that attracts a high-rolling clientele. Take a break at Dean and Deluca, just down the street, or get a sugar fix at Mrs. Field's in the mall. (Allow 30 minutes to 2 hours.)

6. Detour down M Street (west toward Key Bridge) a few blocks to 36th Street. See the steep stairway on the right? Those are the nasty steps immortalized in the blockbuster novel and movie, *The Exorcist.*

7. Backtrack to **Wisconsin Avenue.** Turn left and walk uphill along Wisconsin, lined with scores of shops and restaurants, for about 8 blocks to R Street. Fans of leather, metal, and nose rings shop at Commander Salamander. For kitchenware and home furnishings, nothing beats **Little Caledonia.** (Allow 1 to 2 hours.)

8. If it's lunchtime, drop into one of the restaurants listed in chapter 10, or drop into one that strikes your fancy. I've never had a bad meal in Georgetown, but I recommend checking the prices before you sit down. Two standbys for a juicy hamburger, tasty soup or sandwich, or a hot entree are **Chadwick's,** 3205 K St. NW (☎ **202/333-2565**), and **Clyde's,** 3236 M St. NW (☎ **202/333-9180**). Both have been in business forever, the food is consistent, and you can count on efficient service. If you need a pick-me-up, guzzle an ice-cream soda or another

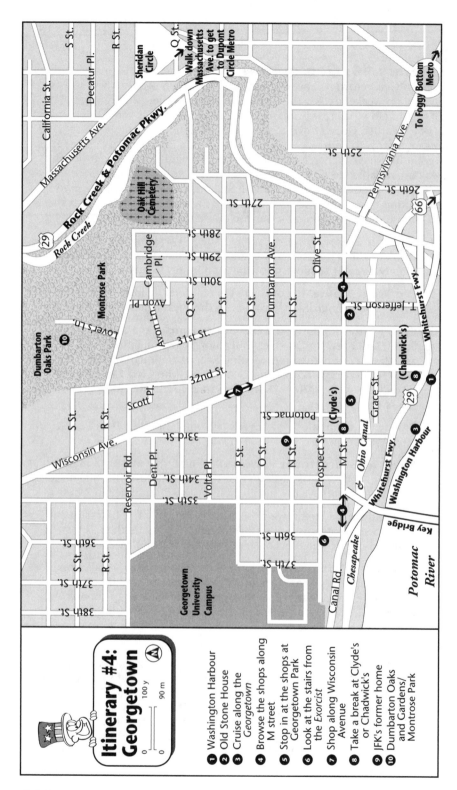

Itinerary #4: Georgetown

0 — 100 y
0 — 90 m

1 Washington Harbour
2 Old Stone House
3 Cruise along the *Georgetown*
4 Browse the shops along M street
5 Stop in at the shops at Georgetown Park
6 Look at the stairs from the *Exorcist*
7 Shop along Wisconsin Avenue
8 Take a break at Clyde's or Chadwick's
9 JFK's former home
10 Dumbarton Oaks and Gardens/ Montrose Park

fountain treat at **Thomas Sweet,** at the corner of Wisconsin Avenue and P Street.

9. As you wend your way up Wisconsin, detour to **3307 N St. NW,** the home of John F. Kennedy from shortly after Caroline's birth in 1957 until he moved into larger quarters at 1600 Pennsylvania Avenue on January 20, 1961.

10. From Wisconsin Avenue, make a right at R Street for **Dumbarton Oaks and Gardens** and/or **Montrose Park.** If the weather is stinky, skip these in favor of shopping. You'll probably spend more, but you'll stay dry. From here, you're closer to the **Dupont Circle Metro** station, but it's still a hike.

Itinerary #5: White House Area

A tour of the president's neighborhood will fill 5 to 7 hours—depending on how many museums you visit and whether you take shopping breaks. Earlybirds may want to start the day with breakfast at **Sholl's Cafeteria** (open at 7am), a Washington institution nearly as well known as the Smithsonian. Otherwise, take Metro to the Federal Triangle stop and walk to the White House Visitors Center. A tour of the presidential mansion, including waiting in line, will eat up the morning, assuming you get in. Take a lunch break, then resume your tour of the area with stops (depending on your interests) at the Renwick Gallery, Corcoran Gallery, or Octagon House. When you're too pooped to peep, rest in historic Lafayette Park and feed the squirrels—or ogle the protestors and dark suits.

1. If you want to breakfast at **Sholl's,** 1990 K St. NW, take Metro to Farragut North or Farragut West (30 minutes). Otherwise, go to the Federal Triangle stop, closer to the . . .

2. **White House Visitors Center** in the Department of Commerce on Pennsylvania Avenue between 14th and 15th streets. Show up as early as 7:30am for White House passes. Pick up other tourist information, to be read while waiting your turn to enter the nation's most famous residence. (Allow 15 minutes to 1 hour.)

3. Tour the **White House** with the other cattle, er, visitors (2 to 4 hours includes waits in line. Now you know why I favor VIP tickets). Alternatively, you can wait in line to get your White House tickets and then have breakfast at Sholl's while you wait for your turn on the tour. When you're done with the tour, cross Pennsylvania Avenue to . . .

4. **Lafayette Square,** sight of numerous protests over the years. The area of Pennsylvania Avenue between the White House and the park is open to foot traffic only, and has become a favorite haunt of in-line skaters. Little wonder that extra care is taken to maintain the trees and flower beds in Lafayette Square. This is, after all, an extension of the president's front yard. (Lucky for him that he doesn't have to cut the grass.)

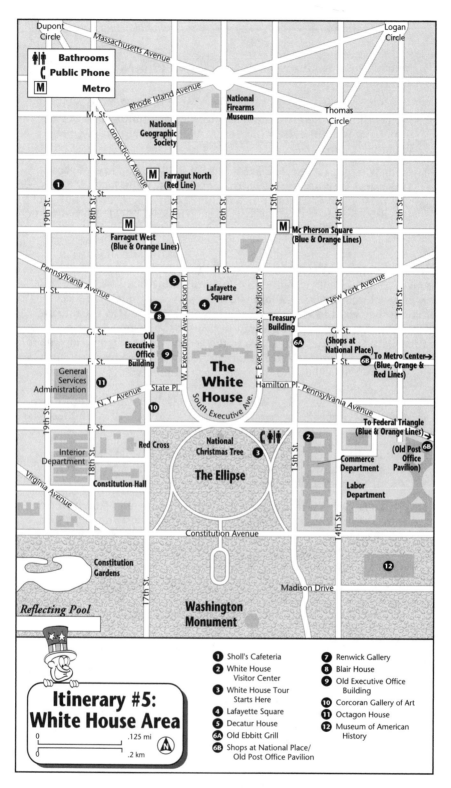

Bathrooms

Public Phone

M Metro

Dupont Circle

Massachusetts Avenue

Logan Circle

Rhode Island Avenue

National Firearms Museum

Thomas Circle

M. St.

Connecticut Avenue

National Geographic Society

L. St.

M Farragut North (Red Line)

❶

K. St.

19th St.

18th St.

17th St.

16th St.

15th St.

14th St.

13th St.

J. St.

M

Farragut West (Blue & Orange Lines)

M Mc Pherson Square (Blue & Orange Lines)

H St.

Pennsylvania Avenue

H. St.

❺ Jackson Pl.

Lafayette Square

❹

Madison Pl.

New York Avenue

13th St.

❼

❽

Treasury Building

G. St.

(Shops at National Place)

❻ᴬ

To Metro Center→

(Blue, Orange & Red Lines)

G. St.

Old Executive Office Building

W. Executive Ave.

E. Executive Ave.

F. St.

❻ᴮ

The White House

❾

F. St.

General Services Administration

❶❶

N.Y. Avenue

State Pl.

South Executive Ave.

Hamilton Pl.

Pennsylvania Avenue

❿

To Federal Triangle **(Blue & Orange Lines)**→

19th St.

E. St.

Red Cross

National Christmas Tree

(♀♂

(Old Post Office Pavilion) ❻ᴮ

Interior Department

18th St.

❷

15th St.

Commerce Department

❸

Virginia Avenue

Constitution Hall

The Ellipse

Labor Department

Constitution Avenue

14th St.

❶❷

Constitution Gardens

17th St.

Madison Drive

Reflecting Pool

Washington Monument

Itinerary #5: White House Area

0 ———— .125 mi

0 ———— .2 km

Ⓝ

❶ Sholl's Cafeteria

❷ White House Visitor Center

❸ White House Tour Starts Here

❹ Lafayette Square

❺ Decatur House

❻ᴬ Old Ebbitt Grill

❻ᴮ Shops at National Place/ Old Post Office Pavilion

❼ Renwick Gallery

❽ Blair House

❾ Old Executive Office Building

❿ Corcoran Gallery of Art

❶❶ Octagon House

❶❷ Museum of American History

234

Opposite the park is **St. John's Episcopal Church,** popularly known as the "Church of the Presidents."

5. Head west on H Street to Jackson Place, where you'll see **Decatur House,** a Federal-style home built in the early 19th century for naval hero Stephen Decatur. By now your stomach should be growling big-time.

6A. Have lunch at the **Old Ebbitt Grill** (you *did* remember to make a reservation, didn't you?).

6B. If the wait at Old Ebbitt is too long, head to the food courts in the **Old Post Office Pavilion** or **Shops at National Place,** both about a 10-minute walk from the White House, or one of the numerous restaurants and quick-turnaround coffee shops in the area. If you're in a shopping frame of mind, you can dish in the food and dish out the money in the multilevel Shops at National Place. (Allow 1 to 2 hours.)

7. After lunch, walk to the **Renwick Gallery,** a Smithsonian museum devoted to American crafts anchoring the northeast corner of 17th Street and Pennsylvania Avenue. (Allow 1 hour.)

8. Next door is **Blair House,** where visiting heads of state stay when the Lincoln Bedroom is occupied.

9. Head south on 17th Street, passing the **Old Executive Office Building,** where presidential staffers work and where Ollie (North) and Fawn (Hall) made mincemeat of Iran-Contra documents. Next stop is the . . .

10. **Corcoran Gallery of Art,** on 17th Street, between E Street and New York Avenue. Enjoy an English tea or dessert break in the Corcoran's **Cafe des Artistes** (also open for lunch). (Allow 30 minutes to $1\frac{1}{2}$ hours.)

11. Nearby is the **Octagon House,** which was recently restored to its 1815 appearance and serves as the museum of the American Architectural Foundation.

12. Walk east on Constitution Avenue for a view, on your left, of the **Ellipse** and back door of the **White House.** Continue past the **Museum of American History**—hey, you can go in if you want; it's a free country—and turn left at 12th Street to the Federal Triangle Metro station. (Allow 30 minutes.)

Itinerary #6: Doing the Mall Crawl

It's too difficult to recommend a single itinerary for the National Mall. There are so many attractions, and a lot depends on your interests and energy level. One recommendation I make without qualification: Don't even think about visiting more than four major museums in a day; fewer if you have kids under 10. Take a break *at least* every few hours to eat, enjoy a brisk walk outdoors, or change the tempo with shopping, a siesta, or some other no-brainer. Here are a few more tips for crawling the Mall:

➤ Look through chapters 13 and 14 and circle your top choices.

➤ Use the map of the Mall on p. 159 to direct you to the **Smithsonian Information Center** in the Smithsonian Castle, open daily from 9am to 5:30pm. Gather brochures. Check out the large lighted map of D.C. sights and the display monitors for daily special events. Take advantage of the multilingual staff who are there to answer questions.

➤ Note that at the busiest museums (**Air and Space, American History, Natural History**) it's best to show up first thing in the morning or after 3pm.

➤ Wear comfortable shoes and layer clothing, except in summer when you should wear the minimum allowed by law.

Chapter 17

Designing Your Own Itinerary

In This Chapter

➤ How to decide what you're going to do

➤ How to determine if you're staying in the neighborhood that's right for you

➤ How to pace yourself

As any traveler will tell you, there is never enough time to see everything. I'm the type who usually starts planning a return visit before the first day of my vacation has ended. I've learned through trial and error to organize and pay attention to details. How frustrating to show up at a museum on the one day it's closed or get on a subway going the wrong way. (Don't even ask how many times I've done this!) The worksheets in this chapter will help you zero in on what to see and how to organize your time.

Back to the Drawing Board—Your Top Attractions

Go back to chapter 13, where you rated the top attractions from 1 to 5. Use this list and break down the sights by number. Then write in all the #1s, all the #2s, and so on.

#1 Picks

➤ _____

➤ _____

➤ _____

➤ _____

➤ _____

#2 Picks

➤ _____

➤ _____

➤ _____

➤ _____

➤ _____

#3 Picks

➤ _____

➤ _____

➤ _____

➤ _____

➤ _____

➤ _____

#4 Picks

➤ _____

➤ _____

➤ _____

➤ _____

➤ _____

Now, go back to chapter 14 and pick up the "other fun stuff" that fits your particular interests. Tag these attractions with a number and incorporate them into the preceding lists. You're probably wondering why there are no spaces for the #5s. Here's why. There are probably so many 1s, 2s, and 3s that you won't need the 5s. You may not even have time to visit the 4s. Suppose your #1 list says "White House, Air and Space Museum, Museum of Natural History, National Gallery of Art, U.S. Capitol, and Union Station"? Whoa! Forget it. Visiting all those would eat up 2 days, if it didn't kill you first. On Day 1 you would stick to the Mall, visit the Air and Space Museum in the morning, have lunch in the museum, then cross the Mall to the National Gallery, take a breather (read, "dessert break") and browse through the gift shop, then head over to the Museum of Natural History. Day 2 would start with a tour of the White House, lunch, then taking Metro to the Hill to visit the Capitol, walking to Union Station for souvenir shopping and, perhaps, an early dinner.

Budgeting Your Time

Plan on 2 hours to visit the major sights, an hour or less for the lesser ones (see the box below for specific time suggestions). For the National Zoo, so you won't feel rushed and because the zoo is a 15-minute Metro ride from downtown, plan on the better part of a day. If you have the stamina, you can visit three or four sights in a day.

Add up the number of 1s and 2s in the above list and divide the total by the number of days in your trip. If the result is larger than four, you may have a problem. At best, you can only see six or more sights per day superficially. Now what? How do you pare down the number of sights per day?

➤ **Extend your visit.** Call the boss or baby-sitter and beg for more time.

➤ **Split up.** If you're traveling as a couple or group, split the days in half and strike out on your own.

➤ **Bury the 3s.** It's better to see fewer attractions and see them well. This is a vacation, so don't schedule something for every second of the day.

Time Savers

Here's a general idea of how much time should be allotted to see the major attractions. This should give you an idea of how best to plan your day.

➤ **Major Mall museums** (Air and Space, American History, National Gallery of Art, Natural History) require 1 to 2 hours each.

➤ **Off-the-Mall sights** (Bureau of Engraving and Printing, Capitol, FBI, Holocaust Memorial Museum, White House) will take 2 to 3 hours each. This includes waiting in line.

➤ **Presidential monuments and memorials** (FDR, Jefferson, Kennedy Center, Lincoln, Washington) can all be done in the span of 2 to 3 hours; otherwise, 15 to 30 minutes each, with the exception of the Washington Monument, where lines are the rule (the wait can be up to an hour).

➤ **National Zoo** should take 3 hours or more (this includes travel time).

Am I Staying in the Right Place?

Take your lists of attractions and plug them into the following geographical areas. If your hotel is in the area with the most entries, good; you'll be able to get to the first item with ease, even if you oversleep. If you can walk to it, so much the better. If, however, you're staying in a hotel that's close to only a few of the things you want to see, you'll waste lots of time commuting. So you may want to change your hotel.

National Mall

➤ _____

➤ _____

➤ _____

➤ _____

➤ _____

Capitol Hill

➤ _____

➤ _____

➤ _____

➤ _____

➤ _____

Downtown

➤ _____

➤ _____

➤ _____

➤ _____

➤ _____

Dupont Circle

➤ _____

➤ _____

➤ _____

➤ _____

➤ _____

Georgetown

➤ _____

➤ _____

➤ _____

➤ _____

➤ _____

Getting Your Ducks in a Row

Making your plan concrete will help make your trip more doable. On a map, mark the locations of all the sights you've listed so far. Then mark your hotel. Try to find clusters of activities (think grapes) that bunch together naturally. You'll wear yourself out traipsing from Capitol Hill to Georgetown to the Mall. Stick to one neighborhood for at least half a day, then have lunch before traveling to another part of the city.

Fill-Ins

Fill-ins are things to do on your way to someplace else. Shopping comes readily to mind. Go back to chapter 15 and pick out the specific stores and neighborhoods in which you want to spend time. List them here.

Time Savers

Have a back-up plan in case the weather is uncooperative. If it's raining or cold, you'll probably want to forgo a walk around the Tidal Basin or through Georgetown. Also take into consideration that night arrives as early as 5pm in December and as late as 9pm in June. If you want to take an after-dark tour in summer, you may need a nap first.

Shopping

➤ _____

➤ _____

➤ _____

➤ _____

➤ _____

Locate these shopping haunts on a map, and figure out what sights lie in between. Allow different amounts of time depending on whether you're just browsing or planning an all-out attack. If you want to window shop all the windows at a mall or do your holiday shopping, this could become a half- to full-day enterprise.

Dining is another fill-in. Let's start with lunch for now. If there are specific restaurants you want to try, locate them on the map. Are they close to your clusters of sights? If you have no "musts," use the listings in chapters 10 and 11 and pick out a few options for each of the clusters. As my grandmother used to say, "Eat, dolly." You must refuel regularly to keep the engine running. List the restaurants below:

Lunch

➤ _____

➤ _____

➤ _____

➤ _____

➤ _____

Time Savers

If you find list-making a drag, deep-six the recommended itineraries in the last chapter. It's okay to mix and match or substitute activities in the same neighborhoods, but keep the basic structure.

Nighttime Is the Right Time

Washington is not a late-night town, but there are numerous places to catch a live performance, listen to music, or shake your bootie. Although the hot restaurants require advance reservations, there's no need to schedule every meal ahead of time. At the end of an exhausting day, you'll probably seek a little down time before beginning your evening's activities. I suggest you return to your hotel, kick back with a cold drink or cocktail, and maybe catch a nap. Think of your nighttime plans as a mini-itinerary. There's no need to be so organized that at 7am you know where you're going to dine 12 hours later. Spontaneity is key here. Check out the nightlife recommendations in the following chapters and see what strikes your fancy. Of course, you'll want to keep track of any dinner reservations or theater tickets you've booked in advance. Jot them down here:

Night #1

➤ _____

➤ _____

➤ _____

Night #2

➤ _____

➤ _____

➤ _____

Night #3

➤ _____

➤ _____

➤ _____

242

Night #4

➤ _____

➤ _____

➤ _____

For any nights that are blank, you might want to write in tentative options, such as "dinner in [neighborhood]; go to [club/bar] afterward?"

Last, but not least, keep geography in mind so that you don't end up at the National Zoo an hour before you have to be at the Kennedy Center for a performance. Remember to leave time for freshening up, changing clothes, and phoning home. Then slow down and go with the flow.

Part 6

On the Town—Nightlife & Entertainment

By day Washington brims with so many things to do and see, no mortal could possibly take in everything. The nighttime scene is not much different. Whether you want to catch a play, tap your foot in a jazz club, or check out the bar scene, there are after-dark activities to suit every taste and budget.

Theater is alive and very well, thank you, in the nation's capital. Pre- and post-Broadway runs play at several venues, and the area is home to several acclaimed repertory companies, the Kennedy Center's six stages, and a handful of theaters on D.C.'s Great White Way, centered around the National, Shakespeare, and Warner theaters. (For information on reserving tickets, see chapter 4.)

Those on a limited budget—and who isn't these days?—will find plenty to do. For openers, free concerts are as integral to Washington as spin doctors and humidity. The Kennedy Center offers "pay what you can" tickets and free performances on the Millennium Stage in the Grand Foyer, at 6pm daily. Like the beat, the list goes on. If you have any doubts, see chapters 18 and 19.

HELP ME
BECOME PRESIDENT

Chapter 18

The Performing Arts

In This Chapter

➤ Getting tickets for shows

➤ A night at the theater

➤ Opera, dance, classical music, and other good-natured entertainment

---

Over the last 20 years Washington's stature as a cultural capital has blossomed, nearly equaling its reputation as a hub of international political power. Today the dazzling array of music, dance, cabaret, and other live performances is second only to the performing arts scene in New York. Remember the old Avis commercial? Well, like Avis, we're #2, so we try harder.

The Kennedy Center is the home of the National Symphony and the Washington Opera, as well as a host of internationally acclaimed guest artists and star-studded companies like American Ballet Theatre and Alvin Ailey. A cornucopia of cultural treats provides not-to-be-missed opportunities for residents and visitors alike.

Due to the stellar caliber of performances, competition for tickets is keen. To get the best seats (or any seats) for a popular performance, buying tickets in advance becomes a necessity.

Finding Out What's Goin' On

Before you leave home, call the **Washington, D.C., Convention and Visitors Association** at ☎ 202/789-7000 or visit the Web site at **www.washington.org**. Or call the **D.C. Committee to Promote Washington** at ☎ 800/422-8644 or 202/724-5644. The *Washington Post*'s Web site at **www.washingtonpost.com** is also a useful resource.

Once you get into town, check the *Washington Post*'s daily "Guide to the Lively Arts" and the Friday "Weekend" pull-out section. Here you'll find previews and reviews of the performing and visual arts and films. For listings and articles about what's goin' on, pick up the free *City Paper* (published every Thursday), in street corner bins, at area book and video stores, restaurants, coffee shops, and the like. You'll probably pick up a copy of *What's Happening* (and any other free information that's not nailed down) when you check in at your hotel. Pick the concierge's brain too. It's what they get paid for! Also see the "City Lights" section of the monthly *Washingtonian* magazine and consult the list of information sources in chapters 1 and 4.

Hear Ye! Hear Ye!

For on-line theater information, click onto these Web sites:

➤ Arena Stage: **www.arenastage.org**

➤ Ford's Theatre: **www.fordstheatre.org**

➤ John F. Kennedy Center for the Performing Arts: **www.kennedy-center.org**

➤ National Theatre: **www.national theatre.org**

➤ Shakespeare Theatre: **www.shakespearedc.org**

➤ Washington Post: **www.washingtonpost.com**

➤ Warner Theatre: **www.warnertheatre.com**

Tickets, Please

Ticket companies such as Ticketmaster allow you to order tickets before you leave home. All you need are a telephone, credit card, and the name and date of the performance. There's a surcharge for this service, usually $1.50 per ticket.

Protix (☎ 703/218-6500), with outlets in selected Waxie Maxies, takes reservations for events at Arena Stage, Ford's Theatre, and Signature Theatre.

Full-price tickets to most city events are sold through **Ticketmaster** (☎ 202/432-SEAT) at Hecht's, 12th and G streets NW at Metro Center. You can enter Hecht's from Metro without going outside.

If you're hanging loose, you can purchase same-day, half-price tickets through **TicketPlace** on the mezzanine of the Old Post Office Pavilion, 11th Street and Pennsylvania Ave. NW (☎ 202/TICKETS). More than 60 institutions participate in the service cosponsored by the Cultural Alliance of Greater Washington and the Kennedy Center. Half-price tickets (with a 10% service charge) are sold for same-day performances. Since TicketPlace is open every day but Sunday and Monday (Tuesday through Friday from noon to

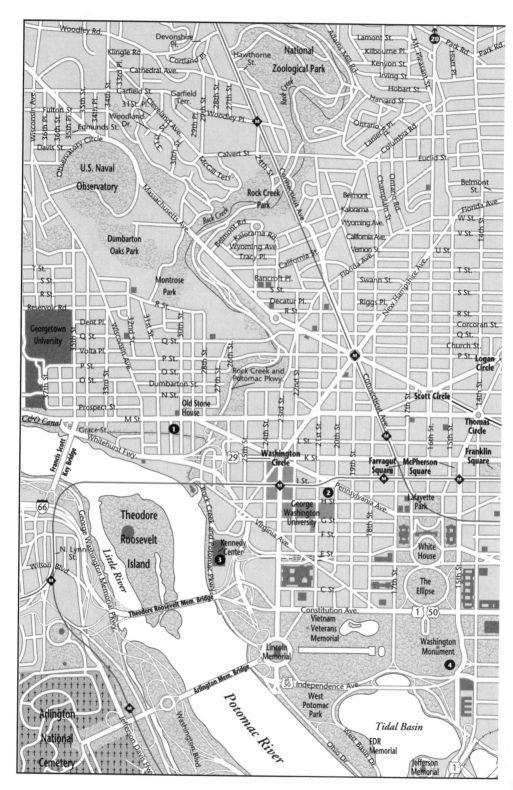

The
Performing
Arts Scene in
Washington,
D. C.

0   .25 mi
0   .4 km

American Film Institute **3**
AMC Union Station 9 **17**
Arena Stage **16**
Carter Barron Amphitheater **20**
Catholic University's
   Hartke Theater **18**
Concerts on the Canal **1**
Discovery Theater **13**
Ford's Theatre **8**
Front-Running Dance Place **19**
Hirshhorn Museum **14**
Kennedy Center **3**
Samuel P. Langley Theater
   (in National Air and
   Space Museum) **15**
National Archives **11**
National Theatre **7**
Shakespeare Theatre **10**
Sylvan Theatre **4**
Ticketmaster **5**
TicketPlace **9**
Top Centre Ticket Service **2**
U.S. Navy Memorial Plaza **12**
Warner Theatre **6**

Hear Ye! Hear Ye!

If you order tickets from your hotel room, open the Bell Atlantic Yellow Pages to the InfoScene section in the front. Here you'll find seating diagrams for several theaters and sports arenas. If the only available seats are in the boonies, ask if the view is obstructed. This may not be a problem if your vision is 20–20 and you're attending the symphony or a hockey game, but it's Hell at a dance performance.

6pm, Saturday from 11am to 5pm), tickets for Sunday and Monday are sold on Saturday. Cash, traveler's checks, and debit cards are accepted for half-price tickets; credit cards are not. TicketPlace is also a full-price Ticketmaster outlet, and you can pay for these with a credit card. To reach TicketPlace, take Metro to the Federal Triangle station. If you don't see the Old Post Office when you exit, you got off at the wrong stop.

Another last-minute strategy is to call, or go to, the box office where an event is taking place. You can find the addresses of lesser-known venues in the *Washington Post*'s "Guide to the Lively Arts." If you're a gambler, arrive a half hour before curtain time. Sometimes unclaimed reserved tickets are available.

Getting Scalped

If all else fails, and you're dying to see something, you may be tempted to go to a scalper (known as a ticket broker in polite circles). Many advertise in the *Washington Post* classifieds and in the phone book. The old rule of supply and demand is at work here, so be sure to nail down the broker's commission before you share your credit-card information. Let the buyer beware!

The following brokers sell tickets to concerts, theater performances, and sports events. Since the Redskins' miserable showing in 1998 (their worst season ever), you may be able to snare tickets, usually scarcer than parking in Adams–Morgan.

Top Centre Ticket Service (☎ 202/452-9040) is only a few blocks from the White House in Foggy Bottom at 2000 Pennsylvania Ave. NW.

Asc Ticket Co. (☎ 301/984-6005) answers the phone 24 hours a day and offers free delivery service. You may want to click onto their Web site **www.oscticket.com**.

The **Ticket Connection,** the area's oldest ticket agency, has an office in Silver Spring, Maryland (☎ 301/587-6850). You don't have to go there, however. Just call and they'll Fed-Ex your tickets or deliver them by courier.

Seasonal Considerations

The performance season chugs along pretty much year-round. While the majority of performances takes place from September to June, exceptions abound. One of the summertime delights in Washington is the series of free outdoor concerts by military service bands and nationally televised concerts by the National Symphony on the West Lawn of the Capitol on Memorial Day and Labor Day weekends and on July 4. More about these and other freebies later on.

Metro It

The shortest distance between two points is still Metro. But if you're coming from or going to an iffy neighborhood, or Georgetown (the Foggy Bottom station is a hike), or it's very late, take a taxi. Here are directions for getting to the major destinations.

Hear Ye! Hear Ye!

If you're visiting during the summer, catch one of the free concerts by bands from all four branches of the military on Monday, Tuesday, Thursday, and Friday evenings at the **Capitol, Washington Monument,** and other sites. Call ☎ **202/767-5658,** 202/433-2525, or 202/ 433-4011 for information.

Time Savers

Night owls should keep in mind that the Metro closes at midnight. After that, it's best to take a taxi. If you can't find a taxi, flip to the box on p. 93 in chapter 8, for a list of telephone numbers of reliable taxi companies.

➤ **Kennedy Center for the Performing Arts,** F Street NW and Rock Creek Parkway: Metro to Foggy Bottom, then ride the free Kennedy Center shuttle bus, departing every 10 minutes.

➤ **Arena Stage,** 6th Street and Maine Avenue SW: Take a taxi.

➤ **Ford's Theatre,** 511 10th St. NW: Metro to Metro Center, then walk east (addresses decrease) on G Street, right at 10th Street.

➤ **National Theatre,** 1321 E St. NW: Metro to Metro Center, walk west 1 block on G Street to left at 13th Street 2 blocks.

➤ **Shakespeare Theatre,** 450 7th St. NW: Metro to Archives, north (away from Mall) on 7th Street 2 blocks.

➤ **Warner Theatre,** 13th and E streets NW: Metro to Federal Triangle, north on 12th Street, cross Pennsylvania Avenue, continue 1 block, left at E Street, right at 13th Street.

Making an Entrance—What to Wear

A big night at the theater used to mean a suit and tie for men, a dress and high heels for women. (I don't want to get into gender reversals here.) Most Washington theatergoers are happy not to subscribe to that code. By all means, get gussied up if you feel like it, but it's not necessary. The usher will take your ticket if you're wearing jeans. Just wash behind your ears, comb your hair, and look presentable. Shorts and flip-flops are always déclassé. Slacks or a skirt, a clean shirt or blouse, and jacket are A-okay, and you'll blend in with the crowd.

Balancing the Budget

Several restaurants offer prix-fixe pretheater dinner specials. If you have tickets for a show, consider dining at one of the following: **Aquarelle,** near the Kennedy Center (☎ **202/298-4455**), offers a prix-fixe from 5 to 7pm for $38. **Le Rivage,** near the Arena Stage (☎ **202/488-8111**), has a $17.95 pretheater special from 5:30 to 6:30pm.

701, near the Shakespeare Theatre (☎ **202/393-0701**), has a pretheater menu available for $22.50 from 5:30 to 7pm. The **Roof Terrace Restaurant** (☎ **202/416-8555**) at the Kennedy Center offers a prix-fixe, pretheater special from 5:30 to 6:30pm for $35. For a complete list of dining options near the most popular theaters, consult the "Most Convenient Pretheater Dining" box on p. 126 in chapter 10.

Missing the Curtain

The curtain usually goes up on time in Washington. There are exceptions, however. I've been to a couple of performances where the president was in attendance. We had to pass through metal detectors and have our purses rifled through by security guards. Thank heavens they didn't confiscate my M&Ms. Those evenings the curtain rose late. Otherwise, it's a good rule of thumb to arrive at the theater 15 minutes before a performance so that you'll have time to visit the rest room and settle in your seat. If you're late, you may have to wait until intermission to be seated.

Tipping the Balance

Ushers at most theaters are paid—so you don't need to tip them. They do it out of love for the performing arts. If you buy a cocktail or snack (other than candy), tipping is appropriate. You'll probably see a large glass on the bar for gratuities.

The Best of Beethoven, Mozart, Mahler & All the Rest

Washington's own **National Symphony** (and the world's top orchestras) plays in the Kennedy Center Concert Hall. Here and elsewhere (museums and galleries, for the most part), you can listen to a slew of chamber ensembles and soloists.

The National Symphony plays in the Kennedy Center Concert Hall, F Street and Rock Creek Parkway NW (☎ **202/416-8100;** Metro: Foggy Bottom). The season runs from September to June and performances are frequently sold out. A $10 obstructed view ticket is the cheapest way to hear, though maybe not see, the musicians. The orchestra plays for free on the West Lawn of the Capitol on Memorial Day and Labor Day weekends, and on July 4; and at the Carter Barron Amphitheater in summer (☎ **202/426-6837**).

Balancing the Budget

If you're determined to attend a performance that's sold out, ask about SRO (Standing Room Only) tickets. These usually go for $20 or less. If someone leaves at intermission, you may get lucky and snag a seat.

A Night at the Opera

The **Washington Opera** presents seven productions (with English supertitles) in the Kennedy Center Opera House, F Street and Rock Creek Parkway NW (☎ **800/876-7372** or 202/416-7800). Although performances are usually sold out to subscribers, you can purchase returned tickets an hour before curtain time. SRO tickets are sold at the box office Saturday at 10am for the upcoming week's performances.

The **Summer Opera Theater Company** stages two operas in June and July at Catholic University's Hartke Theater (☎ **202/526-1669**). The theater is on the campus of the Catholic University of America, 620 Michigan Ave. NE (☎ **202/319-4000** for the box office). The Brookland–CUA Metro station is across the street.

Choral Music

The **Choral Arts Society of Washington**—180 voices strong—performs varied programs of classical works, mostly at the Kennedy Center, from September to June. The ever-popular Christmas sing-alongs sell out every December (☎ **202/244-3669**). Except for the December concerts and the January tribute to Martin Luther King Jr. (usually the second week of January), some tickets are usually available up to showtime. For the Christmas concert, I recommend that you purchase tickets when they go on sale, usually in early November. Tickets are sold through the number listed above and sometimes at the Kennedy Center box office.

More Beautiful Music

The **Smithsonian Associates Program** (☎ 202/357-3030) offers musical performances—everything from barbershop to zydeco—at several museum sites throughout the year. Ticket prices range from $15 to $25.

Dance

Besides supporting a professional ballet company and numerous top-flight contemporary troupes, Washington welcomes to its stages the best companies from all over the world.

Ballet lovers need look no further than our very own **Washington Ballet** (☎ 202/362-3606). The ensemble company presents a fall, winter, and spring series of classical and contemporary works at the Kennedy Center and Warner Theatre. The company's *Nutcracker* has been dishing out holiday cheer to area audiences for generations. Tickets can be purchased through Ticketmaster (☎ 202/432-SEAT).

Balancing the Budget

Many theaters set aside tickets for seniors and full-time students that go on sale the day of the performance. If you don't ask, you don't get!

Front-running **Dance Place,** 3225 8th St. NE (☎ 202/269-1600) presents a broad array of modern, postmodern, and ethnic dance in an unbuttoned setting near Catholic University on weekends throughout the year. The *Washington Post* calls Dance Place "the preeminent center for contemporary dance in Washington, D.C." To get here, take Metro to the Brookland–CUA Metro station (but not after dark! take a cab after sundown), exit Metro at Monroe Street, and go right on Monroe. Continue 2 blocks, go left at 8th Street, and continue 2 blocks to Dance Place.

Taking Your Children to the Theater

To get information on performances of special interest to children, pick up *Frommer's Washington, D.C. with Kids,* or check the "Children's Events" column in the "Weekend" section of the Friday *Washington Post.*

Depending on their ages and interests, children may enjoy the same entertainment that you do. For top-quality productions geared to youngsters, investigate the following:

➤ **Discovery Theater,** in the Smithsonian's Arts and Industries Building, 900 Jefferson Dr. SW (☎ 202/357-1500).

➤ The **Kennedy Center's Theater for Young People,** F Street NW and Rock Creek Parkway (☎ 202/416-8830).

Other children's favorites—all free, except for the *Nutcracker*—include the Kennedy Center's Millennium Stage project (free performances daily at 6pm in the Grand Foyer), F Street NW and Rock Creek Parkway (☎ **202/467-4600**).

➤ Summer evening Military Band Summer Concerts take place from Memorial Day to Labor Day (☎ **202/433-4011**) at several outdoor venues including the West Terrace of the U.S. Capitol; Sylvan Theatre on the Washington Monument grounds; the Ellipse, behind the White House; and on the U.S. Navy Memorial Plaza, 701 Pennsylvania Ave. NW.

➤ Summer Sunday Concerts on the Canal, Foundry Building, below M Street NW, between 30th and Thomas Jefferson streets (☎ **202/ 653-5190**).

➤ Washington Ballet's *Nutcracker* (late November through December) at the Warner Theatre, 1299 Pennsylvania Ave. NW (☎ **202/432-SEAT**).

➤ Pageant of Peace (beginning in early December and continuing though January 1) on the Ellipse, between the White House and Constitution Avenue NW (☎ **202/619-7222**). At 5pm on an early December evening, the president lights the national Christmas tree on the Ellipse. The celebration continues with Disney characters, concerts, and festivities for all. Every night thereafter until the first of January, visitors can enjoy choir music between the hours of 6 and 8pm.

D.C. Dirt

Before heading west to Stanford University, Chelsea Clinton studied ballet at the Washington School of Ballet and danced in the Washington Ballet's *Nutcracker.* Maybe that's where she developed all that poise.

Movie Madness

Besides being the subject of several movies—from *Mr. Smith Goes to Washington* (1939) and *Advise and Consent* (1962) to *All the President's Men* (1976) and *Wag the Dog* (1998)—Washington loves the movies. Maybe it has to do with Hollywood and the capital city's affinity for plots and power. Washington has more than its share of first-run theaters. Most are bunched like radishes around Dupont Circle, Georgetown, and Upper Wisconsin Avenue NW. On Capitol Hill, the nine-screen **AMC Union Station 9** (☎ **202/842-3757**) has (you guessed right) nine theaters, and all those tempting Union Station food stalls near the entrance.

But enough about stale popcorn and testosterone thrillers. Diehard lovers of the silver screen frequent the following. The **American Film Institute,** in the Kennedy Center (☎ **202/785-4600**), screens two to four movies a day—

Hear Ye! Hear Ye!

The Biograph, an 8-screen multiplex art house at 555 11th St. NW is due to open early in 2000. We can hardly wait! Local filmgoers have been in mourning since the original Biograph (in Georgetown) was turned into a CVS drugstore in 1996.

classics, contemporary, national, and foreign—from its collection of 700. Lectures and workshops often accompany the screenings.

First-run documentaries, features, and shorts air weekly in the **Hirshhorn Museum** (☎ **202/357-2700**). And the shows are free. Daily showings of historical films take place in the **National Archives** (☎ **202/501-5000;** Metro: Archives). The National Archives is located at Constitution Avenue and 8th Street NW. Walk south 1 block on 7th Street, right at Constitution Avenue to Archives Building (it's the first building on your right). Spectacular flight-related films alternate daily on the IMAX screen of the **Samuel Langley Theater** at the National Museum of Air and Space, south side of the Mall at Independence Avenue SW and 7th Street (☎ **202/357-2700;** Metro: L'Enfant Plaza).

And, as we fade out to the credits, note that the nation's capital is the site of the **D.C. International Film Festival,** affectionately known as Filmfest, every spring. For information, call ☎ **202/724-5613.**

Chapter 19

Hitting the Clubs & Bars

In This Chapter

➤ The best bars

➤ The best places to hear live music

➤ The best dance spots

➤ Comedy clubs

➤ The gay nightlife scene

Going to a show at the Kennedy Center or catching the *Nutcracker* at the Warner Theater may quench your thirst for cultural events, but if it's libations or live music or a dance party that you're thirsting for, this chapter has something in store for you.

The entertainment scene is well documented in the "Weekend" section of the Friday *Washington Post* and free *City Paper,* available in bookstores, restaurants, bars, and cafes all around town. This being Washington, several venues for international sounds reflect the large number of residents and visitors who hail from faraway. When it comes to dance clubs and watering holes, there are plenty of places to shake your booty or wet your whistle during your visit.

If You Want to Go Bar Hoppin'

The Washington bar scene is, in a word, hoppin'. Whether your favorite drink is a virgin colada or a boilermaker, you'll find places to order your favorite poison. **Café Milano,** 3251 Prospect St. NW (☎ 202/333-6183), is a Georgetown magnet for local celebs and wanna-bes. And then there's the

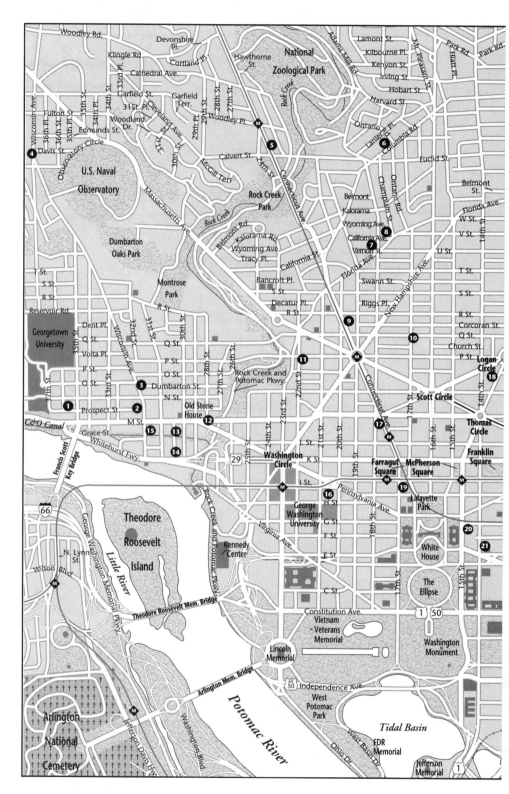

Washington, D. C. Bars & Clubs

0   .25 mi
0   .4 km

Au Pied du Cochon **3**
Black Cat **18**
Blues Alley **15**
Bombay Club **19**
Brickskellar **11**
Café Milano **2**
Capitol City Brewing Company
  (Convention Center) **24**
Capitol City Brewing Company
  (Union Station) **26**
Chelsea's **13**
Chief Ike's Mambo Room **6**
Circle Bar & Tavern **9**
Coco Loco **23**
Dubliner **27**
Four Seasons **12**
Improv **17**
Irish Times **28**
J.R.'s **10**
Kiliminjaro **8**
Kinkead's **16**
Madam's Organ **7**
9:30 Club **25**
Old Ebbitt Grill **20**
Old Europe Murder
  Mystery Theater **4**
Petitto's **5**
Remington's **29**
Round Robin **21**
701 **22**
Sequoia **14**
Tombs **1**

quintessentially collegiate **Tombs,** 1226 36th St. NW (☎ **202/337-6668**), on the campus of Georgetown University, where a certain leader of the free world (initials WJC) hung out when he was a Hoya undergrad.

When the weather is favorable, nothing beats a drink on the riverfront terrace of **Sequoia,** 3000 K St. NW (☎ **202/944-4200;** Metro: Foggy Bottom), in the Washington Harbour complex.

In the Dupont Circle neighborhood, sip suds as other brewhounds have for 40 years at the **Brickskeller,** 1523 22nd St. NW (☎ **202/293-1885;** Metro: Dupont Circle), purveying several hundred international beers, light fare, and grungy charm coming out the kazoo. Speaking of beer, D.C.'s first brew pub, the **Capitol City Brewing Company,** has two locations: 1100 New York Ave. NW (☎ **202/628-2222;** Metro: Metro Center), near the Convention Center; and 2 Massachusetts Ave. NW (☎ **202/842-2337;** Metro: Union Station), in the Post Office Building—site of the National Postal Museum—across the street from Union Station. Try a sampler if you're undecided, and don't overlook the char-grilled burgers and crunchy fries, or chili that'll leave you begging for another icy mug.

Hear Ye! Hear Ye!

Remember to be careful when walking around the city late at night. For all night spots that are accessible to the Metro, I have included a Metro station. If you don't see any Metro stops listed for a certain place, that means take a taxi. The Metro closes at midnight, so if you stay out late anywhere, it's wise to take a taxi back to your hotel.

When all is said and done, my favorite places for bellying up to the bar (after many years of scrupulous research) remain the **Old Ebbitt Grill,** 675 15th St. NW (☎ **202/347-4800;** Metro: Metro Center), and the **Four Seasons,** 2800 Pennsylvania Ave. NW (☎ **202/ 342-0444;** Metro: Foggy Bottom), where cocktails are served in a sumptuous gardenlike lounge off the lobby.

If You Want to Hear Some Rock, Pop, or R&B

The standout, I am told, among the clubs springing up in the area around 14th and U streets NW (a not-so-hot neighborhood, so please take a taxi), is the **9:30 Club,** 815 V. St. NW (☎ **202/393-0930;** Metro: U Street–Cardozo). Sheryl Crow, Smashing Pumpkins, and Shawn Colvin have played in this converted warehouse that's open only when there's a show. The state-of-the-art sound system, three dance floors, and four bars evidently don't hurt the club's popularity.

Cool cats groove at the **Black Cat,** 1831 14th St. NW (☎ **202/667-7960;** Metro: U Street–Cardozo), a premier showcase for new and alternative bands. Think grunge lounge, pinball machines, jukebox (mostly alternative and classic rock) in one room; dance floor for 400; live music (alternative, classic rock, punk) in the other, with occasional poetry readings. Poetry readings? Since you've made it safely to the last chapter of the book, I don't want to lose you now, so please don't wander around this neighborhood.

Where to Go for Jazz & Blue Notes

Georgetown and D.C.'s premier club, **Blues Alley,** rear of 1037 Wisconsin Ave. NW (☎ 202/337-4141), has been presenting top names in jazz and blues since 1965. Sometimes a third show is added at midnight on weekends. Otherwise, book the 8pm or 10pm show as soon as the guest artist's name is announced, and show up by 7pm for first-come, first-served seating. The likes of Nancy Wilson, Wynton Marsalis, and Maynard Ferguson don't come cheap. The cover will run you about $15 to $40, and there's a $7 food or drink minimum.

Charming and romantic, the **Round Robin** nestles in a cozy corner of the elegant Willard Inter-Continental, 1401 Pennsylvania Ave. NW (☎ 202/637-7319; Metro: Metro Center). Well-known jazzers perform in the intimate space. For the ambience and talent, expect to pay a cover of $10 to $20; there's a two-drink minimum. Tell Jim I sent you!

It's worth the trip to **Madam's Organ** (a play on Adams–Morgan, where it's located), 2003 18th St. NW (☎ 202/667-5370), to say you've been there and to hear blues guitarist/singer Bobby Parker, on duty most evenings. Of course, you'll want to check out the second-floor bar, Big Daddy's Love Lounge & Pick-Up Joint. It's a scene.

When You're Hungry Late at Night

Even though heartburn usually follows late-night eating binges, there is something decadent and wonderful about slipping into a restaurant after a show, a movie, or a night on the town.

Au Pied du Cochon, a funky bistro in Georgetown at 1335 Wisconsin Ave. NW (at Dumbarton Street; ☎ 202/335-5440), is open 24 hours for omelets, eggs Benedict, and such. Otherwise, check out the following, which are mentioned in chapters 10 and 11: **Bistro Français** (until 4am), Georgetown; **Full Kee** (until 3am), Downtown (Chinatown); **Kramerbooks & Afterwords** (until 1am Monday through Thursday; 24 hours Friday morning to early Monday morning), Dupont Circle; **Meskerem** (until 2am), Adams–Morgan; **Music City Roadhouse** (until 1am), Georgetown; **Old Ebbitt Grill** (until 1am), Downtown.

261

Where to Go If You're in the Mood for a Melody

Looking for a classy place to kick back and enjoy a cocktail while listening to someone play a mean or gentle piano? Near the downtown theaters and anchoring the south end of the 7th Street Arts Corridor is gracious **701,** 701 Pennsylvania Ave. NW (☎ **202/393-0701;** Metro: Archives/Navy Memorial), where live piano music emanates from the dimly lit lounge nightly from about 5:30 to 10:30pm (later on weekends).

Sip a Pimm's Cup at the opulent, days-of-the-raj-inspired **Bombay Club,** 815 Connecticut Ave. NW (between H and I streets; ☎ **202/659-3727;** Metro: Farragut West), evenings from 6:45 to 10:30pm in the lounge area. Due west several blocks in Foggy Bottom, a pianist holds forth (or is it *forte?*) in the lively lower-level bar area of **Kinkead's,** 2000 Pennsylvania Ave. NW (enter on I Street between 20th and 21st streets; ☎ **202/296-7700;** Metro: Foggy Bottom), from 6:30 to 10 or 10:30pm (sometimes later on weekends).

Where to Go for International Sound Bites

At **Coco Loco,** 801 7th St. NW (☎ **202/289-2626;** Metro: Gallery Place), Thursday through Saturday night, the scene is hot, hot, hot at this eatery in the shadow of the Shakespeare Theatre. When it gets late in the evening, a provocative floor show by Brazilian dancers stops diners dead in their tapas. Stay until 2am on Thursday, 3am on Friday and Saturday, and you can join the conga line and limbo contest.

At **Irish Times,** 14 F St. NW (opposite Union Station; ☎ **202/543/5433;** Metro: Union Station), you can join local students who are swillin' and spillin' their Guinness at the folk sing-a-longs Thursday through Saturday evenings from 9pm to 1am or later. Live Irish music cuts through boisterous customers' conversations nightly at the **Dubliner,** Phoenix Park Hotel, 520 N. Capitol St. NW (opposite Union Station; ☎ **202/737-3773;** Metro: Union Station), from around 9pm (except for Sunday when the action begins at 7:30pm) 'til the wee small hours of 2 or 3am.

Where to Go to Shake Your Booty

Take your dancin' feet to **Coco Loco** (see listing under "Where to Go for International Sound Bites" above) or **Chief Ike's Mambo Room** in Adams–Morgan, 1725 Columbia Rd. NW (☎ **202/332-2211**), where a mostly young crowd boogies Thursday through Saturday nights to deejay-spun contemporary and Latin tunes. Also check out the above-mentioned music clubs, many of which have crowded dance floors.

If You're Looking for Something Different

"Who done it?" is the question on patrons' minds at the **Murder Mystery Theater** in the **Old Europe** restaurant, 2434 Wisconsin Ave. NW (a mile north of Georgetown; ☎ **202/333-6875**), Saturday evenings at 7pm. At

Petitto's, 2653 Connecticut Ave. NW (near Calvert Street; ☎ **202/667-5350**), diners feast on *Pagliacci* with their pasta Friday night when singers perform opera selections. Saturday the mood changes and the sounds of Broadway fill the restaurant.

Where to Go for a Laugh

Top stand-ups on the comedy club circuit perform nightly at **The Improv,** 1140 Connecticut Ave. NW (between L and M streets; ☎ **202/296-7008;** Metro: Farragut North). Biggies like Ellen de Generes, Jerry Seinfeld, and Robin Williams have stepped up to the Improv's mike.

Hear Ye! Hear Ye!

When they're not on tour, members of the nationally known **Gross National Product** (☎ **202/783-7212**) spoof D.C.'s major players at different venues. They're a not-to-be-missed hoot!

Chelsea's, 1055 Thomas Jefferson St. NW (in the Foundry Building on the C&O Canal in Georgetown; ☎ **202/298-8222**), is home of the satirical **Capitol Steps.** Comprising former congressional staffers who know whereof they speak, they deflate Washington institutions with needle-sharp lyrics.

Where to Find the Gay & Lesbian Bars

The Dupont Circle neighborhood has the greatest concentration of gay bars in the District, with most activity centered around 21st and P streets, and on 17th Street between P and R streets NW. Try the **Circle Bar & Tavern,** 1629 Connecticut Ave. NW (between Q and R streets; ☎ **202/462-5575;** Metro: Dupont Circle), with a mixed clientele of under-40 gays and lesbians. Special events—gay proms, rodeos, and the like—take place on the dance floor of the three-level club. An oldies-filled jukebox and pool table share space with two bars on the main floor. Music videos play on big-screen monitors in the upstairs terrace, open to the stars for sipping and supping, weather permitting.

Hear Ye! Hear Ye!

For more information on gay bars and clubs, check the weekly newspaper the *Washington Blade*, which has a Web site at **www.washblade.com**. And while you're surfing, tap into *Jame's Guide to Gay Washington* at **www.alliance. net/-jame/bars/htm**.

Around the corner, **J.R's,** 1519 17th St. NW (between P and Q streets; ☎ **202/328-0090;** Metro: Dupont Circle), attracts an upscale, all-male crowd and is less of a production than the Circle Bar & Tavern. A balcony pool table oversees the tin-ceilinged, exposed-brick bar area. J.R.'s sponsors an annual Drag Race in Dupont Circle.

Fans of Reba and Garth two-step over to **Remington's,** 639 Pennsylvania Ave. SE (☎ **202/543-3113;** Metro: Eastern Market), on Capitol Hill, where country and western disco nights are the rage with the (mostly) gay patrons. If you go to a bar or club on Capitol Hill or near the Navy Yard in the Southeast sector of the city, pleeeeeze take a cab.

Washington, D.C.—
Facts at Your Fingertips

AAA: The local AAA in Washington is located at 701 15th St. NW (☎ 202/331-3000). For emergency road service, call ☎ 800/763-5500.

American Express: There are two American Express offices in the district. One is located at 1150 Connecticut Ave. NW (☎ 202/457-1300; Metro: Farragut North). The other is at Mazza Gallerie, 5300 Wisconsin Ave. NW (☎ 202/362-4000; Metro: Friendship Heights). You can also get American Express traveler's checks over the phone by calling ☎ 800/221-7282.

Babysitters: Wee Sit provides hotel child care by bonded sitters (☎ 703/764-1542), as does **White House Nannies** (☎ 301/652-8088).

Camera Repair: If you're having problems with your camera, head to **Penn Camera,** 915 E St. NW (between 9th and 10th streets; ☎ 202/347-5777), or 1015 18th St. NW (between K and L streets; ☎ 202/785-7366); or **ProPhoto,** 1919 Pennsylvania Ave. NW (mezzanine between 19th and 20th streets; ☎ 202/223-1292).

Congresspersons: To locate a senator or congressional representative, call the **Capitol Switchboard** (☎ 202/224-3121).

Doctors: Prologue (☎ 800/DOCTORS) is a referral service of doctors and dentists. **Physicians Home Service,** Suite 401, 2311 M St. NW (between 23rd and 24th streets; ☎ 202/331-3888), will come to your hotel or treat you in the M Street office during regular hours.

Emergencies/Hot Lines: For police, fire, and ambulance, dial ☎ 911; the 24-hour poison control hot line is ☎ 202/625-3333; the 24-hour crisis line is ☎ 202/561-7000; Drug Abuse/Action Health for alcohol and drug problems is at ☎ 800/234-0420. The 24-hour hot line for Alcoholics Anonymous is at ☎ 800/222-0828.

Hospitals: In life-threatening emergencies, dial ☎ **911.** For emergency-room treatment, call one of the following. If you need emergency treatment, it is no time to practice your map-reading skills. Take a taxicab.

Children's Hospital National Medical Center, 111 Michigan Ave. NW (near Catholic University and the National Shrine; ☎ **202/884-5000**); **George Washington University Hospital,** 901 23rd St. NW (entrance on Washington Circle; ☎ **202/994-3211**); **Georgetown University Hospital,** 3800 Reservoir Rd. NW (☎ **202/784-2118**).

Information: For tourist information, call the **Washington, D.C., Convention and Visitors Association,** 1212 New York Ave. NW (between 12th and 13th streets; ☎ **202/789-7000**). For telephone directory information, dial ☎ **411** or (outside of Washington) the **area code plus 555-1212.**

Liquor Laws: The minimum drinking age is 21. Establishments can serve alcohol from 8am to 2am Monday through Thursday, from 8am to 2:30am Friday and Saturday, from 10am to 2am Sunday. Liquor stores are closed on Sunday, but grocery stores and convenience stores often sell beer and wine 7 days a week.

Maps: Free city maps are available at most hotels and tourist sites and at the Washington, D.C., Convention and Visitors Association, 1212 New York Ave. NW (between 12th and 13th streets; ☎ **202/789-7000**).

Newspapers/Magazines: The two major daily newspapers are the *Washington Post* and *Washington Times.* A weekly newspaper, *Washington City Paper,* is distributed free on Thursday. The *Washingtonian* magazine is published monthly.

Pharmacies: CVS has more than 40 stores, with two 24-hour locations at 14th Street and Thomas Circle (at Vermont Avenue); ☎ **202/628-0720,** and at 67 Dupont Circle (☎ **202/785-1466**).

Police: In an emergency, dial ☎ **911.** For a nonemergency, call ☎ **202/727-1010.**

Rest Rooms: Rest rooms can be found in restaurants, bars, hotels, museums, shopping malls (including Union Station), and service stations. You'll also find bathrooms at the **FDR Memorial** (on the Tidal Basin) and **John F. Kennedy Center for the Performing Arts** (in Foggy Bottom). When nature calls on the Mall, there are **public bathrooms** at 15th Street and Independence Avenue SW (near the Washington Monument and Holocaust Memorial Museum); between Constitution Gardens and the Reflecting Pool (near the Lincoln Memorial and Vietnam Veterans Memorial); and near the Smithsonian Metro station (12th Street and Jefferson Drive SW). While the bathrooms at the White House are for emergencies only, there are public rest rooms on the **Ellipse,** behind the presidential mansion.

Safety: The major tourist areas and presidential monuments are safe zones. Late at night it's advisable not to stray from the Adams–Morgan blocks of

18th Street and Columbia Road NW. When you're done partying, take a taxi back to Metro (remember, Metro trains stop running at midnight) or to your hotel. Other areas in which to sharpen your antennae after dark are Capitol Hill, the Southwest waterfront area around Arena Stage, and anywhere in Southeast D.C. To play it safe, take a cab to or from restaurants, theaters, and clubs in these neighborhoods in the evening, and deep-six any thoughts of a late-night stroll.

Taxes: The sales tax on merchandise is 5.75%. The tax on restaurant meals is 10%. The sales tax on a hotel room is 14.5%.

Taxis: D.C. cabs operate on a zone system. The minimum fare (between two points in the same zone) is $4, regardless of the distance traveled. Drivers are allowed to pick up as many passengers as they can squeeze into the cab. There's a $1.50 charge to call a taxi.

Time Zone: Washington, D.C., is on Eastern Standard Time (EST). On the first Sunday in April, we set our clocks ahead 1 hour and observe Daylight Saving Time (DST) until the last Sunday in October. For the correct time, call ☎ 202/844-2525.

Transit Information: For **Metrorail** (subway) and **Metrobus** information, call ☎ 202/637-7000. If you've left something on the Metro, call **Lost and Found** at ☎ 202/962-1326.

Toll-Free Numbers & Web Sites for Airlines, Car-Rental Agencies & Hotel Chains

Airlines

Air Canada
☎ 800/776-3000
www.aircanada.ca

AirTran
☎ 800/247-8726
www.airtran.com

Alaska Airlines
☎ 800/426-0333
www.alaskaair.com

America West Airlines
☎ 800/235-9292
www.americawest.com

American Airlines
☎ 800/433-7300
www.americanair.com

British Airways
☎ 800/247-9297
☎ 0345/222-111 in Britain
www.british-airways.com

Canadian Airlines International
☎ 800/426-7000
www.cdnair.ca

Continental Airlines
☎ 800/525-0280
www.flycontinental.com

Delta Air Lines
☎ 800/221-1212
www.delta-air.com

Kiwi International Air Lines
☎ 800/538-5494
www.jetkiwi.com

Midway Airlines
☎ 800/446-4392

Northwest Airlines
☎ 800/225-2525
www.nwa.com

Southwest Airlines
☎ 800/435-9792
www.iflyswa.com

Tower Air
☎ 718/553-8500 in New York
☎ 800/34-TOWER outside New York
www.towerair.com

Trans World Airlines (TWA)
☎ 800/221-2000
www.twa.com

United Airlines
☎ 800/241-6522
www.ual.com

US Airways
☎ 800/428-4322
www.usairways.com

Virgin Atlantic Airways
☎ 800/862-8621 in
Continental U.S.
☎ 0293/747-747 in Britain
www.fly.virgin.com

Car-Rental Agencies

Advantage
☎ 800/777-5500
www.arac.com

Alamo
☎ 800/327-9633
www.goalamo.com

Auto Europe
☎ 800/223-5555
www.autoeurope.com

Avis
☎ 800/331-1212 in
Continental U.S.
☎ 800/TRY-AVIS in Canada
www.avis.com

Budget
☎ 800/527-0700
www.budgetrentacar.com

Dollar
☎ 800/800-4000
www.dollarcar.com

Enterprise
☎ 800/325-8007
www.pickenterprise.com

Hertz
☎ 800/654-3131
www.hertz.com

Kemwel Holiday Auto
☎ 800/678-0678
www.kemwel.com

National
☎ 800/CAR-RENT
www.nationalcar.com

Payless
☎ 800/PAYLESS
www.paylesscar.com

Rent-A-Wreck
☎ 800/535-1391
rent-a-wreck.com

Thrifty
☎ 800/367-2277
www.thrifty.com

Value
☎ 800/327-2501
www.go-value.com

Major Hotel & Motel Chains

Best Western International
☎ 800/528-1234
www.bestwestern.com

Clarion Hotels
☎ 800/CLARION
www.hotelchoice.com/cgi-bin/res/webres?clarion.html

Comfort Inns
☎ 800/228-5150
www.hotelchoice.com/cgi-bin/res/webres?comfort.html

Courtyard by Marriott
☎ 800/321-2211
www.courtyard.com

Days Inn
☎ 800/325-2525
www.daysinn.com

Doubletree Hotels
☎ 800/222-TREE
www.doubletreehotels.com

Econo Lodges
☎ 800/55-ECONO
www.hotelchoice.com/cgi-bin/res/webres?econo.html

Embassy Suites
☎ 800/362-2779
www.embassy-suites.com

Hampton Inn
☎ 800/HAMPTON
www.hampton-inn.com

Hilton Hotels
☎ 800/HILTONS
www.hilton.com

Holiday Inn
☎ 800/HOLIDAY
www.holiday-inn.com

Howard Johnson
☎ 800/654-2000
www.hojo.com/hojo.html

Hyatt Hotels & Resorts
☎ 800/228-9000
www.hyatt.com

ITT Sheraton
☎ 800/325-3535
www.sheraton.com

Marriott Hotels
☎ 800/228-9290
www.marriott.com

Motel 6
☎ 800/4-MOTEL6

Quality Inns
☎ 800/228-5151
www.hotelchoice.com/cgi-bin/res/webres?quality.html

Radisson Hotels International
☎ 800/333-3333
www.radisson.com

Ramada Inns
☎ 800/2-RAMADA
www.ramada.com

Red Carpet Inns
☎ 800/251-1962

Red Roof Inns
☎ 800/843-7663
www.redroof.com

Residence Inn by Marriott
☎ 800/331-3131
www.residenceinn.com

Super 8 Motels
☎ 800/800-8000
www.super8motels.com

Travelodge
☎ 800/255-3050

Wyndham Hotels and Resorts
☎ 800/822-4200 in Continental U.S. and Canada
www.wyndham.com

Index

Page numbers in *italics* refer to maps.

273

281